MODERN
AMERICAN
DIPLOMACY

MODERN AMERICAN DIPLOMACY

Revised and Enlarged Edition

edited by

JOHN M. CARROLL
GEORGE C. HERRING

A Scholarly Resources Inc. Imprint
Wilmington, Delaware

Scholarly Resources Inc.
104 Greenhill Avenue
Wilmington, DE 19805-1897

Sources for Cover Illustrations

Woodrow Wilson, *courtesy Seeley G. Mudd Manuscript Library, Department of Rare Books and Special Collections, Princeton University Libraries*; Franklin D. Roosevelt, *courtesy Library of Congress*; Harry S. Truman, *courtesy U.S. Army, Harry S. Truman Library*; John F. Kennedy, *courtesy John F. Kennedy Library*; Ronald Reagan, *courtesy Mary Anne Fackelman-Miner, The White House*

Library of Congress Cataloging-in-Publication Data

Modern American diplomacy / edited by John M. Carroll and
    George C. Herring. — Rev. and enl. ed.
        p.   cm.
    Includes bibliographical references (p.   ) and index.
    ISBN 0-8420-2554-5 (alk. paper). — ISBN 0-8420-2555-3
(pbk. : alk. paper)
    1. United States—Foreign relations—20th century. I. Carroll,
John M. (John Martin), 1943–   . II. Herring, George C., 1936– .
E744.M589   1995
327.73'009'04—dc20   95-8681
                                                                          CIP

⊗The paper used in this publication meets the minimum requirements of the American National Standard for permanence of paper for printed library materials, Z39.48, 1984.

Contents

Preface to the Revised and Enlarged Edition

When *Modern American Diplomacy* was first published in 1986, we were pleased by the favorable reviews in scholarly journals, but we were even more gratified by the positive response from diplomatic historians who found it a useful instructional tool in their courses. In recent years, we have received inquiries from colleagues concerning the possibility of updating and revising the book in order to serve better the needs of teachers and students alike as the twentieth century comes to a close. A number of professors were kind enough to provide specific criticisms of the text and overall organization of the contents and to make suggestions for improving *Modern American Diplomacy* as it related to their teaching needs. We thank them for their interest and effort. In that spirit, and mindful of the many excellent suggestions, we set forth to rework the original volume without undermining the basic conceptual framework that diplomatic historians and students have found useful.

In the new edition of *Modern American Diplomacy*, ten essays held over from the first edition have been revised and updated to reflect new scholarship and interpretations concerning the subject at hand. The authors have added the most important recent scholarship regarding their subject to the Sources and Suggested Readings in their chapters. Some of the original contributors have made only minor changes in their essays while others, especially those authors dealing with issues and events of the late twentieth century, have substantially recrafted their work. The Introduction also has been revised, and the Afterword was rewritten.

The addition of three new contributions gave us an opportunity to provide an infusion of new energy and ideas to stand alongside the high-quality essays with which readers of *Modern American Diplomacy* are familiar. MARC GALLICCHIO has written on the origins of the Cold War in Asia, bringing to his subject a fresh viewpoint and some new twists to this important post-World War II development. The second essay, on U.S. nuclear and strategic policy from 1945 to the present by WALTER L. HIXSON, brings coverage of the Soviet-American confrontation into the mid-1990s. The author analyzes the background and unfolding of events that led to the collapse of Soviet-style communism in Eastern Europe and in the USSR, and he also raises questions about what the end of the Cold War might mean in the future for the United States and the world.

The third new essay is on the topic of the American policy of "containment" of communism in the two crucial decades following the Second World War. Among the suggestions that we received concerning *Modern American Diplomacy*, a number of readers pointed out that in the classroom they normally study, immediately after completing coverage of World War II, the origin of the Cold War as well as U.S. containment policy, particularly as it related to the Mediterranean area and Western Europe. In the first edition of *Modern American Diplomacy*, the treatment of U.S. containment policy is fragmented as a result of being discussed in several different chapters. MARK H. LYTLE now has contributed an essay that traces the origin and development of containment from 1945 through the mid-1960s, thereby raising questions regarding the relative success or failure of this policy. We believe that this essay on the beginning of the Cold War and the strategy of containment of communism will better serve the needs of both teachers and students engaged in the exploration of U.S. diplomatic history.

We would like to thank all the authors for their diligence, punctuality, and commitment, for without their cooperation this project never could have gone forward. In addition, special thanks also are extended to the readers who have offered suggestions or criticisms of the book, and to the many other diplomatic historians who have helped to make this new edition of *Modern American Diplomacy* possible.

John M. Carroll
George C. Herring

Introduction: The Course
of American Diplomacy

John M. Carroll

Beginning in the colonial era, Americans showed a strong interest in foreign policy in order to protect their survival against the larger French and Spanish empires in the New World. During the early years of the Republic, a wise and prudent diplomatic strategy was necessary to preserve independence. Presidents George Washington and John Adams were determined to avoid unnecessary European entanglements while the nation gained strength and stability in the decade after the American Revolution. Although the United States stumbled into war with Britain in 1812, it emerged from that conflict with its national territory intact and with a sense of pride and confidence that helped to stimulate an aggressive policy of continental expansion. This westward thrust consumed much of the nation's energy during the nineteenth century.

The end of the War of 1812 and the larger Napoleonic Wars in Europe marked a change in American and global history. Between 1815 and 1914 the world continued to experience a number of major wars but none matching the intensity and duration of the Napoleonic conflict. Isolated from the mainstream of international affairs by two oceans and the usually benevolent umbrella of the British navy, America enjoyed a period of growth and progress. Despite the traumatic and costly Civil War during the 1860s, the country pulled together to complete the task of continental development and emerged as one of the leading industrial nations by the end of the century.

On the eve of the new century the United States embarked on a course of imperial conquest. Certainly a policy of aggressive expansionism was not new for Americans. What was new was that the territories were noncontiguous lands abroad. JOSEPH A. FRY points out some of the factors that helped propel the United States along the road to imperialism. The economic boom of the late nineteenth century was extremely uneven, and it resulted in poor wages and working conditions for many factory laborers. Some capitalists feared a crisis as unemployment spread, workers became more militant, and production exceeded consumption. With the "safety valve" of the frontier supposedly closing, some industrialists looked to overseas markets as a way out of their predicament. Beyond this, American leaders were impressed by the attainments of European imperial powers and were convinced that the United States also had a mission to protect and uplift backward peoples. Religious groups, sea power enthusiasts, some businessmen, and a large segment of the social elite formed a small but powerful force in favor of overseas expansion. When conditions were ripe in the 1890s, Americans willingly embarked on an imperialistic adventure.

The "splendid little war" with Spain marked the emergence of the United States as a world power, and in just a few months it acquired a modest but sprawling empire. European nations recognized that the United States would play an increasingly important role in international affairs, and by the beginning of the new century America was making its influence felt from the Caribbean to China. President Theodore Roosevelt epitomized the raw and exuberant energy of the rising world power. He sometimes spoke brashly and acted impetuously, but for the most part he was as pragmatic and realistic as the nation itself. The young president bullied the weaker nations in Latin America but acted cautiously in confronting the major powers in Asia. William Howard Taft and Woodrow Wilson were not as successful as their predecessor in properly balancing both American objectives and power in these areas.

America's experience as an imperial nation produced mixed results. Some Americans basked in the prestige that accompanied great-power status. Others were more concerned with the negative side of imperialism: a brutal guerrilla war in the Philippines, the tarnishing of America's anticolonial heritage, the expense of maintaining colonies, and the failure of sizable foreign trade to develop in colonial areas. Above all, Fry maintains that the policies of imperialism often put the United States at cross-purposes with the current of nationalism, which would become the dominant international force in the twentieth century.

At the outset of the new century some optimistic Americans boasted that the next one hundred years would be a period of world leadership for their country. The beginning of World War I in August 1914 offered the United States the opportunity to exert increasing influence in international affairs. As the leading neutral, America could tip the balance between the evenly matched Allied and Central powers. MELVIN SMALL explores both the practical and idealistic reasons that caused President Wilson to lead the nation into war in 1917. The decision to intervene marked what Daniel Smith has called a "Great Departure" in American diplomacy. It reversed a century-long effort by the nation's leaders to remain largely aloof from European problems and conflicts. To mobilize the country for such a radical break with tradition, Wilson characterized the war effort in the most idealistic terms. He succeeded in bringing American power to bear on the western front at an early date and ensured the German defeat which came in November 1918. He also raised hopes and expectations that were difficult to realize at the Paris Peace Conference. WILLIAM C. WIDENOR focuses on the Versailles treaty of 1919, which he maintains proved disappointing for all the major powers involved. It was based on idealistic objectives that were simply unattainable amid the bitterness and chaos of postwar Europe. Wilson came away from the peace conference in an optimistic mood because he believed that his League of Nations could rectify many of the injustices that had crept into the treaty. His design for world peace remains a hotly disputed issue. Historians continue to debate the merits of his League and the "what ifs" regarding Senate ratification of the Treaty of Versailles and U.S. participation in the international organization.

The defeat of the treaty by the Senate in 1919–20 marked still another shift in American diplomacy. America would attempt to remain aloof from European affairs, but policymakers could not ignore the fact that the United States had become the leading creditor nation. JOHN M. CARROLL examines how Republican administrations during the 1920s tried to bridge this gap between isolationism and activism in world affairs by emphasizing economic diplomacy and disarmament. Their hope was that general prosperity and stability, orchestrated through American leadership, would bring lasting peace. These hopes were dashed by the paralyzing effects that the Great Depression had on the victors of World War I. JANE KAROLINE VIETH explores why the 1930s were a decade characterized by an intense mood of isolationism in the United States. She maintains that even a staunch Wilsonian such as Franklin D. Roosevelt seldom attempted to buck the prevailing currents of the depression years. Only the threat posed by the Axis powers allowed Roosevelt to move the nation toward war in 1940–41 to protect America's vital interests.

JONATHAN G. UTLEY traces the complex chain of events resulting in the Japanese attack on Pearl Harbor in December 1941, which swept away American isolationism and allied the nation with Britain and the Soviet Union against the Axis. This strange alliance between Communist Russia and the two capitalist powers was strained from the start, but it held together because of the mutual objective of defeating Nazi Germany. ROBERT L. MESSER views the origins of the Cold War as an outgrowth of the wartime tension between the Soviet Union and the United States. During the war it became clear that Roosevelt and Russian dictator Joseph Stalin were the senior partners in the alliance. Both leaders were content to postpone the discussion of difficult postwar problems in order to preserve a united front against the Axis. Roosevelt, who did not reveal his postwar plans, even to his closest aides, believed that he could successfully negotiate with Stalin after the war was over. His untimely death in April 1945 bequeathed to Harry S. Truman, who had not been kept well informed by Roosevelt, the awesome task of ending the war and negotiating a peace settlement. At the Yalta and Potsdam summit meetings and subsequent postwar conferences, it became evident that a wide gulf separated the British and Americans from the Soviets on a number of important issues, including the political future of eastern Europe.

Not long after the end of the Second World War, U.S. and Western relations with the Soviet Union deteriorated rapidly, giving rise to what historians have termed the Cold War. As early as 1946 former British prime minister Winston Churchill described Europe as divided by an Iron Curtain which separated the free nations in the West from the captive peoples in the Communist-controlled East. Historians have vigorously debated the reasons for the outbreak of the Cold War. Some have traced the origins of the conflict to the long-standing ideological tension between the two powers and the political collapse of Europe in the wake of World War II. Others, such as Messer, have focused on the decisions made by wartime and postwar leaders in confronting the problems of negotiating a lasting peace.

After an uneasy period of adjustment following World War II, the United States and the USSR became implacable enemies. The main area of confrontation was in Europe, where both nations had recently cooperated in the military victory over Nazi Germany. MARK H. LYTLE traces the development of the Cold War in Europe and the origin and application of America's policy of containment of the Soviet Union. He carefully analyzes policies and events on both sides of the Iron Curtain from 1945 through 1963. The Cold War, however, was not confined to Europe; it spread rapidly in the post-World War II decade to other continents, most notably Asia. MARC GALLICCHIO examines the background of U.S. involvement in East Asia, with special emphasis on the tensions that added to Cold War hostilities. Following the Communist takeover of China in 1949 and the outbreak of the Korean War the next year, the United States mobilized its resources to contain communism on a world-wide basis. As Gallicchio notes, American policymakers often assumed that nations that were pro-Marxist, or simply unfriendly to the interests and aspirations of the United States, were part of a Soviet-led Communist effort to overthrow capitalism.

During the past quarter century the United States has been forced to reevaluate the extent to which its diplomatic, economic, and military power can influence and shape world events. At the height of the Cold War, American leaders assumed that the nation could and must pay any price to oppose international communism. Since that time they have begun to question the axiom that all pro-Marxist or unfriendly nations pose a threat to vital U.S. interests. The Vietnam War, America's longest and in some ways most tragic conflict, demonstrated the limits of its power. GEORGE C. HERRING focuses on the origins of the U.S. involvement in Vietnam, why we gradually took over, and the consequences of the American war effort. He maintains that for more than a decade the nation fought to defeat a Communist-led nationalist movement in Southeast Asia. The protracted conflict resulted in divisiveness at home and a diminution of U.S. power and prestige abroad.

One lesson of the Vietnam War was that the world is not divided into two camps headed by the Soviet Union and the United States. A third camp, or "Third World," of intensely nationalistic and neutralist-oriented nations has emerged since World War II. This phenomenon was apparent long before Vietnam, but that conflict dramatized the importance of the Third World for many Americans. In Latin America, Africa, the Middle East, and Asia, Third World nations, some rich and some poor, exerted an increasing influence on global affairs. The United States has been challenged to adjust its foreign policy to accommodate this sweeping change in international power relationships since 1945. LESTER D. LANGLEY and JAMES W. HARPER analyze American foreign policy in these Third World regions and maintain that the United States will face even more difficult problems and challenges in the near future.

Almost from the beginning of the Cold War the global confrontation between the United States and the Soviet Union became infinitely more dangerous when both powers developed effective atomic weapons. By 1949, when the USSR exploded its first atomic bomb, the superpowers possessed weapons with awesome destructive force. From the early 1950s until the late 1980s, Washington and Moscow engaged in a frantic nuclear arms race that made global destruction a real possibility. WALTER L. HIXSON traces the evolution of U.S. nuclear policy and its role in the fall of Soviet-style communism in Russia and Eastern Europe by the last decade of this century. He warns, however, that the end of the Cold War has not resolved the nuclear arms race and that current leaders face that challenge.

American foreign policy in the twentieth century has undergone great changes that seem to be accelerating as the century progresses. The nation has achieved important successes in world affairs and also has experienced failures. It has gone from the position of relative novice in international politics to world leader. There is no turning back to the tranquil period of American isolationism of the nineteenth century. The searching question is how America will use its energy and resources to confront the difficult international problems that will challenge the nation in the future.

In Search of an Orderly World:
U.S. Imperialism, 1898–1912

Joseph A. Fry

In 1900, Theodore Roosevelt responded to the critics of American efforts to subdue the Filipino insurgents by asserting that "every argument that can be made for the Filipinos could be made for the Apaches; every word that can be said for Aguinaldo could be said for Sitting Bull. As peace, order and prosperity followed our expansion over the lands of the Indians, so they will follow us in the Philippines." Roosevelt's assumptions of racial, cultural, and institutional superiority; his belief in American mission; his consciousness of economic considerations; and especially his conviction that order and stability were prerequisites for advancing and protecting U.S. interests abroad all typified the thinking that underpinned the nation's imperial policies from 1898 through 1912.

Not all of Roosevelt's countrymen shared his enthusiasm for imperialism. Writing five years later, Moorfield Storey, president of the Anti-Imperialist League, incorrectly declared that "the wave of imperialism which reached this country in 1898 and for a while threatened to drown our people's faith in the great principles of free government has spent its force." Storey equated imperialism with the formal annexation of noncontiguous lands abroad, and this definition has allowed some historians to portray America's end-of-the-century territorial grab as an "accident" or a "great aberration," uncharacteristic of prior and subsequent national behavior. To be sure, the annexation of Guam, Hawaii, the Philippines, and Puerto Rico was unprecedented. Never before had the United States annexed territory located beyond the North American continent, and until this time Americans had proclaimed that newly acquired lands would eventually become states and their inhabitants citizens.

Only by subscribing to this narrow definition of imperialism and ignoring the aggressive, expansionist nature of previous American actions can one characterize late-nineteenth-century expansion as an "aberration." Imperialism may more properly be defined as a relationship in which a stronger nation controls, or consciously attempts to control, the actions of a weaker country or group of people. This control may be formal (via annexations, protectorates, or military occupations) or informal (via economic control, cultural domination, or threat of intervention). The informal species of empire might involve businessmen, missionaries, and other nonstate actors. Viewed from this perspective, the nation's subjugation of Native Americans and their treatment as subjects rather than citizens, the bullying of Mexico in the 1840s, and the evolving cultural and economic domination of Hawaii after 1820 provide compelling examples of earlier imperial actions. Similarly, subsequent U.S. economic domination of Cuba and the Philippines, efforts at cultural transformation in these countries and China, and hegemony over the Caribbean region dispelled Storey's hope that U.S. imperialism was flagging by 1905.

American imperialism from 1898 through 1912 found its bases in diverse intellectual, economic, and strategic concerns. From the time John Winthrop pronounced the Massachusetts Bay Colony a "Citty upon a Hill," Americans were convinced of their mission to mankind. The late-nineteenth- and early-twentieth-century sense of mission embodied a conviction of racial and institutional superiority. Americans, like many western Europeans, perceived a yawning gap between themselves (the "Anglo-Saxons") and the peoples of Africa, Asia, and Latin America (the "barbarians"). Anglo-Saxonism received apparent scientific support from Social Darwinism, which emphasized the "survival of the fittest" and suggested that the United States had been climbing the evolutionary ladder more rapidly than less-developed competitors. Accompanying this conviction of superiority was at least a verbal sense of obligation. According to William Jennings Bryan, the "advanced nations" were bound to put forth "conscious and constant effort for the promotion of the welfare of the nations which lag behind." How, asked Henry Demarest Lloyd, could America "progress from perfection to perfection while [the] Chinese ossified, and the Cubans and Philippine people were disemboweled, and the Africans continued to eat each other?"

Others added a coercive dimension to this "duty." Professor John W. Burgess argued that there was "no human right to the status of barbarism"; uncivilized peoples who failed to cooperate would face compulsion, expulsion, or even extermination. While many contemporary Americans opposed wars among Western, "civilized" nations, they found the use of force on weaker, "uncivilized" countries quite acceptable. In fact, the latter was necessary both to preserve peace and to lay the basis for progress. "In the long run," declared Roosevelt, "civilized man finds he can keep the peace only by subduing his barbarian neighbor." Moreover, he continued, "the most ultimately righteous of all wars is war with savages" since it cleared the path for enlightened progress.

Economic considerations reinforced these notions of mission. During the depression of the 1890s, Americans increasingly attributed the nation's economic problems and social tensions to the overproduction of manufactured and agricultural goods. The key to disposing of this "glut" and ensuring domestic prosperity and order was an enlarged export trade. In 1893, the first year of the depression, the *New York Tribune* characteristically declared: "Today we produce of manufactures more than any two nations of Europe; of agriculture more than any three, and of minerals more than all together. The necessity for new markets is now upon us." Economic expansionists called for a variety of measures to capture world markets: an enlarged navy and merchant marine, island coaling stations, an isthmian canal, government aid for American businessmen, and overseas colonies. Expansionists emphasized that commerce coincided nicely with America's larger mission to mankind. As Albert Beveridge told the National Association of Manufacturers in 1908, every ship carried "American ideas and American ideals, more tangibly than all the speeches that were ever made."

Strategic concerns provided further impetus to U.S. imperialism. When Americans looked abroad in the 1890s, they saw the European states constructing empires throughout Asia and Africa; they saw a "world of empires." Some policymakers believed that to behave as a Great Power the United States needed to emulate the Europeans. Apprehension over the nation's economic and security interests led others to favor a preclusive or preemptive imperialism aimed at seizing the initiative from the Europeans. This was especially true in the Caribbean, where Americans had long been suspicious of British intentions and by the 1890s had come to see Germany as a threatening competitor. Few U.S. policymakers feared the establishment of an outright European colony in the Caribbean; however, the region's chronic financial and political instability provided European nations with the opportunity to encroach upon the independence of smaller nations, while ostensibly protecting property or collecting debts. America's minister to Cuba observed characteristically in 1904 that "the German government never loses an opportunity to impress itself on every community, whether economically or politically." Roosevelt spoke for a generation of U.S. civilian and military leaders when he agonized over the kaiser's possible attempt "to seize some Venezuelan harbor and turn it into a strongly fortified place of arms, . . . with a view to exercising some measure of control over the future of the Isthmian Canal, and over South American affairs generally." Although Americans found no comparable interests in East Asia prior to 1899, U.S. leaders feared being denied access to the fabled but chimerical "China Market"; and, after acquiring the Philippines, they were continually troubled by the strategic vulnerability of the archipelago.

The pursuit of these interlocking ideological, economic, and strategic objectives produced the central characteristic of U.S. imperial policy during the 1898–1912 period: the desire for an orderly and stable world. Policymakers deemed order and stability essential to transplanting American institutions successfully in "uncivilized" areas. Moreover, U.S. policy assumed a circular rationale as American leaders persistently defined the most acceptable "order" as one in which the nation's institutions were being recreated. Economic expansion seemed to require similar conditions. Buoyed by the nation's burgeoning economic strength, Americans were confident of great commercial gains if the country were free to trade and invest in a peaceful, preferably capitalist, setting. Instability not only interrupted trade but also offered the occasion for European colonial powers to seize new colonies or restrict access to old ones. More important, disorder and financial insolvency provided the excuse for European intervention in the strategically vital Caribbean region. Reinforcing the direct linkage of these contemporary interests and assumptions to the search for order and stability was the nation's long-standing aversion to revolution with its "twin . . . bugaboos—violence and radicalism." American leaders objected to the use of violence as a vehicle for political change but failed to recognize that in many societies opposition groups had no other way to gain power. Americans had similar difficulty in empathizing with poorer countries and the violent social change that often shredded these deprived and stratified cultures. Still, as the 1898–1912 period demonstrates, these leaders occasionally tolerated and even encouraged revolutions—but only revolutions they felt able to control or perceived as requisite to achieving subsequent order.

Ironically, the American pursuit of order invariably proved disruptive and destabilizing; a stark incongruity developed between imperial objectives and results. Remaking weaker nations in the U.S. image required the wrenching displacement of indigenous cultures and institutions. This process was especially true when the United States coerced weaker countries into accepting its ideas of order and progress. Economic expansion often led to conflict with imperial rivals or produced explosive economic and social conditions in the exploited countries. Finally, the U.S. imperial presence, whether it was based on strategic, economic, or ideological considerations, helped to stimulate the revolutionary force of anti-imperial nationalism in colonial countries.

The Spanish-American War of 1898 brought the nation's imperial inclinations to the fore. The Cuban rebellion against Spanish rule had begun in 1895, with both sides pursuing strategies that destroyed crops and left thousands of Cubans dead of disease and starvation. The fighting not only devastated the island's economy and society, but it also impinged directly upon American interests and humanitarian sensibilities. The revolt jeopardized more than $50 million of American investments in Cuba, reduced Cuban exports to the United States from $79 million in 1892 to $15 million in 1898, led to the harassment and imprisonment of U.S. citizens, raised the prospect of European interference in the Western Hemisphere, and stirred the nation's concern for the Cuban people.

The quest for an expeditious end to what Secretary of State Richard Olney termed the "anarchy, lawlessness and terrorism" in Cuba guided the official U.S. response to the rebellion. President Grover Cleveland and Olney believed that this could best be achieved under continued Spanish sovereignty. Dismissing the Cubans as incapable of self-government, Olney feared that a "war of races" would follow Spanish withdrawal. In 1896 he indicated that the United States stood ready to support Spain in a policy combining force and reform in a mixture that offered the "most potential for the termination of hostilities and the restoration of peace and order to the island." Despite this American support for continued Spanish sovereignty and vigorous enforcement of neutrality laws aimed at blocking Cuban expeditions launched from the United States, Spain failed to quell the rebellion, which raged on past William McKinley's inauguration in March 1897.

Elected on an expansionist platform, the new Republican president favored the annexation of Hawaii, construction of an isthmian canal, a stronger navy, and the establishment of "American supremacy in world markets." Like his predecessor, McKinley deemed prolonged instability in Cuba intolerable, and he entered office with a definite policy: if Spain failed to restore order, then the United States would be forced to intervene. From his first note to Madrid in June 1897, McKinley's demands for rapid pacification of the island carried the implied threat of U.S. intervention, and his decision for war one year later followed logically from this policy.

Early 1898 brought clear evidence of Spain's inability to stop the fighting. Mobs rioted in Havana against Spanish autonomy proposals, the *New York Journal* published the letter of the Spanish minister to Washington revealing his country's insincerity in talks with the United States, and the battleship *Maine* exploded and sank in Havana harbor. Reports from Cuba of potential social revolution increased apprehensions in Washington. Cuba Libre included not only the drive for national independence but also the clamor for redress by the politically and economically dispossessed. In November 1897, U.S. consul Fitzhugh Lee had informed the State Department that continued fighting could lead to "a revolution within a revolution." Against this backdrop of unacceptable disorder, McKinley demanded an armistice, the right to mediate the conflict, and Cuban independence. When Spain rejected these demands, war ensued. In calling for a declaration of war, the president based his decision squarely on the aforementioned U.S. interests; he would employ American forces to end the hostilities in Cuba and "to secure in the island the establishment of a stable government, capable of maintaining order and observing its international obligations, insuring peace and tranquility and the security of its citizens as well as our own." Lasting barely four months, the "splendid little war" ended in early August 1898, with the United States in possession of the Philippines and Puerto Rico. (Hawaii had been annexed in July, and Guam would be acquired later.)

Subsequent American actions in Cuba and the Philippines provide case studies of the workings of U.S. imperialism. In declaring war upon Spain, Congress had passed the Teller Amendment, which renounced any intention of annexing Cuba. As Whitelaw Reid wrote to McKinley, there was a critical inconsistency in going to war to restore order in Cuba and simultaneously disclaiming any right of "sovereignty, jurisdiction, and control." To expel Spain and not establish U.S. authority would lead to another unstable "Hayti nearer our own coast." An American withdrawal, according to one correspondent, would "give [Cuba] over to a reign of terror—to the machete and the torch, to insurrection and assassination." McKinley agreed; and, according to historian Louis A. Pérez, his policies transformed a "Cuban war of liberation into a U.S. war of conquest." American generals ignored Cuban commanders, and the United States refused to recognize the insurgents as an independent government or to include them in peace negotiations with the Spanish. At the war's end, U.S. troops remained in Cuba, and in December 1898 the president affirmed that the military occupation would continue until there was "complete tranquility in the island and a stable government."

McKinley and his secretary of war, Elihu Root, resolved the dilemma of control under the Teller Amendment by making Cuba an American protectorate. Prompted by Root, Senator Orville Platt of Connecticut offered an amendment to the Army Appropriations Bill of 1901. This amendment authorized the withdrawal of U.S. soldiers after Cuba had agreed to make no other financial or political agreements compromising its independence, to sell or lease naval bases to the United States, and to accept future U.S. intervention in its affairs. Under heavy American pressure, Cuba wrote the Platt Amendment into its constitution in 1901 and subsequently signed a treaty with Washington in 1903 embodying its terms. General Leonard Wood, the U.S. military commander in Cuba from 1899 to 1902, succinctly observed that the island retained "little or no independence." Although the American army departed in 1903, the marines returned in 1906, 1912, and 1917; and over the first half of the century no government in Havana survived without U.S. approval. Rather than ensuring stability, this foreboding presence actually prompted Cuban politicians to act on the probability of American intrusion and often to invite it.

Just as these intermittent military interventions starkly dramatized the American desire for order in Cuba, the occupation policy from 1899 to 1903 revealed similar objectives. In reform measures akin to the Progressive Movement under way in the United States, General Wood sought to remake Cuba in America's image by constructing a stable, middle-class, business-oriented society that would attract additional U.S. investors. He instituted a new school system, a revised legal code, a revamped structure for municipal governments, and extensive sanitary and public works projects. Few of these reforms yielded salutary results. Cuban students showed little interest in American textbooks that had been translated into Spanish with no regard for the island's history or culture. Habeas corpus and jury trials found no place in the Spanish legal tradition, and the practice of smashing down doors and publicly whipping people to enforce sanitation measures generated little enthusiasm.

Wood's desire for continuing U.S. economic control proved more enduring. In 1903, President Roosevelt complemented the Platt Amendment with a reciprocity treaty that gave U.S. goods a substantial tariff preference in Cuba and funneled its sugar exports to the United States. Over the ensuing twenty years, U.S. investments in Cuban sugar rose from $50 million to $600 million, and American companies came to dominate the island's public utilities, port facilities, and industries. This economic dominance contributed directly to Cuba's overdependence on sugar and to the growth of a large plantation system manned by hordes of impoverished and discontented workers. With control over virtually all sectors of the economy came a highly visible and privileged North American presence in the form of civic and social clubs, newspapers, magazines, missionaries, and tourists. Cubans were hostile and resentful. As early as 1910 a traveler observed that when facing "the sober reality of American domination," Cubans feared that they had simply "made an exchange of masters. . . . It is America who is the enemy, in the mind of the average Cuban."

In the Philippines, no restrictive legislation such as the Teller Amendment hindered McKinley, and his decision to annex the archipelago embodied the various motives behind American imperialism. He judged that returning the islands to Spain would have been "cowardly and dishonorable." Since they were located so close to the enticing China Market, abandoning them to "France or Germany—our commercial rivals in the Orient," would have been "bad business." McKinley also feared that casting adrift any portion of the islands would have created a "golden apple of [international] discord" and set off a scramble leading to war. Both his concern for order and stability and his low regard for the Filipino people further convinced him that they could not be left to themselves; they were "unfit for self-government" and would soon degenerate into "anarchy and misrule." The only alternative was to take all the islands and to "educate the Filipinos, and uplift and civilize and Christianize them."

When Emilio Aguinaldo and his followers proved none too eager to become "civilized," the U.S. quest for order and stability in the islands produced horrifyingly contradictory results. Fighting between the Filipino nationalists and American occupation troops began in February 1899, and three and one-half years of bloody guerrilla warfare followed. In a frank admission of American objectives, General William Shafter told correspondents that it was necessary to kill the guerrillas so that "the remaining half of the population could be advanced to a higher plane of life." Following this dictum, U.S. soldiers tortured and killed captured Filipinos, herded civilians into concentration camps, burned crops, and slaughtered animals. The costs were staggering: 4,200 American lives lost and an expenditure of more than $400 million, 18,000 Filipino battle casualties, at least 100,000 others dead from disease and starvation, and general devastation of land and crops. It is difficult to imagine that any disorder accompanying Philippine independence could have been so costly.

The rebellion having been quelled, U.S. officials and missionaries undertook a reform program even more ambitious than the one attempted in Cuba. The results by 1913 were equally disappointing. Thousands of new schools and teachers failed to raise the literacy rate. In their average attendance of two years, few Filipino children benefited from a curriculum that fluctuated between that of a Massachusetts elementary school and the contemporary industrial training for American blacks. Transplanted political institutions also floundered when restructured municipal and provincial governments and a new national assembly offered a forum for anti-American sentiments but failed to alter previous patterns of corruption and elite rule. Economic measures were on the whole detrimental and unsettling when miles of new roads and extensive harbor improvements did little to relieve the pervasive poverty. The 1909 U.S. tariff ultimately tied the Philippines to the American economy, promoted large landholdings and overreliance on commercial crops, and helped fuel chronic agrarian unrest among landless rural workers. Acting closely with U.S. officials, Protestant missionaries approved of the war to suppress the insurgents and endorsed and aided the government's campaign for cultural change. Often the most aggressive champions of order and stability, these missionaries frequently criticized the government for being insufficiently aggressive militarily or for making too many political concessions to Filipino nationalists. Despite these comprehensive and vigorous efforts, still another "experiment in self-duplication" proved futile, leaving primarily economic domination and resentment of U.S. control.

Even as the United States was annexing and pacifying the Philippines, the China Market appeared to be in jeopardy. The McKinley administration had watched anxiously in late 1897 and early 1898 as France, Germany, Great Britain, Japan, and Russia forced a weak and vulnerable China to grant them spheres of influence and leaseholds within its territory. If these countries were to obstruct U.S. trade within their areas of control, the value of the Philippines as an "American Hong Kong" would be negligible. To avoid this possibility, Secretary of State John Hay dispatched his first Open Door Note in September 1899. He called upon the European countries and Japan to treat all trading nations equally with regard to tariff rates and transportation facilities in their areas of influence.

EXECUTION. The American military hangs Filipino rebels in the early 1900s. (National Archives)

The ambiguous European responses to Hay's note were hardly reassuring, and McKinley and his secretary of state soon had reason to be even more apprehensive over the fate of both American commerce and East Asian stability. In June 1900 the Boxers, a secret society devoted to ridding China of foreign domination, besieged the diplomatic compound in Peking. McKinley readily joined with the European powers in sending an expeditionary force to restore order. The president sought not only to protect endangered American diplomats and businessmen but also to prevent the European powers from utilizing their armies to secure further commercial or strategic advantages. Hay's closest adviser, William Rockhill, typified administration thinking when he pronounced East Asian stability essential to American economic interests and expressed concern that China's complete collapse might even produce the ultimate instability: a war among the rapacious, imperial rivals.

This combination of fears prompted Hay to send his second Open Door Note on July 3, 1900, in which he urged the preservation of "Chinese territorial and administrative entity" and the safeguarding of "equal and impartial trade with all parts of the Chinese Empire." Aware that the United States lacked the power to restrain the European nations, Hay hoped that a clear statement of policy might moderate their actions. When the precariously balanced European rivalry in China prevented a division of the country, Americans renewed their vision of potentially great economic gains.

With McKinley's assassination in September 1901, Theodore Roosevelt assumed the management of the nation's evolving imperial interests. The very embodiment of U.S. imperialism, the Rough Rider had enthusiastically endorsed McKinley's more assertive policies. Once in office he carried these policies to their logical conclusion in the Caribbean; however, he located no interests worthy of comparable effort in East Asia.

Carefully balancing foreign policy objectives against the power available to achieve them, Roosevelt pursued a restrained East Asian policy. Demanding the Open Door for American trade and investment in Manchuria (the Chinese province of greatest commercial interest) or actively supporting Chinese territorial integrity would have necessitated confronting Japan. As he later advised William Howard Taft, the Japanese had vital interests in Korea and Manchuria; the United States did not. The Open Door was an "excellent thing, . . . so far as it could be maintained by general diplomatic agreement"; but Manchuria's history demonstrated that the " 'open

door' policy . . . completely disappears as soon as a powerful nation determines to disregard it, and is willing to run the risk of
war." The president equated Japan's "paramount interest in what
surrounds the Yellow Sea" with U.S. domination of the Caribbean,
and he was willing to grant the Japanese a comparable police power

VOL. XLVII   *New York, Saturday, November 21, 1903*   NO. 2448

"HELD UP THE WRONG MAN." President Theodore Roosevelt deals with
Colombia on the canal issue. (*Harper's Weekly*, 1903, Library of Congress)

as long as they showed "no more desire for conquest of the weak than we had shown ourselves in Cuba." For Roosevelt, an orderly and stable relationship with Japan outweighed the prospect of persistently elusive economic gains in China.

When he turned to the Caribbean, Roosevelt exercised no such restraint; he believed that both American interests and power warranted vigorous action. His acquisition of the Panama Canal route provides a vivid illustration of both this vigor and the often disruptive effect of his quest for order. By 1900, Roosevelt and the nation considered an isthmian canal essential. Reducing the sailing time between the two coasts by one third would enhance the power of the navy and facilitate commercial access to the new island empire, to the west coast of South America, and to the beckoning Asian market. After securing British agreement to exclusive American control and fortification of a canal, Roosevelt settled on the Panama route as superior to an alternate one through Nicaragua.

To Roosevelt's disgust, Colombia balked at granting a right-of-way through its northernmost province. After threatening to negotiate with Nicaragua, Secretary of State Hay wrung a treaty from the Colombian chargé to Washington, Tomás Herrán. Signed in January 1903, the Hay-Herrán Treaty granted the United States sovereign control over a six-mile-wide zone for ninety-nine years. In return, Colombia was to receive $10 million and rent payments of $250,000 per year. Eager to "make the dirt fly," Roosevelt became irate when Colombia rejected the treaty, demanding an additional $5 million from the United States and $10 million from the French-owned New Panama Canal Company. After fulminating privately that the "foolish and homicidal corruptionists in Bogotá" could not "be allowed permanently to bar one of the future highways of civilization," he publicly reiterated the persistent imperial linkage of U.S. interests and international order and stability: "The Government of Colombia, although wholly unable to maintain order on the Isthmus, has nevertheless declined to ratify a treaty . . . which opened the only chance to secure its own stability and to guarantee permanent peace on, and construction of a canal across, the Isthmus."

Even though Colombia had simply exercised its right as an independent nation, Roosevelt seriously considered forceful intervention to seize the coveted passage. This step proved unnecessary when a most opportune revolution occurred in Panama against Colombian rule. Prior to the bloodless coup of November 3, 1903,

Philippe Bunau-Varilla, a French engineer with interests in the New Panama Canal Company and contacts with the Panamanian conspirators, had talked with Roosevelt and several members of the State Department. In each of these conversations, he received the unmistakable impression that the United States would aid the revolution. Roosevelt made no explicit guarantees, but he later admitted that Bunau-Varilla "would have been a very dull man had he been unable to make such a guess." Indeed, an American battleship arrived promptly on November 2, ostensibly to discourage European intervention but actually to prevent Colombia from suppressing the rebellion. Roosevelt justified this action on the basis of an 1846 treaty with Bogotá in which the United States had pledged to uphold, rather than destroy, Colombian sovereignty on the isthmus. When the president asked his cabinet about the effectiveness of this defense, Secretary of War Root responded incisively: "You have shown that you were accused of seduction and you have conclusively proved that you were guilty of rape."

Roosevelt's support for this revolution was a momentary and calculated deviation from his pursuit of order and stability in the Caribbean. Acting with unseemly haste, he recognized the new Panamanian government on November 6 and put Secretary of State Hay to work on a new canal treaty. The product (later characterized as "The Treaty that No Panamanian Signed") was negotiated with Bunau-Varilla and placed Panama alongside Cuba as a U.S. protectorate. For the same payments that originally were offered to Colombia, the United States received a zone ten miles wide (up from six) to administer as if "it were the sovereign." The new lease was to run in perpetuity and included the right to use any rivers, bodies of water, or land outside the Canal Zone that were necessary to the canal's construction. Taft correctly observed that the treaty empowered the United States "to prevent revolutions" in this "Opera Bouffe republic." With this goal in mind, Roosevelt promptly shored up the white-dominated Conservative party's rule and dismantled the Panamanian army. Henceforth, both domestic politics and external security were dependent on decisions made in Washington. Once again, however, this policy hardly guaranteed stability. Panamanian opposition to U.S. sovereignty arose immediately and continued unabated into the 1970s.

"The inevitable effect of our building the canal," Secretary Root asserted, "must be to require us to police the surrounding premises. In the nature of things, trade and control, and the obligation to keep order which go with them, must come our way." Roosevelt agreed; disorder disrupted trade, interrupted America's civilizing mission, and invited European intervention. While still vice president, he had thought it necessary periodically to "spank" unruly Caribbean nations, and in October 1902 the U.S. Navy established a Caribbean squadron charged with enforcing political order. Referring to Venezuela in 1901, one naval officer expressed a general American perception. Diplomacy, he said, had little impact on "the semi-enlightened and uncultivated members of the present administration . . . but they can appreciate the potential presence of a squadron of battleships."

It was the threatening presence of European battleships in Venezuelan waters that strengthened Roosevelt's resolve to impose order on the Caribbean. The Venezuelan dictator, Cipriano Castro, had provoked a combined British-German-Italian blockade and occupation in December 1902 by refusing either to pay or to arbitrate debts owed these nations. While Roosevelt cared nothing for Castro, whom he dismissed as an "unspeakably villainous little monkey," he feared that the Germans would use the incident or similar ones to establish a permanent presence in the Western Hemisphere. To preclude this possibility, the president pointedly warned the kaiser against attempting to annex territory in the Caribbean and dispatched a fleet to the region as an even more tangible deterrent. The Venezuelan crisis was arbitrated in February 1903, but Roosevelt remained apprehensive.

His apprehension intensified as he watched the Dominican Republic "drifting into chaos." Plagued by chronic financial and political difficulties, the country had incurred millions of dollars in debts to both European and American creditors. Roosevelt was reluctant to allow Germany or Great Britain "to act as the policeman of the Caribbean." However, he confided to Root that "if we intend to say 'Hands off' to the powers of Europe, then sooner or later we must keep order ourselves." He put his solution before Congress in December 1904 in what came to be known as the Roosevelt Corollary to the Monroe Doctrine: "chronic wrongdoing" in the Americas could "require intervention by some civilized nation," and adherence to the Monroe Doctrine could force the United States "in flagrant cases of such wrongdoing or impotence" to serve as an "international police power."

Armed with this rationale, he pressured the Dominicans into accepting American loans and permitting the United States to administer its customs system, giving 45 percent of the receipts to the Dominican government and the remainder to its creditors. When the U.S. Senate rejected a treaty embodying this arrangement, Roosevelt ignored the legislators and implemented the plan through an executive agreement. Secretary of War Root reinforced American domination of the country and clearly foreshadowed subsequent attempts to fasten a sterile status quo on Latin America when he assigned U.S. military officers to train a rural police force. Having combined these measures with the presence of the U.S. Navy, Roosevelt announced in December 1905 that "all revolutionary movement" had been "completely discouraged" and that "stability and order and all the benefits of peace" were "at last coming to Santo Domingo."

The imposition of order and stability on the tumultuous Caribbean region also constituted one of the central goals of Roosevelt's handpicked successor, William Howard Taft. Genial and well intentioned, the corpulent Taft had helped to oversee the growth of the American empire while serving as governor of the Philippines and as secretary of war, but he lacked Roosevelt's grasp of, and inclination to dominate, his administration's foreign policy. As a result, Secretary of State Philander C. Knox played a prominent role.

Taft termed the policy that resulted from this collaboration "dollar diplomacy." Acutely aware of the nation's ever-expanding industrial production, he unabashedly declared "that the Government of the United States shall extend all proper support to every legitimate and beneficial enterprise abroad." While he gave greater emphasis to the economic aspects of American imperialism than either McKinley or Roosevelt had done, the quest for order and stability remained central. Taft explained that he preferred to substitute dollars for bullets, and Knox elaborated concerning the Caribbean: "True stability is best established not by military, but by economic and social forces. . . . The problem of good government is inextricably interwoven with that of economic prosperity and sound finance; financial stability contributes perhaps more than any one factor to political stability."

Both Taft and Knox would have preferred "some formal right" such as the Platt Amendment "to compel peace" by knocking Central American "heads together"; failing that, they turned to Roosevelt's Dominican formula and ultimately to military intervention. While the Taft administration meddled in Mexico, El Salvador, and Honduras, its most ambitious attempt at stabilizing Caribbean affairs centered on Nicaragua and that country's aggressive dictator, José Santos Zelaya. Disparaged by Knox as a "blot upon the history of Nicaragua," Zelaya had long aspired to unite Central America, had attacked Honduras militarily in 1907, and thereafter had fomented unrest in El Salvador and Costa Rica. He had further aroused American ire by canceling concessions held by U.S. citizens and by soliciting financial support in Japan and Europe. In May 1909 he concluded a disturbing financial agreement with a European syndicate, which refinanced Nicaragua's national debt and provided for the creditors to control the country's customs receipts in case of default. Zelaya manifested his fierce nationalism and overt defiance in the boast: "I ridicule the United States, laugh at Germany, and spit on England."

When a revolution, partially inspired by American firms, challenged Zelaya's rule in October 1909, Taft and Knox seized the opportunity to expel the independent and troublesome Nicaraguan. As Roosevelt had done in Panama, these U.S. leaders welcomed a revolution which they felt capable of controlling and which they perceived as a necessary interim step toward stability. Zelaya's removal from power was deemed indispensable to order, even if it entailed temporary disorder. The execution of two captured Americans who had been fighting with the revolutionaries provided the pretext for intervention. Knox accused Zelaya of personally ordering the killings and declared that the revolution represented the will of the majority of Nicaraguans. After Knox implicitly recognized Juan J. Estrada, the rebellion's leader, Zelaya perceived the futility of further resistance to U.S. power and fled to Mexico. However, Zelaya's departure did not bring stability. Washington refused to accept his successor, José Madriz, contending that he was a Zelaya puppet, and the fighting continued. American intervention became even more direct the following May when U.S. Navy vessels and marines çordoned off the port city of Bluefields to protect Estrada's forces. After regrouping behind American defenses, Estrada gained tenuous control of the country in August 1910.

The Taft administration promptly moved to apply dollar diplomacy. In return for diplomatic recognition, Washington demanded that Estrada request a loan guaranteed by Nicaragua's customs receipts and appoint customs officers approved by the United States. Estrada reluctantly consented, but, before the treaty was signed in

May 1911, he was replaced as president by Adolfo Díaz, formerly the bookkeeper of an American mining company. All of Taft's efforts went for naught when the U.S. Senate rejected the treaty and the application of the Dominican formula to Nicaragua.

Unable to make Nicaragua a protectorate, as had been done with Cuba, Panama, and the Dominican Republic, Taft and Knox persuaded American bankers to advance funds, intercede with Nicaragua's European creditors, and administer the customs system. But order and stability remained elusive, and in July 1912 a revolution challenged Díaz's rule. Dollar diplomacy having failed, Taft resorted to force, the ultimate American tactic in the Caribbean. He dispatched 2,600 marines and eight warships, stifled the rebellion, and ensured Díaz's reelection in 1913. As an ongoing symbol of Taft's failure to substitute dollars for bullets, American marines remained in Nicaragua until 1925.

Dollar diplomacy proved no more successful in China. At the time of Taft's election, one wag suggested that TAFT might well have stood for "Take Advice From Theodore." Nothing could have been less descriptive of his East Asian policy. Unlike his predecessor, Taft aggressively sought to enforce the Open Door and to increase American investments and trade in China. Together with Knox and key State Department officials Willard Straight and Francis M. Huntington Wilson, the president also believed that large doses of American capital would contribute to a more stable balance of power by strengthening China and countering growing Japanese influence in Manchuria.

The administration initiated this policy in the summer of 1909 by demanding that American bankers be included in the Hukuang Railway loan. China had concluded an agreement in June with English, French, and German bankers for funds to build this road. After nearly one year of pressuring both the Europeans and the Chinese, Taft obtained reluctant agreement for American involvement. Knox explained this persistence, stating that he envisioned both economic benefits and the "right to proportional representation in the influence which attaches to the holding of the credits of the Chinese government." When internal Chinese opposition blocked the project, Knox succeeded only in exasperating the Europeans.

Undeterred, the secretary of state concocted another scheme, described by a British diplomat as "so vast and fantastic as almost to stagger the imagination." In October 1910, Straight, having left the State Department, negotiated an agreement with China to have an Anglo-American banking group finance a trans-Manchurian railway from Chinchou to Aigun. Hoping that this agreement would furnish the leverage he needed to "smoke Japan out" of the region, Knox called for a multinational syndicate to neutralize or internationalize all Manchurian railways. Most particularly, he sought to wrest the East Manchurian Railway from Russia and the South Manchurian Railway from Japan. If these countries refused to cooperate, he planned to proceed with the Chinchou-Aigun railroad. Japan and Russia responded by agreeing in July 1910 to defend the status quo in Manchuria. Knox's plan garnered only conflict with Russia and Japan, thus driving the two rivals together and prodding them to close the Open Door more tightly. When he reverted to the Chinchou-Aigun route, he found that the Chinese had not ratified the agreement and the British were unwilling to alienate Japan, their primary Asian ally.

In violating his earlier resolve not to "let anything so unimportant as China interfere" with his golf game, Knox made a final attempt to apply the Dominican formula. In September 1910 the Chinese approached American bankers for a loan to finance currency reform and Manchurian development. Knox consented but with the stipulation that an American be made the official financial adviser to China. At the urging of U.S. bankers, who had begun to harbor reservations about the Taft-Knox strategies, Britain, France, and Germany were invited to join the consortium. Each country assented but vetoed an American financial adviser to the Peking government. Combined Japanese-Russian opposition further delayed implementation of the agreement until it fell victim to the revolution that overthrew China's Manchu dynasty in October 1911.

These futile, even counterproductive, policies were ironic since America's exports to China in 1912 amounted to only 1 percent of its overall sales abroad. In reality, the cultural and religious "exports" by Protestant missionaries embodied a more significant U.S. influence. The fifteen years after 1900 have been characterized by historian Michael H. Hunt as the "golden age of the China mission movement"; indeed, by 1912, some 3,100 of America's 3,770 Protestant missionaries were working there. Theodore Roosevelt believed that their efforts helped "to avert revolutionary disturbance in China" and reduced the "chance of a dreadful future clash between two radically different and hostile civilizations" by spreading Western ideas. Other U.S. officials contended that Western education, which increasingly became the missionaries' principal endeavor, would augment Sino-American commerce, counterbalance Japanese influence in the country, and move the Chinese toward orderly reform rather than revolutionary chaos.

Roosevelt and his fellow Americans badly misjudged the Chinese response. Just as Washington's pursuit of political and economic order often resulted in precisely the opposite outcome, the American cultural offensive proved equally disruptive. Viewing the Chinese as malleable children akin to the allegedly inferior Cubans or Filipinos, American missionaries had gone as "conscious agents of change, of radical transformation. They came to Asia *to do something to* Asia and Asians." Their efforts to displace indigenous religion, culture, and social practices elicited complex reactions and consequences. As Mark Twain, one of the harshest critics of the missionaries, warned, "Almost every convert runs a risk of catching our civilization [and] . . . *once civilized, China can never be uncivilized again.*" Western ideas of individualism, democracy, progress, and Christianity helped to undermine the old order; at the same time, missionary condescension, privilege, and intrusion helped to stimulate mounting nationalism and antiforeignism. This combustible mix combined with other resentments to produce the 1911 revolution, which starkly symbolized the failure of dollar diplomacy and missionary influence either to stabilize China or to increase America's trade and investments. The U.S. response was also instructive: Straight worried that a republican government would yield "chaos" and "constant disturbance"; and the Taft administration cast its support to Yuan Shih-k'ai, a military strongman previously described by China expert Rockhill as the "chief influence for order, stability and progress in the government."

As the Taft administration ended, the United States looked back over a decade and a half of intense imperial activity. From Cleveland through Taft, policymakers had translated the nation's economic, ideological, and strategic objectives into the quest for an orderly and stable world. However, these policymakers never seemed to grasp the fact that their actions as often as not caused disruption and instability. Throughout the period a persistent dichotomy had haunted U.S. imperial policy, a dichotomy between the goal of order and stability and the frequent result of disorder and conflict.

Indeed, American policies yielded mixed results. In the Caribbean, the United States had expelled the Spanish, stifled European interventions, increased investments from $100 million in 1902 to $1.5 billion in 1912, and imposed a tenuous peace by curbing the warfare between Central American states and reducing the incidence of revolutions. These accomplishments were accompanied by marked failures. Sanitary measures, new roads and buildings, and reformed customs services did little to relieve the pervasive poverty. Efforts to impose a conservative status quo through training rural guards and crushing revolutions did nothing to further representative governments and more often reinforced tendencies toward autocratic, one-party rule. These economic and political consequences were part of the larger, futile effort to export American institutions to Cuba and the Philippines. The contemptuous and coercive treatment of the Latin Americans ignored their pride and nationalistic aspirations, confused stability with progress, and left a legacy of hatred and distrust. José Vargas-Villa, a well-known Colombian writer, graphically conveyed these sentiments when he referred to "the barbarians of the North," whose imperial policies were "the sport of savages" and the "doctrine of plundering, robbery, and conquest."

East Asian policies were even less successful. The costs of imposing order on the Philippines were appalling and the returns negligible. Neither the acquisition of these islands nor the proclamation of the Open Door policy increased trade with China. In fact, U.S. exports to China actually decreased from $53 million to $24 million between 1905 and 1912. Perceptive statesmen such as Roosevelt recognized that the United States lacked both the power and the interests for a policy comparable to the Caribbean efforts. Others, such as Taft and Knox, failed to understand this, and their attempts to strengthen China and augment American commerce served only to alienate European and Japanese competitors. Cultural intrusion was similarly disruptive. While managing to obtain relatively few converts, American missionaries helped to stimulate the intense antiforeignism so central to China's 1911 revolution. Significantly, the U.S. aversion to revolution and search for an orderly, stable world continued well beyond 1912. This emphasis on a status quo patterned after American institutions helped to place the United States on a collision course with a broad spectrum of twentieth-century nations and forces that found existing conditions unacceptable: modern, developed nations such as Germany or Japan; less-developed, revolutionary nations such as China, Cuba, and Vietnam; Russia, which combined characteristics of both of these categories; and terrorist groups such as those who took Americans hostage in Iran in 1985—in short, a remarkably large segment of the international community.

Sources and Suggested Readings

Beisner, Robert L. *From the Old Diplomacy to the New, 1865–1900*. Arlington Heights, IL, 1986.

Burton, David H. *Theodore Roosevelt: Confident Imperialist*. Philadelphia, 1969.

Challener, Richard D. *Admirals, Generals, and American Foreign Policy, 1898–1914*. Princeton, NJ, 1975.

Collin, Richard H. *Theodore Roosevelt's Caribbean: The Panama Canal, the Monroe Doctrine, and the Latin American Context*. Baton Rouge, LA, 1990.

Crapol, Edward P. "Coming to Terms with Empire: The Historiography of Late-Nineteenth-Century American Foreign Relations." *Diplomatic History* 16 (1992): 573–97.

Fry, Joseph A. "Imperialism, American Style, 1890–1916." In *American Foreign Relations Reconsidered, 1890–1993*, edited by Gordon Martel. London, Ont., 1994.

Gould, Lewis L. *The Spanish-American War and President McKinley*. Lawrence, KS, 1982.

Healy, David. *Drive to Hegemony: The United States in the Caribbean, 1898–1917*. Madison, WI, 1988.

Hunt, Michael H. *Ideology and U.S. Foreign Relations*. New Haven, 1987.

———. *The Making of a Special Relationship: The United States and China to 1914*. New York, 1983.

Israel, Jerry. *Progressivism and the Open Door: America and China, 1905–1921*. Pittsburgh, 1971.

LaFeber, Walter. *The American Search for Opportunity, 1865–1913*. London and New York, 1993.

———. *The New Empire: An Interpretation of American Expansion, 1860–1898*. Ithaca, NY, 1963.

Markowitz, Gerald E. "Progressivism and Imperialism: A Return to First Principles." *Historian* 37 (1975): 257–75.

Marks, Frederick W., III. *Velvet on Iron: The Diplomacy of Theodore Roosevelt*. Lincoln, NE, 1979.

May, Glenn A. *Social Engineering in the Philippines: The Aims, Execution, and Impact of American Colonial Policy, 1900–1913*. Westport, CT, 1980.

Miller, Stuart C. *"Benevolent Assimilation": The Conquest of the Philippines, 1899–1903*. New Haven, CT, 1982.

Offner, John L. *An Unwanted War: The Diplomacy of the United States and Spain over Cuba, 1895–1898*. Chapel Hill, NC, 1992.

Pérez, Louis A., Jr. *Cuba and the United States: Ties of Singular Intimacy.* Athens, GA, 1990.

Rosenberg, Emily S. *Spreading the American Dream: American Economic and Cultural Expansion, 1890–1945.* New York, 1982.

Rydell, Robert W. *All the World's a Fair: Visions of Empire at American International Expositions, 1876–1916.* Chicago, 1984.

Scholes, Walter V., and Scholes, Marie V. *The Foreign Policies of the Taft Administration.* Columbia, MO, 1970.

Schoonover, Thomas D. *The United States in Central America, 1860–1911: Episodes of Social Imperialism and Imperial Rivalry in the World System.* Durham, NC, 1991.

Welch, Richard E., Jr. *Response to Imperialism: The United States and the Philippine-American War, 1899–1902.* Chapel Hill, NC, 1979.

Williams, William Appleman. *The Tragedy of American Diplomacy.* New York, 1972.

Woodrow Wilson and
U.S. Intervention in World War I

Melvin Small

When World War I began in August 1914, those Americans who read the front pages of their newspapers clucked their tongues over the latest folly of the Old World. A few even began rooting for their favorites in the lethal contest: the Franco-British-Russian coalition or the Austro-German side. Most Americans, however, went on with their summertime activities and paid scant attention to the cataclysmic events on the Continent.

To a people insulated from the turmoil of Europe by the Atlantic Ocean and unencumbered by alliances, such nonchalance was understandable. But American memories were short. The last time Europe had been at war, from 1792 to 1815, the remote and weak United States became deeply involved economically, politically, and ultimately (in 1812) militarily. In 1914, no longer remote and weak, it was emerging as the most powerful country in the world and was the most important neutral for the major belligerents.

On April 6, 1917, the United States entered the Great War. This involvement had far greater impact on Americans than the War of 1812. When the guns finally fell silent on November 11, 1918, their country was the preeminent power in the world, their president a towering international figure, bringing his influence to bear in such far-flung places as Shantung and Siberia.

How this all came about has been a topic that has intrigued Americans almost from the day that President Woodrow Wilson went before Congress to ask for a declaration of war. The minority that had opposed intervention swelled in the 1920s when the world did not turn out as Wilson had promised and when the archives began to reveal that the "democratic" Allies were almost as disreputable as their enemies. When war clouds again appeared on the European horizon in the late 1930s, so many Americans looked back with distaste to the alleged blunder of April 1917 that Congress passed a series of neutrality acts that, in effect, were designed to keep the country out of the *First* World War.

The eddies of controversy that once swirled around the question of Wilson and his diplomacy from 1914 through 1917 have been forgotten today by all but a few historians. At the same time, the issues of that controversy are still salient, for they involve definitions of national security, the proper role of the president in foreign policy, and, indeed, the control citizens have over that foreign policy. Much of the controversy centers around Woodrow Wilson, who was one of the best prepared of American presidents. A college professor and administrator before he entered politics in 1910, he had written a major textbook on U.S. government and was a noted historian. When he took office in 1913, he anticipated answering the call for reform from the Progressive Movement and devoting himself primarily to domestic politics, an area in which he felt most comfortable. As he commented, "It would be an irony of fate if my administration had to deal chiefly with foreign affairs."

Not the typical politician, Wilson was a deep thinker with a well-developed view of the world and the nature of human interaction. His father was a minister and his mother the daughter of a minister. Although he did not enter the clergy, the spirituality and idealism that infused his thought made him the country's most prominent lay preacher. Concerned above all with principle, he understood the amorality of the game of international politics but never accepted it as the proper way for Christian nations to conduct their business.

Strong-willed and confident in his own vision, Wilson was a powerful leader who by war's end was looked to by people everywhere to guide them out of the ruinous cycle of imperial rivalries, arms races, and war. His idealism and his belief in a world without empires and alliance systems also could be interpreted as a highly realistic policy—that is, in breaking down the barriers to free economic interaction, he could enhance the peaceful expansion of America's informal empire.

Wilson understood the power of the presidency in foreign policy. The Constitution's checks and balances worked fairly well in apportioning power between Congress and the president on the domestic scene. When it came to international relations, the president held most of the cards. With Wilson's power to interpret neutrality law, his command of the armed forces, and the "bully pulpit" that he controlled, it was no contest in the conflict with Congress over American posture toward the belligerents.

At the start of the war, however, a war that many Americans believed would be over before the first snow fell, Wilson did not foresee that his administration would be dominated by foreign adventures. After all, most of the recent European wars had been limited affairs of several weeks or a few months. Thus, the United States could proclaim its traditional neutrality, and Europe would be back to normal in a short time.

America's "traditional neutrality" was easier to proclaim than to practice. In the abstract, neutrality could take three forms. A nation could be strictly neutral in a legalistic sense, apply its laws, treaties, and precedents to specific incidents, and let the chips fall where they may. In that case, legalistic neutrality might aid one belligerent more than another to a point where a neutral could tip the balance in the war. On the other hand, a nation could try to be fair to both sides, not allow its actions to determine the military outcome, and, consequently, decide to ignore legal precedents on occasion. A third, and rather unrealistic, option would be to close up one's ports and economy to belligerents and refuse to have anything to do with them until after the war, in which case a nation would be giving up the bonanza of increased trade that is normally available to neutrals during wartime. Moreover, this third option would be unfair to those belligerents that had every reason to expect that they would be able to buy needed materials in the neutral country.

Throughout the war Wilson maintained that he had selected the first option, that of scrupulous legal neutrality. In reality, although he would not admit it, he also was concerned with the impact of his policy on the military fortunes of the belligerents and, more important, with the maintenance of the lucrative U.S. war trade with the Continent.

When Wilson took office in March 1913, the United States was in a recession that spiraled down toward a depression by the summer of 1914. The war trade gave a much-needed shot in the arm to the ailing American economy and, naturally, to the president's political fortunes. By 1915 hard times were over, and the economy boomed through the end of the war. When confronted with major assaults against American neutrality by the British on the high seas, Wilson could not lose sight of the fact that most of the war trade was with them. Any punitive severance of the economic link to

Britain could lead to a drastic diminution of that trade which, in turn, could lead to a recession or depression.

The impact of economic variables is unmeasurable. Suffice it to say that for whatever reasons, fair-minded observers could conclude that Wilson tolerated many more violations of his country's neutrality from the British, with whom the United States had a most lucrative trading relationship, than he tolerated from the Germans. In his defense it was true that, while British violations involved the loss of property and, to some degree, national prestige, German violations often involved the loss of human life.

Wilson's pursuit of neutrality was affected by general American attitudes toward the belligerents. When the war began, the vast majority of his countrymen, perhaps as many as 80 percent, preferred a British to a German victory. At the same time, those who supported British arms did not feel as strongly about their favorites as did the minority that was fervently anti-British. This minority included many German-Americans, Irish-Americans who hated England, Jewish-Americans who hated England's ally Russia, and Scandinavian-Americans who feared Russian domination of their homelands. In many cases in a democracy, a minority that backs an issue strongly can compete with a majority that is only lukewarm in its support of the opposite side of that issue. In this case, the majority also included the powerful American intellectual, economic, and political elites, almost all of whom were pro-British. For many analysts this is the only group that counts in the formation of opinion, for its views must ultimately influence those of everyone else.

As the war progressed, more and more Americans who were relatively neutral or mildly pro-British became strongly anti-German, owing to the influence of those elites, British propaganda, real and fabricated German atrocities on land, submarine outrages at sea, and bumbling German spies caught in the United States. By 1917 the vast majority of the American population was prepared to join a crusade that would defeat Germany and make the world safe for democracy.

Interestingly, Wilson's attitudes toward the belligerents did not follow those of the general population. At the onset of the conflict, he instinctively blamed Germany for initiating a war against the England that he loved. Upon reflection, he realized that all of the blame was not on one side and that the system was at fault more than any single nation. Through the end of 1916, he was relatively balanced in his judgment, although he never wavered from a fundamental Anglophilia. Yet, when he finally decided on war, he returned full circle to his original position and seemed to catch up with the rest of the population. In the spring of 1917, Wilson again blamed Germany for the entire war. Perhaps he had to convince himself of the rectitude of the British cause before he led his nation into war.

Whatever his personal feelings in the late summer of 1914, Wilson's early neutrality policies appeared to be both neutral and evenhanded in their impact on the belligerents. Rulings that were in the German interest included a refusal to speak out against alleged German atrocities in occupied Belgium, an attempt to increase the number of neutral vessels plying the Atlantic by permitting the sale of German merchant ships bottled up in American waters when the war began, and a ban on the sale of submarine parts to England. Rulings that were in the British interest included the seizure of two German wireless stations in the United States and the refusal to demand that England adhere to the London Naval Treaty of 1909, a treaty it had not signed because it permitted neutral merchant vessels far more freedom to trade with belligerents than Britain could accept.

As the war dragged on, three other major policies tipped the balance toward England. The first is the most controversial. When the war began, Wilson adopted an unusual policy for a neutral. He banned private American loans to belligerents since money, "the worst of all contrabands," according to Secretary of State William Jennings Bryan, bought all others. Historically, it had always been proper for neutral bankers to make loans to belligerents. Now, Wilson took the high road and forbade those loans. Unfortunately for his claim to consistency, he took a lower road in 1915 when the British, whose orders for food and war materials had catapulted the United States from recession to boom, began to run out of cash. Confronted with the prospect of a new recession, Wilson reversed himself and permitted credits and loans that the British used to buy U.S. materials essential to their war effort. On the surface, this policy was entirely legal; all belligerents could make loans in the United States. It was not Wilson's fault that American bankers much preferred doing business with England than with Germany. However, Wilson had gone on record earlier against this sort of traffic, and his reversal belied his claim to a new, highly moral brand of neutrality.

A second major neutrality policy that favored England involved Wilson's acceptance of the American arms trade with the belligerents. Since the British controlled the seas, most of this deadly material arrived in the Allied camp and ultimately was used to kill Germans. As with the American loan policy of 1915, trade in contraband was legal. Moreover, according to the president, were it not permitted, those belligerents that had been less militaristic and thus not so well armed prior to the war would have been at a disadvantage once the war began. As for the one-sided nature of the trade, Wilson noted coolly that the Atlantic Ocean had been around for a long time; it was too bad that the Germans had not taken account of that geographic fact.

Finally, when the British mined the North Sea and made it virtually impossible for neutral vessels to reach Germany without first stopping in England for sailing instructions through the minefields and for inspection, Wilson did not protest. Again, mining was a legal belligerent act, although no nation had ever mined an entire sea before. The Germans questioned the difference between mines, which Wilson accepted, and submarines, which he opposed. There was legal precedent for mining but none for submarine warfare, responded Wilson. More important, since mines were very effective, few neutral vessels dared to enter the fields without stopping in England; thus, loss of life attributable to mines was minimal. Submarine warfare was not as effective. Therefore, neutral vessels took their chances in the German war zone and occasionally were sunk, with consequent loss of life. Had more lives been lost as a result of the mining, Wilson might have been more receptive to German protests against American acceptance of that mining.

Wilson's interpretation of neutrality law was favorable to England. London was able to buy weapons in the United States, using American private loans to finance those purchases. Any neutral vessel that hoped to sell contraband to Germany risked the perils of the mined North Sea. Yet, what should Wilson have done? It was not his fault that the British controlled the Atlantic. Furthermore, the war trade with England was essential to American economic recovery. In any event, all of Wilson's measures could be defended as being within the bounds of international law and historical precedent. Throughout the war he maintained that America was scrupulously neutral and fair to both sides. The Germans were incredulous, for they could well see how the president's brand of neutrality was contributing significantly to the success of Allied arms. One can understand their frustration with Wilson and the United States in 1917 when they finally adopted a submarine policy that led the world's most prominent neutral into war against them.

From the Germans' perspective, Wilson not only erected a pro-British structure of neutrality law, but he also tolerated far too many violations of American rights on the high seas. In the quantitative sense, the Germans were absolutely correct, but how does one equate the loss of human life with the loss of property?

As in previous wars, Britain was mistress of the seas and controlled its domain imperiously. As usual, its navy's definition of neutral rights and the neutrals' definitions of their rights were at odds. Neutrals wanted to be able to sell almost anything to any belligerent without being subject to seizure by the British navy. For their part, the British tried to choke off neutral trade with Germany by using the broadest possible interpretation of contraband and by violating other nations' conceptions of the laws of search and seizure. Knowing the sensitivity of the Americans, the Admiralty did not tighten all of the screws at once. Indeed, had the British been violating American rights in 1914 in the manner in which they were in 1916, Wilson might have been forced to break relations at the outset of the war. Instead, they tightened the screws almost imperceptibly, first adding this item and then another to the contraband list, often changing the rules during periods of major German-American tensions.

Such violations of American neutral rights were not ignored by Wilson. Each resulted in the filing of a formal protest, with such protests increasing in number and intensity until, as one wag noted, the State Department ran out of stationery. There was a point in late 1916 when British violations were so flagrant and frequent (the German submarine warfare was dormant) that Americans finally considered retaliatory legislation against London, including an embargo. In a classic case of cutting off one's nose to spite one's face, such action in late 1916 would not have caused England to cease and desist but would have brought about another American recession. Therefore, Wilson never went any further than strongly worded protests, which London did not take seriously.

The British also were guilty of a variety of other offensive practices, including hovering just outside the three-mile limit in a most unsporting fashion, intercepting mail on U.S. vessels, removing foreign nationals from those vessels, flying the American flag on their own merchant ships to deceive German submarines, and, in

1916, issuing a blacklist of American firms that were trading with Germany and its allies. Protesting against all of these actions, Wilson blustered and threatened but never actually told the British to refrain from such behavior, or else. "Or else" meant the closing down of Anglo-American trade, and by 1916 the United States needed that trade for economic stability as much as England needed U.S. supplies for the war.

To Wilson, the German assault upon American neutral rights was another story. When the war began, control of the seas belonged to England, an island nation that depended upon ocean-going commerce to maintain its economy and supply lines. Even though the German surface fleet was the second largest in the world, it was no match for Britain's. Still, if only the Germans could attack the British on the high seas, their chances on land would improve immeasurably.

Germany did have several submarines in its naval arsenal, new-fangled devices that had not been used in warfare to any extent until World War I. After some tentative experimentation in the fall of 1914, the Germans discovered that submarines were surprisingly effective; they had a new offensive naval weapon. In early February 1915, Berlin announced that, as of February 18, England would be subjected to a submarine blockade. Within a clearly defined war zone, the kaiser's submarines would attempt to sink all British vessels, including merchantmen. The Germans urged neutrals to keep their people and property off ships that flew the British flag. As for neutral merchantmen, German submarine commanders would try their best to avoid mistakes.

The Germans thus began to employ a novel weapon for which no international law existed. In the absence of any precedent, Wilson argued that submarines had to follow the detailed etiquette of naval warfare that had long been applied to surface vessels. For example, when a submarine commander wanted to blow an enemy merchantman out of the water, he first had to surface and warn the merchantman of his intentions. A submarine was therefore virtually worthless once it relinquished attack by surprise. Those small World War I submarines were quite vulnerable to being rammed by surface vessels and were so thin-skinned that the relatively small cannon mounted on merchantmen could destroy them. Obviously, if a submarine behaved like a surface vessel, its value would be significantly diminished. Nevertheless, Wilson maintained that submarines were no different from other ships of the line. If they struck without warning against nonmilitary targets, he would hold them to what he called "strict accountability." However, he never held the British strictly accountable for their violations of neutral rights.

Incidents involving Americans were bound to happen. In late March 1915, one American went down with a British steamer in the war zone, a victim of a German torpedo. While Wilson and his cabinet were hammering out a response, a much larger vessel, the British passenger liner *Lusitania*, was sunk on May 7. This time 128 Americans were among the almost 1,200 who lost their lives. At no point up to 1917 were the American people more outraged at the Germans. To no avail the leaders in Berlin claimed that they had warned neutrals not to travel on the liner because they considered the *Lusitania* to be part of the British war machine. Furthermore, they pointed out that it carried munitions and was heavily armed. The latter charge has never been proved. Whether armed or not, the *Lusitania* was primarily a passenger vessel, and the German submarine commander, who had been publicly honored for his marksmanship, had struck without warning. The unpleasant image of the brutal Prussian, enhanced by atrocity stories associated with the occupation of Belgium, was indelibly etched in American memories. Although German submarines never again sank a passenger vessel with so much loss of civilian life, Americans never forgot the *Lusitania*.

Even before a furious Wilson was able to obtain an apology and settlement from the Germans for the celebrated sinking, the *Arabic*, another British liner, went down with the loss of two American lives. In response, a contrite German ambassador pledged that such occurrences would not happen again and that his nation would pay indemnities. For the remainder of 1915, German submarines operated cautiously and successfully avoided incidents that could enrage the United States. Germany's luck or circumspection ran out in March 1916 when the *Sussex* was sunk, in apparent violation of the *Arabic* Pledge. After strong threats from Wilson, Berlin produced a new document, the *Sussex* Pledge, in which Germany promised not to sink without warning vessels carrying passengers. This promise, however, was conditional upon British acceptance of neutral rights. Later, when the Germans violated the *Sussex* Pledge, they claimed they had every right to do so since the neutrals had not compelled London to alter its illegal practices on the high seas. Wilson rejected the argument, refusing to acknowledge that the *Sussex* Pledge was conditional. This pledge was observed through

January 1917 when Berlin adopted a new submarine policy that forced Wilson's hand. The decision for unlimited submarine warfare was influenced by the failure to develop acceptable mediation plans.

Throughout the war, Wilson engaged in a variety of schemes in which he either would serve as an honest broker or at least bring the warring parties to the peace table. His task became more and more difficult as this first "total war" dragged on. Wilson proposed a peace without victors. How did one make such a compromise peace with an enemy that had to be painted as the Devil incarnate in order to obtain the requisite sacrifices from one's citizenry?

In addition, the Germans were always slightly suspicious about the Anglophilic Wilson's professed evenhandedness. For example, his most serious mediation proposal was the House-Grey Memorandum of February 1916. Colonel Edward M. House, Wilson's chief diplomatic adviser, had journeyed to London, Paris, and Berlin. In London, in conferences with Foreign Secretary Sir Edward Grey, House tried to lure the British to the peace table with a plan that suggested possible American entry into the war if the British agreed to talks and the Germans did not. Berlin was not given the same bargain.

Wilson then offered his final and most impartial mediation proposal in late 1916 when he was far more exasperated with the British than with the Germans. At almost the same time, the German government gave peace one last chance and floated its own program. When the American and German proposals failed, Berlin decided to go for broke. In January 1917 the German High Command made its fateful decision to move from limited to unlimited submarine warfare. As of February 1 all vessels carrying contraband, enemy and neutral alike, were declared fair game in the German war zone around the British Isles. Up to this point, submarine commanders had been relatively genteel in the use of their weapons. With hopes for a German victory fading, the submarine was to be unleashed in a desperate attempt to bring England to its knees. According to the decision makers in Berlin, the balance of power was slowly shifting toward the Allies, especially considering their relative economic strength. The time had come to do all that was needed to obtain a swift victory in 1917.

As for the most prominent neutral, from the Germans' perspective the United States had discriminated against them in its unequal application of neutrality laws. The *Sussex* Pledge had not been violated, they contended, since it was conditional. The Germans knew that unlimited submarine warfare was likely to move the United States from neutrality to belligerency, but they thought that the war would be over before a single American doughboy arrived in France. Their timetable was correct in one respect in that U.S. soldiers did not have an impact until 1918. They erred, however, in thinking that the submarine unleashed would cripple England in a matter of months.

Significantly, Wilson opposed preparedness measures in 1914 and 1915. Only in 1916, an election year during which Republicans assailed his defense policies, did he launch programs to increase the country's military and naval strength. Thus, the Germans knew that the United States was woefully unprepared for war in 1917. Had the nation been better prepared, had its soldiers been ready to jump into troopships that would take them to the battlefields of France, the Germans might have thought twice about risking American belligerency.

Whatever marginal fault one can find with Wilson for not preparing his nation better, he was confronted with a serious crisis not of his own making. He had gone on record against the use of the submarine in the manner announced by the Germans and was wholeheartedly supported in that position by most Americans. Through 1971 ten American vessels had been sunk by mistake; in March nine were sunk on purpose. Each day's newspaper brought a new horror story about Americans lost at sea.

Wilson's move toward war was aided by two other events. First, the Russian revolution of February–March 1917 meant that the tyrannical czar was no longer a member of the alliance led by democratic England and France. The new Russian government was at first decidedly democratic and reformist, according to Wilson a "fit partner" for the United States.

The second and more important event was the Zimmermann Telegram. German foreign minister Arthur Zimmermann sent a message to his embassy in Mexico City, urging his diplomats to try to induce Mexico to join the German side in exchange for the territories taken by the United States in 1848. The telegram was intercepted by the British intelligence service and handed over to the Americans. To make matters worse, when the story leaked out, Zimmermann admitted that he had been the author of the dispatch. Wilson compounded Germany's public relations problem when he released the infamous document to the press. Undoubtedly, by the time he decided to go public with it, he wanted to obtain strong popular backing for his increasingly tough line toward Berlin.

President Wilson had three options in February 1917. The first was to acquiesce in the German policy and ban American vessels and citizens from the war zone. Such a move would have kept the United States out of war. It also would have crippled Anglo-American commerce, and, more important, for Wilson and many of his countrymen it would have represented an unconscionable truckling to an allegedly immoral weapon wielded by a brutal people. In the latter respect, Wilson believed that he not only had to defend the nation's honor but the honor of all of the civilized world as well.

Wilson's second option, midway between turning the other cheek and entering the war, was armed neutrality. Although he was unable to obtain congressional authority to arm merchantmen, he did use executive authority to effect that policy. Armed neutrality, however, was only a stopgap measure. The cannons mounted on American vessels could not contend with submarines that no longer adhered to naval etiquette.

By mid-March, Wilson became convinced that national security could be protected only by entering the war on the Allied side. Moreover, he argued, once on the Allied side, he could use his influence to construct a peace that would establish a new international order. On April 2 he went before Congress to ask for a declaration of war. The six senators and fifty representatives who refused to go along with their colleagues on April 6, the date that war was formally declared, reflected accurately the sizable antiwar minority in the nation at large.

Most of Congress and the country thrilled to Wilson's stirring message. He took the high ground with the immediate cause for his decision—the submarine—serving only as a symbol of the immorality of the German leadership. In oversimplified terms, Wilson blamed Berlin for starting and prolonging the war and promised that democracy would be made safe once the Prussian menace was destroyed. What the president did not choose to discuss in his speech was revealing. He did not mention the European balance of power, the significance of American trade with Britain, the heavy investments that U.S. financiers had made in the Allied cause, or the secret imperialist designs of France and England, among others, in the "democratic" coalition.

On the other hand, by choosing to emphasize the idealistic nature of the U.S. entry into war, Wilson increased the number of Americans who accepted the dramatic deviation from their country's tradition of isolation. It is impossible to determine how much of Wilson's personal rationale was presented in his public request for war. Undoubtedly, he was convinced that German submarine warfare reflected the innate inhumanity of the Prussian character as compared to the Anglo-Saxon. Surely he could not have forgotten his earlier, more sophisticated analyses that emphasized the structural failings of the European international system and British violations of neutral rights.

Whatever Wilson really believed, unlimited submarine warfare was the catalyst that moved him to ask for a declaration of war. One can sympathize with the Germans who were frustrated with Wilson's acceptance of neutrality policies that were skewed toward Britain. After all, unlimited submarine warfare can be interpreted as an understandable response to Britain's unlawful behavior in the Atlantic, unlawful behavior that greatly enhanced its capacity to make war on the Continent against Germany and the Central Powers.

A genuinely pacific man who abhorred war, Wilson was convinced that his country's honor and security and, indeed, the honor and security of the civilized world were at stake. From today's perspective, the picture is less clear, especially when we remember how the Germans linked their policies to Wilson's perceived unneutrality.

According to most analysts, national security can involve three components: a military dimension, an economic dimension, and a prestige dimension. (A fourth, the moral dimension, must be dismissed as irrelevant in the real world of international politics.) In the spring of 1917 the Germans did not pose an immediate military threat to the United States. To be sure, its civilians were assaulted on the Atlantic, but there was no direct threat to U.S. territory and none to American vessels had they chosen to stay out of the submarine-blockaded area. A national security justification for war must be found elsewhere.

The German submarine blockade did pose an economic threat. The health of the American economy was dependent upon trade with Britain. A diminution of that trade could have resulted in a recession. Yet, how much of an economic downturn merited the resort to arms? That is a deep philosophical question for which each observer may have his or her own answer.

In the same vein, the submarine blockade was a clear challenge to American prestige or honor. Supported by his constituents, Wilson had proclaimed early on that his country could never accept unlimited submarine warfare. To back down, according to those who can justify war on the grounds of honor, would be to sully the name of the United States and to make the country look so weak that aggressors might try to get away with even more direct challenges to national sovereignty. Most wars originate in perceived threats to national honor. American involvement in World War I was no exception.

With Wilson's decision for war the United States at last became a full participant in the international system, a position into which it had been slowly moving since the turn of the century. Doubtless, the nation would have taken its place at the table of the mighty sooner or later, given its immense economic power and political and cultural influence. Still, the manner of entry into the system had a major impact on future U.S. behavior.

For the short run, Wilson's simplistic and idealistic public presentation of American policies led to disillusionment and partial retreat from the system once the world did not turn out as he had promised. Also, the perceived mistakes of 1917 crippled the hands of U.S. leaders in the 1930s who wanted to curb Axis aggression before it was too late. Finally, the manner in which Wilson almost singlehandedly determined neutrality policy and defined the international situation for the public served as a dramatic lesson for later presidents who exerted enormous power over their countrymen as they involved them in crises in every corner of the globe. In most cases, American money, diplomats, and sometimes soldiers were sent in the name of Wilson's policy of making the world safe for democracy.

Sources and Suggested Readings

Buehrig, Edward H. *Woodrow Wilson and the Balance of Power.* Bloomington, IN, 1955.

Burk, Kathleen. *Britain, America, and the Sinews of War, 1914–1918.* Boston, 1985.

Clements, Kendrick. *The Presidency of Woodrow Wilson.* Lawrence, KS, 1992.

Coogan, John W. *The End of Neutrality: The United States, Britain, and Maritime Rights, 1899–1915*. Ithaca, NY, 1981.

Devlin, Patrick. *Too Proud to Fight: Woodrow Wilson's Neutrality*. New York, 1975.

Gregory, Ross. *The Origins of American Intervention in the First World War*. New York, 1971.

Karp, Walter. *The Politics of War: The Story of Two Wars Which Altered Forever the Political Life of the American Republic (1890–1920)*. New York, 1979.

Link, Arthur S. *Wilson*. 5 vols. Princeton, NJ, 1947–1965.

———. *Woodrow Wilson: Revolution, War, and Peace*. Arlington Heights, IL, 1979.

May, Ernest R. *The World War and American Isolation, 1914–1917*. Cambridge, MA, 1959.

Small, Melvin. *Was War Necessary? National Security and U.S. Entry into War*. Beverly Hills, CA, 1980.

Smith, Daniel M. *The Great Departure: The United States and World War I, 1914–1920*. New York, 1965.

———. "National Interest and American Intervention, 1917: An Historiographical Appraisal." *Journal of American History* 52 (June 1965): 5–25.

Tansill, Charles C. *America Goes to War*. Boston, 1938.

Woodward, David R., and Maddox, Robert F. *America and World War I: A Selected Annotated Bibliography of English-Language Sources*. New York, 1985.

The United States and the Versailles Peace Settlement

William C. Widenor

In the unstable and dangerous world in which we live, some of us have come to believe that the ethics of actions in international politics can be appraised only in terms of results and not in terms of intentions. No one has ever seriously questioned President Woodrow Wilson's devotion to securing a "just" peace to conclude World War I and constructing a better world. The more important question is whether he possessed true political wisdom, whether he understood how to attain the best results that circumstances would permit.

Whatever the shortcomings of the American peace commission that went to Paris in 1919 to negotiate a treaty to end World War I, it did not lack expert advice. Wilson's oft-heralded commission of expertise, frequently called The Inquiry, studied most of the international problems likely to arise in the course of peacemaking and supplied him with some two thousand reports, most of them quite perceptive. Such knowledge, however, never coalesced into a philosophy of international relations or a coherent approach to the construction of a lasting peace. Reports did not constitute plans, least of all blueprints for a workable international organization. In many ways the United States was as unprepared for bringing about peace as it originally had been unprepared for war. Historically, Americans had little experience in making other than bilateral peace treaties, and they were unaccustomed to thinking in terms of the requisites of a lasting peace.

Both the initial reaction of the American people to the outbreak of war in Europe, and their subsequent efforts to distance themselves from it and to arrange a "peace without victory," had much to do with the manner in which the United States finally went to war in April 1917. That in turn had a profound effect on the American view of a proper peace settlement. As Robert Osgood once put it, "Because neither war nor peace seemed related to any enduring self-interest, the motives which led to war were not adequate for the prosecution of war, and the objects for which the nation fought were not sufficiently compelling to sustain the break with isolation that was necessary for their fulfillment." Into this breach stepped the great idealist and master propagandist, Woodrow Wilson. Essentially, the Wilsonian argument for war was that the United States as a participant, rather than as an onlooker, would be able to exert greater influence on behalf of its ideals in shaping a new world order and a just peace. It was Wilson's moral leadership that finally enabled America's pacifists and idealists to acquiesce in the unpleasant fact of U.S. participation in the war. Only the loftiest motives were capable of reconciling them to such organized violence.

The American people go to war in their own peculiar way. Messianism seems a recurrent propensity of American society in times of international conflict. Only high moral purposes can justify a supposedly moral society's engaging in war; all other conflicts are by definition immoral. As recent history all too strongly attests, the United States has found it extremely difficult to fight wars that are limited in either scope or object. The pity of this is that in consequence only huge wars, and only those raising important ethical issues, are worthy of moral approbation. In 1917 a large minority in the country opposed American entry, and it was necessary to rally them to the cause. Woodrow Wilson knew how.

Both American war aims and expectations with respect to the peace—Wilson's Fourteen Points and Four Principles—were a function of these circumstances, but another important factor also was involved. One's conception of the kind of peace that was required developed rather naturally from one's view of the inception and character of the war itself. Take, for example, the various theories regarding its causes. Merely to state the theories (the French theory that the war was completely Germany's fault, the British theory that it was the result of the breakdown of the Concert of Europe, and Wilson's belief that it was a function of the old order, of the political and social structure of the conservative regimes of Europe) is to understand what profound implications were contained therein for one's perspective as to the kind of settlement necessary for a lasting peace. Essentially, Wilson blamed the "old system," the old way of doing things, and that included the traditional diplomacy of both England and France, countries on whose side the United States would fight but with whom Wilson would only "associate," not "ally," the nation. The old system was variously particularized as the old diplomacy, the old balance-of-power system, and the absence of democratic control over foreign policy. In this view, because the fault lay with the system, however defined, attribution of guilt or innocence to individual belligerents was of little relevance. The need was to change the scheme of things entirely, to democratize and also, unfortunately, to Americanize it. The need was to set the world's peoples free and to encourage self-determination. Only a nation that determined its own destiny could be democratic, and only a democracy could be trusted to love peace and to make a new world order work. This was in essence the view held by Wilson in 1914 and one that he never really abandoned, but still another consideration led to his enunciation of the Fourteen Points. They were designed as a statement of war aims and as an instrument of propaganda, both at home and abroad, intended to cause the Allied peoples to quicken their efforts and to weaken enemy resistance by holding out the seductive hope of a just peace.

For all their obvious attractions and political popularity, Wilson's proposals were not quite the concrete plan for peace that his partisans later depicted them to be. As British economist John Maynard Keynes once complained, Wilson's ideas were very nebulous: "He could have preached a sermon on any of them or have addressed a stately prayer to the Almighty for their fulfillment, but he could not frame their concrete application to the actual state of Europe." His famous fourteenth point, calling for a universal collective security organization, was particularly undeveloped. It was difficult to oppose "a general association of nations to be formed under specific covenants for the purpose of affording mutual guarantees of political independence and territorial integrity to great and small states alike," but that did not mean that there was any agreement as to how those guarantees would be effected. Moreover, in enunciating his program, Wilson had sown many seeds of future difficulty. His extravagant promises of world harmony in the offing were bound to come back to haunt him as it became clear that he had no magic formula for reconciling the claims of competitive nation-states. In addition, his was a peace program conceived in pacifist abstention from the war and probably much better suited to a "peace without victory," but the very act of entering the war meant that the United States would sit at the peace conference not as a disinterested mediator but as a victorious ally. The transition was a difficult one, and Wilson's task as peacemaker was formidable.

When in October 1918 the war was going badly for the Central Powers but (and this is important to note) before their armies had been completely defeated and before there were substantial Allied troops on German soil, the Central Powers sued for peace on the basis of the Fourteen Points. Their application was accepted by Wilson, and an armistice was finally concluded on November 11, 1918, even though the Allies themselves did not agree upon the meaning of the Fourteen Points (indeed, several of them had been drafted to be deliberately vague). The British insisted on an important modification and the French on a significant clarification. The modification was that the Allies should retain complete liberty in the matter of the freedom of the seas. In other words, they would not be bound by Wilson's pledge and would be free to institute blockades in the future. The clarification was that the restoration of evacuated territory by Germany should include compensation for damages to the civilian population. To any but the uninitiated that clearly meant reparations. These emerging ambiguities in the Allied peace program, portentous as they were, paled in significance before the fact that the manner in which the war was concluded left considerable doubt as to whether the peace was to be imposed or negotiated. The Germans certainly expected a negotiated peace, and in that they were to be gravely disappointed.

In what frame of mind and with what expectations did Wilson approach the peace conference? On November 18, 1918, two weeks after the mid-term election in which his party lost its majorities in both houses of Congress (with the result that Wilson's critics both at home and abroad could henceforth claim that he was the only one of the leading statesmen at Paris who did not command a legislative majority in his own country), the president startled the nation with the announcement that, contrary to precedent, he personally was going to Paris as the head of the U.S. peace delegation. He apparently believed that only by appearing in person and using the weight of his enormous prestige could he secure the just and lasting peace which he had been advocating. What is unfortunately all too clear is that Wilson held an exalted view of both his own role and that of the United States. While en route to France in December, he not only claimed that "we would be the only disinterested people at the Peace Conference" but also boldly told the other members of the delegation that the European leaders did not really represent their respective peoples (which was false) and that, if they did not do what he wanted, he would appeal to their people over their heads (which naturally did not work). Just as his partisans among historians would later depict the struggle, Wilson himself actually believed that he was engaged in a contest to determine whether his principles of a new world order would prevail over the dictates of reactionary nationalism. Americans are particularly inclined to think that they have principles, whereas other countries have only ambitions.

Wilson faced a task far more difficult than he knew. The war had destroyed the traditional European order and had resulted in what Raymond Sontag has so aptly called "a broken world." Unfortunately, speed was at a premium. Europe was not only exhausted but also hungry. Anxiety was at a fever pitch. As Herbert Hoover put it, "The wolf is at the door of the world." The image was undoubtedly meant both figuratively and literally. There was a widespread fear, inflamed by temporary Bolshevik successes in both Bavaria and Hungary, that the Red menace was spreading westward, and there were many at the peace conference who sought to turn that fear to their own national advantage. As Ray Stannard Baker once claimed, "Paris cannot be understood without Moscow."

The changing nature of international politics also presented problems. Expectations ran dangerously high, and Wilson was not without responsibility for that state of affairs. This was to be the first great peace conference at which the diplomats were expected to conduct their negotiations in the open and with due consideration for public opinion. Wilson arrived in Paris on December 13 and was greeted with such an enthusiastic reception, not only in France but in England and Italy as well, that it was easy for him to misinterpret European public opinion and to assume that his version of a peace settlement would meet with nearly universal acclaim. Public opinion, however, was never unitary, and it was soon divided into thirty-two separate opinions, the number of nations in actual attendance at the conference.

The absence of Germany and Russia did not mean that harmony would prevail. Neither did Wilson's realization that open diplomacy was the enemy of negotiation and compromise, and that the important decisions had to be reserved for consideration by the Big Four (David Lloyd George of Great Britain, Georges Clemenceau of France, Vittorio Orlando of Italy, and Wilson himself). Both his ascendant popularity, which invited jealousy, and the feeling that Wilson and the United States did not deserve their preeminent position at the peace table, due to their tardy if still crucial participation in the war, invited problems with the European leaders.

Moreover, those same leaders operated from an entirely different philosophical basis. They were suspicious of American intentions, believing that a conflict of interest was inevitable, both because all states had interests and could not be trusted to act contrary to them and because America, protected by the Atlantic, might be more bent on satisfying its self-righteous image of itself than in undertaking real commitments to enforce the peace in Europe. Clemenceau, remembering that the Germans had been turned back by bayonets and bullets, not by idealism, was particularly skeptical and could not think of Wilson without a derogatory reference to his messianic complex. As he told Wilson's adviser and close friend Colonel Edward M. House, "You are practical, I understand you, but talking to Wilson is something like talking to Jesus Christ." In specific reference to the Fourteen Points, Clemenceau reportedly said that "God gave us his Ten Commandments and we broke them. Wilson gave us his fourteen points—well, we shall see." The French and the Italians were, on the whole, much more skeptical than the British, but then they had a history of opposition to Anglo-Saxon cant. As Harold Nicolson, a member of the British delegation, once described their attitudes,

> They [the Latins] observed, for instance, that the United States, in the course of their short but highly imperialistic history, had constantly proclaimed the highest virtue while as constantly violating their professions and resorting to the grossest materialism. They observed that all Americans liked to feel in terms of Thomas Jefferson but to act in terms of Alexander Hamilton. They observed that such principles as the equality of man were not applied either to the yellow man or to the black. They observed that the doctrine of self-determination had not been extended either to the Red Indians or even to the Southern States. They were apt to examine "American principles and American tendencies" not in terms of the Philadelphia declaration, but in terms of the Mexican War, of Louisiana, of those innumerable treaties with the Indians which had been violated shamelessly before the ink was dry. They observed that, almost within living memory, the great American Empire had been won by ruthless force. Can we blame them if they doubted, not so much the sincerity as the actual applicability of the gospel of Woodrow Wilson? Can we blame them if they feared lest American realism would, when it came to the point, reject the responsibility of making American

idealism safe for Europe? Can we wonder that they preferred the precisions of their own old system to the vague idealism of a new system which America might refuse to apply even to her own continent?

The traditional and Wilsonian explanation emphasizes two essential goals. First, Wilson wanted a peace settlement of justice based, with respect to territorial adjustments, upon the principle of self-determination, a settlement that would leave no sores to serve as centers of infection productive of future wars. Second, he desired the creation of a League of Nations to ensure permanent peace. Revisionist critics have charged that his real interest lay in the construction of a peaceful, liberal, capitalist world order designed to ensure both the moral and economic preeminence of the United States. Although one might quibble with the latter interpretation and insist that personally Wilson seemed much more intent on claiming moral preeminence, the virtue of the revisionist argument lies in its recognition that the United States was an ordinary country intent, as were all others, on the protection of its own interests. Moreover, it too was represented at Paris by men who had reputations to protect and constituencies to serve.

Wilson's principal antagonist at the peace conference, and his intellectual opposite in all matters pertaining to the assessment of the behavior of men and nations, was Clemenceau. From the French premier's conservative, skeptical point of view, conflicts among states were inevitable, and, although his country had prevailed over Germany on this particular occasion by assembling a powerful coalition against it, German resources and potential military power were such that even in victory France found itself in a precarious position. From the French perspective a Wilsonian peace would likely result in shortening the interval of Germany's recovery and hastening the day when that nation would seek to avenge its temporary defeat. The only security for France lay in the reduction of German power and the exaction of guarantees against its rising again. As Keynes once explained,

> So far as possible, therefore, it was the policy of France to set the clock back and to undo what, since 1870, the progress of Germany has accomplished. By loss of territory and other measures her population was to be curtailed; but chiefly the economic system, upon which she depended for her new strength, the vast fabric built upon iron, coal, and transport, must be destroyed. If

France could seize, even in part, what Germany was compelled
to drop, the inequality of strength between the two rivals for
European hegemony might be remedied for many generations.

Such a program, Carthaginian in both philosophy and effect,
represented a challenge to Wilson's conception of what was likely
to make for a lasting peace at every fundamental point: disarmament of Germany as against general disarmament, a league of victors determined to prevent that country from ever "breaking out"
again as against a universal collective security organization, indemnities designed to cripple Germany as against simple reparations, and some dismemberment of Germany as against a peace
based on the principle of self-determination. In fact, just beneath
the surface of practically every problem confronting the peace conference lay the question of how France could best be protected
against its defeated enemy.

Wilson had advantages on his side but also serious obstacles in
his path. One advantage was the extraordinary position of moral
leadership to which he had risen. His eloquent statements of idealistic war aims had made him a hero to liberals everywhere and had
led war-weary and oppressed populations throughout the world to
hail him as their deliverer, as the one person capable of making a
just peace. This moral leadership, however, was bound to decline
as ideals were forced to give way to practical considerations and as
the aspirations of different national groups, such as the Italians and
Yugoslavs, proved to be mutually incompatible. Inevitably, justice
had a different face to every one of the nations concerned. But, in
addition to this moral influence, all the traditional instruments of
power lay in Wilson's hands. His severest critics, Keynes and
Nicolson, always made much of this point. As Keynes expressed it,

> The American armies were at the height of their numbers, disci-
> pline, and equipment. Europe was in complete dependence on
> the food supplies of the United States; and financially she was
> even more at their mercy. Europe not only already owed the
> United States more than she could pay; but only a large measure
> of further assistance could save her from starvation and bank-
> ruptcy. Never had a philosopher held such weapons wherewith
> to bind the princes of this world.

However, it is easy to overstate the efficacy of the weapons in
Wilson's diplomatic arsenal. Only rarely can one nation force another to do things that seem to run deeply counter to its own interest in self-preservation.

One significant obstacle to a Wilsonian peace was the group of secret treaties and agreements that the Allies had made among themselves before the United States entered the war. France had been promised by Russia, although not by Great Britain, not only the return of Alsace-Lorraine but also possession of the Saar valley and the conversion of German territory west of the Rhine into an independent buffer state. Italy had been assured of large accessions of Austrian territory in the southern Tyrol and about the head of the Adriatic Sea, and Japan had been promised the German islands in the North Pacific and the inheritance of German rights in Shantung, a particularly important province of China. The French and Italian claims in Europe and Japan's claim to Shantung were destined to be the real headaches.

A second obstacle in Wilson's path was the vindictive spirit prevalent among the peoples of the Allied countries, including the United States, a spirit that, because these were democratic countries, had to be taken into account. The domestic politics of Britain (witness the so-called Khaki Election of December 1918) and France were such that few politicians could resist the temptation to seek domestic political advantage by upping the ante as to what should be demanded from the Germans by way of compensation. Thus, the very democracy that Wilson thought a safeguard against war proved to be a barrier to a statesmanlike peace. The people were bloodthirsty and wanted retribution.

Still a third obstacle to Wilson's program was the awareness on the part of the other negotiators that he and his party were in political difficulty at home, and that Wilson himself had long ceased to be a prophet among his own people. As Nicolson once stated, "The tragedy of the American delegation in Paris was that they represented something which America had felt profoundly in 1915 and would again feel profoundly in 1922. They did not, however, represent what America was feeling in that January of 1919."

Perhaps the principal reason why Wilson was unable to translate American power into a settlement that would have conformed to the Fourteen Points was that he was not as disinterested as he pretended to be. All of his actions in Paris point to the conclusion that the League of Nations was what he really cared about; all other considerations were secondary. To get the League Covenant adopted was an achievement so precious that Wilson was willing to pay for it with concessions on other issues which in many cases contravened the principles of the Fourteen Points. He was almost obsessed by the conviction that the League Covenant was to be his personal monument and the solution to all human difficulties. What mattered some injustices here and there if the world had permanent machinery in the League to prevent war and to correct wrongs by peaceful process?

While it is certainly questionable whether the machinery incorporated in the League Covenant provided any guarantees that henceforth war would be prevented and that wrongs would be corrected by peaceful process, there is no gainsaying the fact that Wilson had succeeded in weaving the League into the fabric of the whole peace settlement in such a way as to make them virtually inseparable. Many of the provisions of the treaty (for example, those respecting the future of the Saar) were to be supervised, monitored, and even carried out by the instrumentality of the League. For this reason, Wilson could not but oppose Republican attempts to separate the League Covenant from the rest of the treaty. His failure lay in his inability to explain that his position was not just obstructionist, not just one of shoving the League down reluctant Republican throats, but rather was one based on the necessities of the negotiations that he had undertaken.

Clemenceau first and foremost, but the other Allied leaders as well, let it be known, just as did the Soviets at the end of World War II, that they would swallow the American plan for international organization, but at a price. Therein may lie the key to understanding how to find one's way through the labyrinthine negotiations that led to such a complex and inconsistent peace treaty. As Colonel House, who had to go about the dirty business of purchasing support for Wilson's League, once explained the ensuing pattern of negotiations: "The fact is that the League of Nations in which he [Wilson] has been more deeply interested than anything else from the beginning . . . has been played to the limit by the French and Japanese in extracting concessions from him; to a certain extent by the British too, and the Treaty as it stands is the result."

Before his vision of what could be achieved by a League of Nations he sacrificed his Fourteen Points one by one. Suffice it to say that at the outset Wilson conceded the South Tyrol to Italy for supposedly strategic reasons, thereby incorporating 225,000 Austrians into Italy and violating the principle of self-determination. From there on, it was all downhill. In order to convince France to give up its plans for an independent buffer state on the Rhine, Wilson was forced to sign a special treaty pledging the United States to protect France against invasion, a treaty derogatory of the League idea since it implied that the League might not be effective and that separate and special guarantees were required. The Japanese threatened not to join, and as a result Wilson gave in on Shantung despite the long tradition of American concern for the preservation of the territorial integrity of China. The Germans were not only deprived of all their colonies and of considerable territory in Europe that contained large German populations, but they also were saddled with an exceptionally high bill for reparations and forced, in a war-guilt clause that was both anathema to the German people and ran contrary to the common sense of most Americans, to accept exclusive blame for starting the conflict.

Assessments of the peace settlement vary greatly. One of the most influential books of the post-World War I period was written by Keynes, who had served as a member of the British delegation. It was a severe indictment of the Treaty of Versailles, particularly its economic sections. Keynes considered the treaty a failure and blamed Wilson, who was unsuited by qualities of character and temperament to overcome the guiles of the experienced European statesmen who demanded a vindictive peace. The president, according to Keynes, lacked sufficient intellectual equipment, had come to Paris without detailed proposals, demonstrated incompetence in the agilities of the council chamber, and had an arrogant, egotistical, and obstinate personality. This "blind and deaf Don Quixote," who before the treaty had appeared to the world as the savior of mankind, simply did not measure up to the challenge. Wilson, the Presbyterian theocrat, was easily "bamboozled" by Clemenceau and Lloyd George. Together, in Keynes's opinion, they wove a "web of sophistry and Jesuitical exegesis that was finally to clothe with insincerity the language and substance of the whole treaty."

Keynes's indictment of Wilson exhibits all the characteristics associated with the disappointed idealist, and it often has been dismissed on precisely those grounds. From our perspective in time it appears so harsh and personal that one is inclined to reject it out of hand. To do so, however, might be to deprive ourselves of the best explanation we have for the fact that a peace, which had so many Carthaginian features, was disguised by a kind of Wilsonian liberal rhetoric that even today creates an impression of fairness in unsophisticated readers. Wilson's attitude, as depicted by Keynes, was: "I see your difficulties and I should like to agree to what you propose; but I can do nothing that is not just and right, and you must first of all show me that what you want does really fall within the words of the pronouncements which are binding on me." Keynes's point is that European draftsmen were up to the challenge and that as a result a certain hypocrisy pervaded the whole treaty.

On the other hand, Paul Birdsall, an American scholar, in his book *Versailles Twenty Years After* (1941), called Keynes's account "caricature, not history." To Birdsall, Wilson was the only man of real stature at the peace conference. He insisted that the president had not failed; the League of Nations was, after all, to be accounted a victory for the Wilsonian approach to peace. Moreover, the record of what Wilson prevented was equally important. Had his moderating influence on Clemenceau and Lloyd George been removed, the treaty would indeed have been Carthaginian. Birdsall admits that the settlement contained many unfortunate provisions but claims that they must be considered in the light of conditions over which Wilson had no control. He believes that on every major question, except that of reparations, the Treaty of Versailles would have been worse had Wilson remained in Washington. Pointing to the fact that the principle of self-determination prevailed to a considerable extent and that the political map of postsettlement Europe came closer to coinciding with an ethnographic map than ever before in European history, other scholars have observed that the surprising aspect of the negotiations is that Wilson was able to save as much of his program as he did. Even Birdsall admits that the treaty was a compromise between Anglo-American and French conceptions of a stable international order and contained Carthaginian as well as Wilsonian features. Although not going as far as Keynes, who stressed the Allies' economic subjugation of their defeated enemy and claimed that little was overlooked which might impoverish Germany or obstruct its future development, most scholars (Birdsall included) still condemn the reparations settlement, if not for its injustice then for its lack of economic sense and because "it combined an egregious breach of faith with an impolitic accusation of moral turpitude."

The question here is by what standards one assesses the treaty. If it is judged by the standards of American idealism, then Birdsall is probably right that without Wilson it would have been a worse treaty, but by any objective historical standard it is difficult to imagine how it could possibly have been worse. Certainly it did not last, and certainly it did not bring peace to Europe. In this regard, it compares unfavorably with the peace constructed at the Congress of Vienna in 1815, a peace that except for short and relatively minor wars lasted almost one hundred years.

As Julius Pratt once reminded us, Machiavelli, the Italian political philosopher, thought that there were only two prudent ways to deal with a defeated enemy: "Either destroy him altogether or treat him so generously that he will become your friend." Any middle course, Machiavelli believed, was perilous. It seems difficult to escape the conclusion that, at Paris, Wilson and the Allies chose a middle course. Either a hard Carthaginian peace or a peace of reconciliation probably would have stood a better chance of survival. It is not easy to read the German criticism of the treaty without deriving the impression that the Paris Peace Conference was indeed guilty of disguising a hard Carthaginian peace under the cloak of Wilsonian idealism and liberalism. Nicolson even went so far as to claim that "seldom in the history of man has such vindictiveness cloaked itself in such unctuous sophistry." Hypocrisy was the overwhelming and inescapable outcome, and as a result the settlement never had the moral authority so necessary to a lasting peace.

Moreover, as Henry Kissinger has argued, it also was unsuccessful from a balance-of-power viewpoint.

> If there was any real purpose to World War I, it was that of destroying German hegemony, but the Versailles peace settlement was probably more favorable to German expansion than the world that existed previously. Before the war Germany had France on one side and Russia on the other, with Britain commanding the seas. After the peace conference, Germany came to be surrounded by weak successor states of uncertain strength, none of whom were capable of resisting Germany.

In short, the diplomats paid precious little attention to the power structure of the postwar world. They made no provisions for the economic rehabilitation of Europe, ignored the Soviet Union, and did little to stabilize and strengthen the new states of eastern Europe.

Even Wilson's strongest defenders now agree that the treaty was imperfect and that it contained many unfortunate provisions, but they would insist that such problems pale before the great achievement of the League of Nations. Arthur Link, for example, has long argued that Wilson in the League was "able to create the machinery for the gradual attainment of the kind of settlement he would have liked to impose at once," and that things would have turned out very differently if only the United States had joined. As a result, in recent years the debate among scholars has tended to focus on the structure of the League and its capabilities with respect to preserving the peace and the reasons underlying the American failure to join.

It is probably true, as Wilsonians then claimed and have claimed ever since, that in the spring of 1919 the majority of the American people favored U.S. membership in a League of Nations. Thirty-two state legislatures had endorsed the idea, and thirty-three governors had gone on record in favor; a *Literary Digest* poll of newspaper editors indicated the same trend. It was very difficult to be against a league to preserve the world's peace.

What happened to change public opinion and why did the United States never join the League? There have been several principal explanations. Many historians have argued that Americans wished to return to what President Warren G. Harding called "normalcy," the result of the slump in idealism which naturally follows in the wake of war. Wilson's inspiring leadership during the war raised the American people to a spirit of self-sacrifice that even brought them to accept the prohibition of alcoholic beverages, but with victory came an emotional letdown. America, many thought, had received little or nothing at the peace table but opposition and ill will. The country was weary of war. Hundreds of thousands of American boys were returning from Europe homesick, irritated by the treatment that they had received in France, and generally disgusted with the whole affair. As one commentator wrote in the *New York Globe*, they were "only too glad to shut the front gate and stay at home for a while."

Another group of historians has accepted the explanation offered by Wilson and his friends and contained in the Democratic party platform of 1920. Henry Cabot Lodge, Republican majority leader in the Senate and chairman of the Senate Foreign Relations Committee, was singled out by name in that platform for his alleged inconsistency and partisanship on the League and peace issue. The Republican Senate also was condemned for "its refusal to ratify the treaty merely because it was the product of Democratic statesmanship, thus interposing partisan envy and personal hatred in the way of peace and renewed prosperity of the world." It is true that the Republicans in the Senate, humiliated by six years of rather iron-handed Wilsonian rule and now again in the driver's seat politically, had their knives sharpened for Wilson. Congress, as invariably happens after a war during which the executive branch has run the show, also was determined to reexert its control over the nation's foreign policy.

These explanations are not necessarily wrong, but they may be incomplete. They tend to ignore the fact that it was no simple matter to construct a workable collective security organization. The Wilsonian interpretation has inhibited rational consideration of the real issues involved in Article X of the League Covenant concerning the role of force in international affairs, and it is precisely on that point that American thinking has often tended to imprecision. We will, as Senator Lodge recognized, always have with us "those who wish to have the world's peace assured by force, without using force to do it." The best of recent American scholarship now concludes that differences of opinion as to how to achieve a lasting peace did play an important, even decisive, role in the struggle over the League. It served the interests of many of those involved to present the struggle as essentially one of partisan politics and personal hatred, but the real problem seems to have been that Americans could not agree upon the nature of the League they wanted or upon the arrangements necessary to make it succeed.

Both Wilson and former president William Howard Taft, leader of the pressure group League to Enforce Peace that advocated U.S. membership, occupied a position fraught with tension. As Walter Lippmann later came to recognize, "In them the idealism which prompts Americans to make large and resounding commitments was combined with the pacifism which causes Americans to shrink from the measures of force that are needed to support the commitments." Wilson, like many of his constituents, believed that idealism was a self-fulfilling proposition, and that the moral force of world public opinion was the best guarantee of peace. Consequently, he came to minimize the very exertions that were so important to the Europeans (the commitment to come to their aid with troops) and implied that the United States would never in practice be called upon to fulfill its commitment to use force on behalf of the territorial integrity of the other members of the League. He was trapped, in short, by the contradiction inherent in his own desires, a contradiction laid bare by Senator William E. Borah when he so pointedly asked: "What will your league amount to if it does not contain powers that no one dreams of giving it?"

Even the actual language of Article X betrayed much of the ambiguity of Wilson's statements:

The Members of the League undertake to respect and preserve as against external aggression the territorial integrity and existing independence of all Members of the League. In case of any such aggression the League Council shall advise upon the means by which this obligation shall be fulfilled.

That left the precise obligation of any particular individual state rather vague, and that was a serious problem. Collective security systems are dependent on perceptions that their guarantees will be automatically invoked. When guarantees become nebulous and fail to engender confidence that they can be relied upon, collective security systems are prone to weaken and dissolve.

As Wilson's principal antagonist Lodge put it, the idea of a League was "all right—fine—but the details were vital." Lodge himself never thought that either world conditions or the nature of the American political system were conducive to the formation of an effective League. He believed in the necessity of enforcing the peace with Germany, as did other conservative internationalists such as Theodore Roosevelt and Elihu Root, men who cannot be classed as isolationists because they were quite willing to support the French guarantee treaty and to undertake similar specific commitments. At the heart of their position was the conviction that there was no halfway measure, no way of constructing an effective League without putting an international military force behind it. As Lodge told the Senate,

If, however, there is to be a league of nations in order to enforce peace, one thing is clear. It must be either a mere assemblage of words, an exposition of vague ideals and encouraging hopes, or it must be a practical system. If such a league is to be practical and effective, it cannot possibly be either unless it has authority to issue decrees and force to sustain them. It is at this point that the questions of great moment arise.

It was, Lodge insisted, "easy to talk" about a League of Nations and the beauty and necessity of peace, but the hard, practical demand is: "Are you ready to put your soldiers and your sailors at the disposition of other nations?" In public he left the answer open, but, well aware of the strength of both the pacifist and isolationist blocs in Congress, Lodge was firmly convinced that a plan for an international army could never get through the Senate. It could not in 1919, it could not in 1945, and it could not today. There were insuperable obstacles to the formation of an effective collective security organization. Those obstacles lay deep in the American character and in the nature of the U.S. political system. What was required for the construction of an effective League of Nations was never politically feasible at home. It was a dilemma from which Wilson found it difficult to escape.

The Covenant that Wilson brought home was an uneasy compromise; it was not quite the "definite guarantee of peace" that Wilsonians, then and later, pictured it to be. It begged even the most basic of questions. It was not even clear whether it was meant to be an instrument of reconciliation or a means of giving permanence to the Allied victory, whether it was to be a truly universal association or only an organization of "free" nations. The fault was not entirely Wilson's but lay in the nature of things. As Brooks Adams once trenchantly observed, "To attain to a relation among its parts in which physical force could be used by a League, would imply an effort of collective thought of which we have no adequate notion." On the all-important question of the precise nature of the obligation incurred under Article X, the Covenant was particularly equivocal. This confusion was but the inevitable consequence of the peacemakers' efforts to preserve national sovereignty while nevertheless suppressing its consequences. This is the classic problem confronting those who would construct a universal collective security organization, and it was not solved either at Paris in 1919 or at San Francisco in 1945.

Wilson always found it difficult to give a compelling interpretation of American responsibilities under Article X. Although claiming that this article was "the very backbone of the whole Covenant," he dared not claim that the League Council's advice derogated from "the right of our Congress under our Constitution to exercise its independent judgment in all matters of peace and war." Actually, either the council had the last word or Congress had it, but Wilson could not politically admit that. Consequently, he was left to try to resolve the contradictions inherent in American participation in the Covenant's version of universal collective security in the following unsatisfactory fashion. The engagement under Article X, he claimed, "constitutes a very grave and solemn moral obligation. But it is a moral, not a legal, obligation, and leaves our Congress absolutely free to put its own interpretation upon it in all cases that call for action. It is binding in conscience only, not in law."

To Wilson and his supporters the moral obligation was a real one, and their objection to Lodge's reservation to Article X was that it specifically removed that moral obligation. This was not a minor point but perhaps the major obstacle to ratification, for the nature of the obligation assumed by member states would of necessity determine just what kind of organization the League was going to be. Since the success of a collective security organization would seem to rest on the absence of doubt as to the intentions of its members—that is, on the credibility of their commitments—Lodge's reservation stating that the United States assumed no obligation was, in effect, a denial of the whole theory on which collective security rested. His reservations, although they would have preserved the League as a useful instrument of collaboration and international cooperation, would nevertheless have transformed it into a noncoercive or intermediate type of international organization, which is essentially what it became. The problems involved in constructing a workable collective security organization without derogating from national sovereignty proved insuperable; Canada tried to have Article X suppressed in 1920, and in 1923 the League Council could not even decide whether its advice was binding. Like the United States, most of the countries involved were unwilling to sacrifice their traditional policies or vital interests to secure a more satisfactory peace. It seems doubtful that U.S. membership in the League, with or without the Lodge reservations, could have solved these fundamental constitutional questions.

The final argument of those who would defend the peace settlement and the American role therein is that it did manage, for all its imperfections, to create a new international order that functioned rather well for some years. Link would still insist that "it failed not because it was imperfect, but because it was not defended when challenges arose in the '30s." In this opinion, Link echoes the sentiments of Lloyd George, who once remarked that many of the ills blamed on the treaty were not intrinsic but rather the fault of the oncoming generations of leaders who failed to execute it. That argument, however, only raises the question of why the Versailles treaty was not defended. Root always believed that a great opportunity had been wasted at Paris, and that the American people could have been persuaded to undertake a specific and binding obligation to defend France, such as was incorporated in the French guarantee treaty, but that Wilson's League left too many loopholes to stand the test of time. Moreover, a good argument can be made that the treaty's hypocrisies and inconsistencies contributed much to its demise, instilling in the Germans the belief that they were being judged by standards that did not apply to other nations and hence lending a sense of righteousness to their revanchism and undermining in the minds of the Allies the idea that this was a legitimate and moral peace, deserving of respect and of being forcefully upheld.

The unhappy results can probably best be attributed to a confusion of purpose, to ongoing problems in the whole American approach to the conduct of foreign policy. Peace, a stable international order, and justice are not necessarily synonymous ends. Justice is a particularly troublesome and fleeting, time-bound concept. Wilson was sincerely determined to arrange a just peace, but that very preoccupation may have prevented both a peace of accommodation with Germany and a peace designed to keep Germany permanently in check. Either of these alternatives might have been preferable to the actual result.

Sources and Suggested Readings

Ambrosius, Lloyd. *Woodrow Wilson and the American Diplomatic Tradition.* Cambridge, MA, 1987.

Bailey, Thomas A. *Woodrow Wilson and the Great Betrayal.* New York, 1945.

———. *Woodrow Wilson and the Lost Peace.* New York, 1944.

Birdsall, Paul. *Versailles Twenty Years After.* New York, 1941.

Buehrig, Edward H., ed. *Wilson's Foreign Policy in Perspective.* Bloomington, IN, 1957.

Floto, Inga. *Colonel House in Paris: A Study of American Policy at the Paris Peace Conference, 1919.* Copenhagen, 1973.

Gelfand, Lawrence E. *The Inquiry: American Preparations for Peace, 1917–1919.* New Haven, CT, 1963.

Huthmacher, J. Joseph, and Susman, Warren, eds. *Wilson's Diplomacy: An International Symposium.* Cambridge, MA, 1973.

Keynes, John Maynard. *The Economic Consequences of the Peace.* New York, 1920.

Knock, Thomas J. *To End All Wars: Woodrow Wilson and the Quest for a New World Order.* New York, 1992.

Kuehl, Warren F. *Seeking World Order: The United States and International Organization to 1920.* Nashville, TN, 1969.

Levin, N. Gordon, Jr. *Woodrow Wilson and World Politics: America's Response to War and Revolution.* New York, 1968.

Link, Arthur S. *Wilson the Diplomatist: A Look at His Major Foreign Policies.* Chicago, 1965.

Mayer, Arno. *Politics and Diplomacy of Peacemaking: Containment and Counterrevolution at Versailles, 1918–1919.* New York, 1967.

McDougall, Walter A. *France's Rhineland Policy, 1914–1924*. Princeton, NJ, 1978.

Nicolson, Harold. *Peacemaking, 1919: Being Reminiscences of the Paris Peace Conference*. Boston, 1933.

Schwabe, Klaus. *Woodrow Wilson, Revolutionary Germany, and Peacemaking, 1918–1919*. Chapel Hill, NC, 1985.

Smith, Daniel M. *The Great Departure: The United States and World War I, 1914–1920*. New York, 1965.

Stromberg, Roland. *Collective Security and American Foreign Policy: From the League of Nations to NATO*. New York, 1963.

Tillman, Seth P. *Anglo-American Relations at the Paris Peace Conference of 1919*. Princeton, NJ, 1961.

Trachtenberg, Marc. *Reparations in World Politics: France and European Economic Diplomacy, 1916–1923*. New York, 1980.

Vinson, John Chalmers. *Referendum for Isolation: The Defeat of Article Ten of the League of Nations Covenant*. Athens, GA, 1961.

Walworth, Arthur. *Wilson and His Peacemakers*. New York, 1986.

Widenor, William C. *Henry Cabot Lodge and the Search for an American Foreign Policy*. Berkeley, CA, 1980.

Yates, Louis A. *The United States and French Security, 1917–1921: A Study in American Diplomatic History*. New York, 1957.

American Diplomacy in the 1920s

John M. Carroll

In recent years a debate concerning the nature of American foreign policy in the 1920s has stirred considerable controversy among historians. Reduced to its simplest terms, the debate has centered on the question of whether or not America followed a policy of isolationism. Historians such as Selig Adler and Foster Rhea Dulles, who admire President Woodrow Wilson and his vision of a League of Nations that would ensure international peace and security through the collective action of its members, have argued that U.S. foreign policy was largely one of aloofness and withdrawal from world affairs during the 1920s. They maintain that the Senate's rejection of the Treaty of Versailles and membership in the League, as well as the subsequent refusal of Republican administrations to make political commitments to preserve the peace, led to a policy and sentiment that can be properly characterized as isolationism. These historians view American diplomacy in the 1920s as weak, halting, and timid and claim that it contributed significantly to the breakdown of the international order in the 1930s which, in turn, resulted in World War II.

Revisionists such as Carl Parrini and Melvyn P. Leffler, who have followed the lead of radical historian William A. Williams, maintain that America was extremely active in international affairs in the 1920s and that its diplomacy was not isolationist. Its leaders, they claim, vigorously pursued international objectives of peace, stability, and prosperity but through economic diplomacy rather than through binding treaties and political commitments.

The debate over whether or not American diplomacy in the 1920s was isolationist is of limited usefulness because it is more semantic than real. The defeat of the treaty in the United States and the persistent instability in Europe after the war did cause the sense of despair and hopelessness that gripped the American public and prompted many citizens to reject Wilsonianism and its advocacy of political commitments. To this extent, a mood of isolationism existed in the United States which affected diplomacy and disappointed Wilsonian internationalists, who wanted their country to play a direct political role in world affairs. It is also clear, however, that except from 1917 to 1920, America was never more active in international affairs until the eve of World War II than it was during the 1920s. This apparent paradox helps to explain why the controversy focusing on isolationism has raged for so long without producing a consensus on the nature of American foreign policy in the 1920s.

Recent scholarship on the diplomacy of the postwar decade has provided several clues which help to clarify the nature of U.S. foreign policy. These studies indicate that the 1920s were a transitional decade in the shaping of twentieth-century American diplomacy. Republican policymakers rejected the traditional aloofness from international affairs associated with the nineteenth and early twentieth centuries but were not prepared to embrace the kind of international commitment that has characterized the post-World War II era. Policy in the 1920s simply took on a new form, making it difficult for observers then, as well as now, to characterize: America was restrained yet active in foreign affairs during the 1920s. Three basic elements combined to shape Republican foreign policy. First, the treaty debacle in the United States and the public disillusionment with Wilsonianism created what Adler has called an "isolationist impulse." Policy-makers were aware that close association with the League, or any indication of political commitment in international affairs, would bring a sharp reaction from Congress and the public. Thus, they avoided political commitments and what became known as collective security.

Second, officials in Washington had great faith in the theory that economic, rather than political, forces would be the key to maintaining peace and stability in the postwar world. This view was based on the optimistic premise that advances in technology, communication, and transportation were making the world more interdependent and would lead to greater mutual trust among peoples. By solving economic problems and creating greater prosperity, these leaders hoped to build an international community in which the benefits of peace would be so evident that war would be unthinkable. The American strategy of economic diplomacy relied on two concepts that were in evidence throughout the decade: 1) that independent business experts should help shape diplomacy because of their skill in this area and their objectivity in the face of political pressures; and 2) that economic and political agreements should be voluntary, based on mutual benefit and the enforcement power of public opinion.

Third, policymakers believed that the United States enjoyed basic economic and military security and should not pursue any policy that might endanger either. This conception of its place in the world was a restraining force in foreign policy because it limited the sacrifices America would make or the risks it would take to ensure world stability. To many leaders of the era, the nation was an unassailable economic and military fortress. The United States would be active in international affairs in the 1920s so long as no

"WHY THIS CHICKEN CROSSED THE ROAD." (Rochester *Herald*, 1921, Library of Congress)

political commitment was required or economic concession sought that might weaken its presumed security. The historian Joan Hoff-Wilson has aptly named this policy "independent internationalism," while others have called it "continentalism."

The debate over the Treaty of Versailles, with its controversial League of Nations section, dominated American foreign policy in the early 1920s. In retrospect, Wilson's statement that the 1920 election should be "a great and solemn referendum" on the League issue proved to be a costly error. The election results turned out to be not just a landslide for the Republicans but what Democratic national chairman Joseph P. Tumulty termed an earthquake. Although Vice President-elect Calvin Coolidge doubted if Warren G. Harding's overwhelming victory meant that the American people opposed membership in the League of Nations, most politicians and media representatives believed otherwise. In early 1921, President Harding, who had equivocated on the issue during the recent campaign, declared that the question of membership in the League was as dead as slavery. Republican leaders realized that they would have to distance themselves from the tarnished mantle of Wilsonian internationalism or face the wrath of many in Congress who boasted with Senator Henry Cabot Lodge that they had "torn up Wilsonianism by its roots."

Republican presidential leadership during the 1920s reflected both the party and the public's desire to repudiate the missionary zeal and strong personal authority in foreign affairs associated with Wilson. Harding, who possessed at best a second-rate mind, made it clear that his secretary of state would run the State Department and make vital decisions. The Ohio president was content to allow Charles Evans Hughes (1921–1925), Secretary of Commerce Herbert Hoover (1921–1928), and Secretary of the Treasury Andrew Mellon (1921–1932) make most foreign policy decisions. Coolidge, who served as president for most of the decade, followed a similar policy, although his secretary of state, Frank B. Kellogg (1925–1929), was not as capable as Hughes. Both Harding and Coolidge were better informed and more astute in foreign affairs than historians have generally conceded, but they deliberately chose to play a subordinate role in that area. President Hoover, who is considered one of the most knowledgeable of all public officials in diplomatic matters during the 1920s, did not initiate any bold policies in foreign relations. For all his experience and expertise in diplomacy, Hoover, perhaps more than either Harding or Coolidge, feared and disliked encountering congressional opposition and usually avoided diplomatic measures likely to stir up Congress against his administration. For the most part, presidential leadership in foreign affairs was weak in the 1920s, and most of the initiative in that field devolved on the secretary of state, his department, and other interested cabinet members who often confronted a suspicious Congress.

Secretary of State Hughes was largely responsible for shaping the nation's diplomacy in the early part of the decade. A confirmed internationalist, he sought to reestablish American influence in the critical task of reconstructing Europe. Sensitive to charges that he was a "bewhiskered Wilson," Hughes appointed U.S. diplomats to sit on important League-affiliated bodies, such as the Reparations Commission and the Supreme Council, as "unofficial observers." These observers participated in discussions and outlined American policy but did not vote. Nevertheless, the influence of unofficial diplomats such as Roland Boyden was considerable because of America's dominant financial position in the world and the desire of European leaders to mobilize U.S. capital to help solve the pressing problems of reconstruction. After snubbing the League of Nations in the early days of the administration by failing to answer official communications from Geneva, Hughes and Harding began to cooperate with the League on a variety of humanitarian matters. By mid-decade American delegates served on committees and conferences relating to such problems as the opium trade, white slavery traffic, and improving world health. Later in the decade the United States participated in League deliberations that were more clearly economic and political, including conferences on world disarmament.

The main thrust of America's European diplomacy, however, was directed toward the problem of postwar reconstruction. Europe had been devastated by the Great War. Its economy was shattered, political tensions were high, rearmament was under way, and the future political and economic stability of the Continent was in doubt. Hughes and other Republican leaders recognized that European instability directly affected U.S. interests. They addressed the question of European reconstruction by drawing on the experience gained in the Progressive Era, the war, and the recent peace settlement.

American foreign policy leaders in the 1920s placed great emphasis on economic diplomacy. Stunned by the tragedy of the

recent war, they questioned whether dependence on political commitments, military alliances, or large expenditures on armaments
would prevent a future world conflict. Many argued that these very
policies had led to the outbreak of the Great War. Instead, policymakers held that economic prosperity and stability might lead to
future peace. Hughes emphasized this point when he stated that
"there will be no permanent peace unless economic satisfactions
are enjoyed." Business as well as political leaders stressed that the
scientific advancements in communication, transportation, and technology made in the early part of the century and accelerated by the
war would lead to a prosperous world society linked together in
peaceful effort. Economic, rather than political, forces would shape
the future, and governments should pursue policies that conformed
to the movement of economic forces rather than impeded them. As
the leading industrial and creditor nation, the United States would
play a vital role in shaping post-war events if a coherent policy of
economic diplomacy could be implemented.

The country's leaders also insisted that policy objectives should
be pursued through voluntary agreements and with the aid and counsel of independent business experts. Both measures were brought
about in part by the defeat of the Versailles treaty and the reaction
against Wilsonianism. They were expedients designed to camou-
flage American diplomacy from the eyes of the Senate and deflect
criticism that the nation was entangled in the affairs of Europe.
The use of voluntary agreements also reflected the view that political commitments and military alliances did not prevent wars, or at
least had not in 1914. Hughes once remarked that "the alternative
of friendly settlements is resort to coercion, and if you wish peace
you must pursue the methods of friendly intercourse between governments . . . there is no other way." The use of independent business experts to implement diplomacy was based in part on the
experience of the Progressive Era and the war, which showed that
scientific management of governmental problems was more efficient, more equitable, and served the public interest. As Michael
Hogan has pointed out, this form of public/private power sharing
in diplomacy "conformed with the American political economy,
avoided wasteful and undemocratic state capitalism, and guaranteed a more efficient and peaceful management of world affairs."
In confronting the problem of European reconstruction along with
many other diplomatic issues of the 1920s, American leaders relied

heavily on economic diplomacy, voluntarism, and the use of business experts to achieve their goals.

This diplomatic strategy was first put to the test in confronting the problems associated with European reconstruction. Much of the Continent was devastated by both the military and economic effects of the war. Parts of France and Belgium, as well as areas in eastern Europe, were destroyed by the advancing and retreating armies. The economies of most major nations were plagued by heavy indebtedness and persistent inflation. Germany, which had the strongest prewar economy, was saddled with a reparations debt under the Versailles treaty which was set in 1921 at $33 billion, an enormous sum at that time. Although some recent historians such as Marc Trachtenberg maintain that Germany could have repaid the debt, American leaders were heavily influenced by the British economist John Maynard Keynes, who held that Germany was the key to European reconstruction and that it could not recover unless the reparations debt was reduced substantially. The United States had a vital stake in German and European recovery because without it America's trade, foreign investment, and eventually its entire economy were bound to suffer. Beyond this, the continuing economic paralysis on the Continent might trigger social upheaval and the spread of bolshevism into central and western Europe. The unresolved reparations dispute also heightened tensions between Germany and France and indirectly threatened political stability in all parts of Europe.

The United States had an indirect stake in the reparations controversy in that major Allied nations owed it more than $10 billion in war debts. Beginning in 1919, Allied leaders urged the United States to cancel these debts in exchange for a commensurate reduction in German reparations. Although some reductions were made in the war debt payment agreements of the 1920s, American leaders refused to cancel them. Leffler has argued persuasively that domestic political considerations were the main cause of the U.S. stance on war debts. Cancellation would have meant higher taxes for Americans because the original war loans were raised by selling wartime bonds. The Republican administrations of the 1920s placed a high priority on aiding in the economic rehabilitation and political pacification of Europe but not to the extent that it might cause undue sacrifice or political turmoil in the United States. The refusal to cancel the war debts is an example of the domestic restraint under which American diplomats had to pursue foreign policy objectives.

Their approach to the problem of European reconstruction was to use patience and economic diplomacy. As the United States was the world's leading creditor nation, its capital would be needed to bring about European recovery. Working in cooperation with U.S. international banking firms, the State Department made it clear that capital would not be available for European reconstruction until the German reparations debt had been scaled down to a reasonable figure. Although recent studies indicate that France's reparations policy was more flexible than previously thought, its leaders considered a substantial reparations debt as a kind of ransom to ensure their nation's security and a safeguard to protect the Treaty of Versailles. The growing revisionist view of the treaty touched off by Keynes's *The Economic Consequences of the Peace* (1919), Berlin's refusal or inability to meet reparations quotas, and the general British and American sympathy for the German position combined, however, to undermine French policy. In desperation, France jeopardized its entente with Britain by occupying the German Ruhr valley in January 1923 in order to collect reparations. During the months and days prior to the French military move, Hughes offered to establish an independent conference of business experts to set reparations within what he described as Germany's "capacity to pay." The French military gamble temporarily sidelined the so-called Hughes Plan. Hughes responded philosophically by declaring "that each side would probably have to 'enjoy its own bit of chaos' until a disposition to a fair settlement had been created."

The Ruhr occupation resulted in the near collapse of the German economy and frustration for France's attempt to collect reparations. By November 1923, Premier Raymond Poincaré, with American encouragement, authorized the Reparations Commission to summon financial experts to study the reparations question. The Dawes Committee convened in Paris in January 1924 and included Owen D. Young, chairman of both General Electric and RCA, and Chicago banker Charles G. Dawes, who were selected with the advice and consent of the State Department. Although ostensibly independent experts, Young and Dawes worked in close cooperation with the State and Commerce departments. During early 1924 the Dawes Committee turned out a report which suggested a major revision in the reparations system. The report called for a year-by-year schedule of payments, the reorganization of Germany's financial structure under an independent expert called the Agent General for Reparations, and a sizable private loan for Germany to help revitalize its economy. The plan was to be a temporary system to determine how much Berlin could actually pay.

During the summer of 1924, American leaders, including Young and Ambassador to Britain Frank B. Kellogg, lobbied to gain French and German acceptance of the Dawes Plan. This was accomplished at the London Conference of July 1924. The powerful New York banking firm of J. P. Morgan and Company agreed to underwrite a substantial portion of the German Dawes loan after it was agreed that France would evacuate the Ruhr and that the power of the Reparations Commission to declare German defaults on reparations would be restricted.

The Dawes Plan, which went into effect in the fall, had an immediate positive impact on European economic and political conditions. American capital began to flow into Germany, and, through the office of the Agent General for Reparations, payments were transferred to the Allies. On the surface the German economy prospered, but its recovery was fueled by a torrent of short-term loans, mainly from America, which overly optimistic investors poured into the country. Contrary to the advice of Dawes Plan architect Young, German leaders failed to use the loans for productive purposes that would ensure a future trade surplus capable of meeting the reparations debt from solely domestic resources. Instead, the foreign loans were largely used for nonproductive purposes and to meet current reparations quotas. This created a dangerous situation because the Dawes Plan now rested squarely on the willingness of foreign investors to provide Germany with a continuous supply of short-term capital.

Despite the dangerous economic conditions developing in Germany, European leaders greeted the Dawes Plan and the anticipated economic recovery in a spirit of trust and conciliation. In 1925, Allied and German leaders met in Locarno to discuss a series of agreements designed to guarantee the existing borders in parts of Europe. During the course of the discussions, President Coolidge made it plain that the continued flow of American capital to Europe was dependent on some kind of security agreement on the Continent. On December 1, 1925, the Locarno treaties were signed by German and Allied leaders. The most important of these treaties was an agreement confirming the inviolability of the Franco-German and Belgo-German frontiers and the demilitarized zone of the Rhineland. A feeling of euphoria swept Europe which contemporary observers hailed as the "spirit of Locarno." To many it appeared that the hatred and bitterness associated with the war were over, and a new era of peace and conciliation was at hand. For American policymakers the Dawes Plan and resulting Locarno pacts appeared to be a singular triumph of their economic diplomacy.

The new era proved to be more an illusion than a reality. The spirit of Locarno only disguised the fact that Germany was thoroughly determined to revise the Versailles settlement by conciliation if possible, or by force if necessary. So long as Europe was relatively prosperous and the former enemies remained strong, Foreign Minister Gustav Stresemann was content to unchain his country through diplomacy. German and European prosperity, however, largely depended on the Dawes Plan and the American short-term loans that supported it. By the end of the decade, Germany was finding it difficult to meet the increasing yearly reparations quotas stipulated in the plan. European leaders agreed in 1928 that it was time to establish a final reparations plan that would set Germany's total debt as well as a new yearly payment schedule. Such a plan would allow it to assess its total obligation to the Allies and presumably work harder to put its economic affairs in order.

In February 1929 the Young Committee of financial experts, which included Young and Thomas W. Lamont of J. P. Morgan and Company, met in Paris and hammered out a new reparations plan. The resulting Young Plan set German reparations at about $8 billion and reduced yearly payments below Dawes Plan levels. Subsequent agreements which helped implement the plan in 1930 called for the early military evacuation of the Rhineland and the establishment of the Bank of International Settlements, which would facilitate reparations transfers. German payments were to run for fifty-nine years, the same time span as the Allied war debt obligations to America, and during the last twenty-two years the two debts exactly corresponded. This linkage between war debts and reparations angered President Hoover, who became wary of the new reparations agreement and ultimately refused to ratify the Young Plan. Young, who had earlier urged Hoover to cancel the war debts and reduce American tariff barriers, was frustrated by the president's lack of support. He hoped that the new reparations plan, in combination with the Bank of International Settlements, might make it possible to commercialize all the wartime debts and thus put the whole issue out of the realm of future political conflict. Young maintained that Hoover was afraid to take the initiative on the war debt and tariff issues because he might incur the wrath of domestic interests that were well represented in Congress. The cancellation of war debts and tariff reductions, in Young's view, would stimulate world trade and facilitate the removal of the war debt and reparations questions from the political arena. Hoover held firm in his position and even signed a higher tariff law, the Hawley-Smoot Act, in 1930.

The conflict in views between Hoover and Young indicated one of the liabilities of using private business experts to carry out public policy. It also showed that Hoover, like Coolidge and Harding before him, pursued a policy of continentalism, which put domestic priorities far ahead of economic sacrifices that might have ameliorated international tensions during the 1920s. The Great Depression, which was triggered by the Wall Street crash of 1929, curtailed short-term lending to Germany and undermined the Young Plan. By 1932, Berlin defaulted on reparations, with Allied acquiescence, and this led to a series of German initiatives that struck at the heart of the Versailles system and destabilized international politics in the 1930s.

In addition to their reliance on economic diplomacy, American leaders believed that international disarmament would help guarantee worldwide security and stability. Their emphasis on disarmament in the 1920s was a reaction to the massive slaughter of the Great War and conformed to the prevailing view that economic progress, rather than military might, was the best safeguard against future wars. In fact, the two threads of American policy were linked. The cost of armaments in many countries caused both domestic and international economic problems and often led to political instability. Disarmament would help to eliminate wasteful expenditures and in the process promote commercial expansion and peace. Beyond this, most Americans believed that the prewar arms race had been a major cause of World War I.

The advocates of disarmament were active both in government and in the society as a whole. Reacting to the devastation of the war and its aftermath, disarmament advocates "fired the formation of the most dynamic peace movement in American history," Charles DeBenedetti has written. The peace seekers founded a variety of organizations supported by internationalists, pacifists, and liberal reformers. Such groups as the League of Nations Non-Partisan Association, the War Resisters' League, and the National Council for

the Prevention of War thrived during the 1920s. One of the most
striking successes in terms of publicity was the American Peace
Award offered by millionaire publisher Edward W. Bok in 1923.
The $100,000 award was to go to the author of the best brief plan
to involve the United States in maintaining world peace. Veteran
peace activist Charles H. Levermore won the award in 1924, but
his plan was never adopted. Despite the lack of unity in the peace
movement, it did have an impact on government policy.

In the spring of 1921 a coalition of peace groups, including
feminists, Protestants, and internationalists, gathered to force President Harding to take the initiative in world disarmament. As a result of their efforts and with the support of Senator William E. Borah,
Harding convened the Washington Conference of 1921–22. Although the agenda was limited, it offered an opportunity to stop the
naval arms race and stabilize political affairs in the Far East. Delegates from the Big Three naval powers—America, Britain, and
Japan, along with French and Italian representatives—assembled
in Washington in late 1921 to open the first postwar disarmament
conference.

Secretary of State Hughes stunned the delegates at the opening
session by calling for an immediate end to the naval race. He proposed that Britain, America, and Japan reduce the number of their
capital ships to conform to a relative power ratio of 5:5:3, respectively, and that no new battleships be constructed for ten years.
France and Italy were assigned a ratio of 1.75 in the Hughes formula. In all, the secretary called for the major powers to scrap more
than sixty ships. One British admiral was purported to have remarked that Hughes was preparing to scrap more English ships than
the navies of the world had sunk in "a cycle of centuries." The
Five-Power Treaty, signed the following year, incorporated the
Hughes proposal and stipulated that neither the United States nor
Britain could build new bases or strengthen existing ones in the
Far East. The latter concession guaranteed naval superiority in Asian
waters to Japan. The delegates, largely because of French opposition, were unable to negotiate a disarmament agreement to cover
submarines and cruisers.

Although the disarmament negotiations received most of the
headlines, the conference was equally concerned with establishing
a new order in Asia. As a result, two multinational pacts were signed
to replace the imperialistic system symbolized by the Anglo-
Japanese alliance of 1902. A Four-Power Treaty, signed by Britain,

France, America, and Japan, abrogated the former alliance and called for its signatories to maintain the status quo in Asia. Under the Nine-Power Treaty, signed by all nations having an interest in Asia with the exception of the Soviet Union, it was agreed to respect the integrity of China in conformity with the Open Door policy. The treaties contained no provisions for enforcement and thus rested on the goodwill of the signatories and the presumed weight of world opinion.

In light of the events of the 1930s and 1940s, many historians have criticized the noncoercive, voluntary nature of the Washington treaties. Since voluntarism was a vital aspect of Republican policy, which also included an emphasis on economic diplomacy and disarmament, it would be fairer to evaluate the Washington Conference in view of the totality of American foreign policy of the 1920s. It can be argued that the treaties failed to provide lasting security not because of their voluntary nature per se but because American economic diplomacy did not generate an expanding commercial system in which economic satisfactions were enjoyed by all nations. Japan, it should be remembered, started on its aggressive course mainly in response to the deteriorating state of the world's economy in the early 1930s.

Further attempts at naval disarmament were not as successful as the Five-Power Treaty. The Geneva Conference of 1927 failed to reach an agreement on cruisers because of an Anglo-American dispute over the desirability of limiting light, as opposed to heavy, vessels. At the 1930 London Naval Conference the United States, Japan, and Britain reached an agreement concerning their relative strengths in terms of light and heavy cruisers and submarines, but it was seriously undermined by an escape clause that allowed any of the three powers to suspend the agreement if they felt threatened by a nonsignatory nation.

The most highly publicized peace initiative in the 1920s was the Kellogg-Briand Pact. This treaty, which called for states to renounce war as an instrument of national policy and to settle all disputes by peaceful means, was eventually ratified by sixty-three powers. The origins of the pact can be traced to the early 1920s when Chicago lawyer Salmon Levinson organized the American Committee for the Outlawry of War and insisted that war was like collective murder and should be considered a crime before the law. In 1927, Columbia University professor James T. Shotwell took up the theme and urged Paris to sign with Washington a bilateral treaty outlawing war. French foreign minister Aristide Briand, desiring an understanding with the United States that might bolster French security, cautiously endorsed Shotwell's plan. Pressured by various peace groups and the Franco-American amity resulting from Charles A. Lindbergh's solo flight to Paris in May 1927, the Coolidge administration began to consider the plan seriously. Secretary of State Kellogg took the lead in early 1928 by offering to France and other countries a treaty to outlaw offensive war as an instrument of national policy. The multilateral agreement was much less significant to the French, who had hoped for a private security understanding with America, but France, the United States, and thirteen other nations signed the officially named Paris Peace Pact in August 1928. The U.S. Senate ratified the treaty in January 1929 by a vote of 85 to 1.

By any standards the Kellogg-Briand Pact was a weak instrument for preventing future wars. Senator Carter Glass remarked that it was not "worth a postage stamp" in terms of maintaining permanent peace. The pact divided the numerous peace groups. Some peace activists such as Shotwell maintained that it was the first step in revising America's neutrality status in time of war and opening the way for cooperation with the League of Nations in imposing sanctions on aggressor nations. Other peace reformers noted that the pact was ratified at the same time that Congress was increasing naval strength and U.S. Marines were invading Nicaragua. They saw the pact as a smoke screen camouflaging the more pressing problems that stood in the way of maintaining a lasting peace. At best the Kellogg-Briand Pact was a voluntary agreement which the United States might interpret as a justification for taking indirect action against aggressors in time of war. Above all, the pact was a clear manifestation of America's independent internationalism in the 1920s.

The Latin American diplomacy of the United States stood in contrast to its relations with the rest of the world. American leaders still paid homage to the Monroe Doctrine and the Roosevelt Corollary to that document and considered Latin America a U.S. sphere of influence. As a result of the war, American trade and investments expanded rapidly and supplanted those of European powers that previously had had an important economic stake in the region's republics. With the support of Secretary of Commerce Hoover's Bureau of Foreign and Domestic Commerce, American businessmen gained dominance over markets and economies in Latin

America during the 1920s. In contrast to the Open Door style of economic diplomacy practiced in other parts of the world, however, the U.S. government encouraged closed door techniques in Latin America. The same cartels and special trading agreements that Washington objected to in Europe, the Middle East, or Asia formed the basis of inter-American trade. Under the doctrine of continentalism, Latin America was considered a special province of the United States, and different economic and political rules applied in that region.

During the early part of the century the United States had maintained stability and thwarted outside intervention in Latin America through the use of military force. By 1920 the Central American trouble spots—Santo Domingo, Cuba, Panama, Haiti, and Nicaragua—had been stabilized through U.S. military efforts. This policy of direct intervention and a commitment to preserve political stability contrasted sharply with America's economic diplomacy in other parts of the world.

By the early 1920s the threat of foreign intervention in Latin America receded, and this encouraged U.S. policymakers to pursue a less interventionist strategy in that region. The rise of intense nationalism and the undermining of old-style imperialism, which came about as a result of World War I, also caused Washington to reevaluate its interventionist policies. Secretary of State Hughes took the initiative by making several goodwill tours in South America and by terminating the U.S. military occupation in Santo Domingo. America's attempt to live down its image as the Colossus of the North, however, was at best halting during the postwar decade. In 1926, President Coolidge ordered marines into Nicaragua to quell internal disturbances, even though American forces had been withdrawn as recently as the previous year. Under pressure from peace groups and congressional critics, he moderated his policy toward Nicaragua and appointed a special troubleshooter, Henry Stimson, to work out a nonmilitary solution to the crisis.

Although U.S. forces remained in Nicaragua until 1933, Coolidge's action indicated a new direction in the nation's approach to Latin American problems. In a similar vein, he responded with caution and restraint to a crisis in Mexico triggered by the recent revolution in that country and to a dispute over subsoil mineral rights. Pressed again by peace activists and congressmen weary of the old-style interventionist tactics, the president appointed former Amherst College classmate Dwight Morrow as ambassador to

Mexico. Morrow charmed his Mexican hosts and negotiated a satisfactory settlement on the issue of subsoil mineral rights, thereby averting a serious crisis. Taken as a whole, the nation's Latin American policy conformed with the overall thrust of U.S. diplomacy in the 1920s, despite the important exceptions cited above. Washington's policymakers, for the most part, eschewed the use of military force and attempted to stabilize the region through the use of eco-

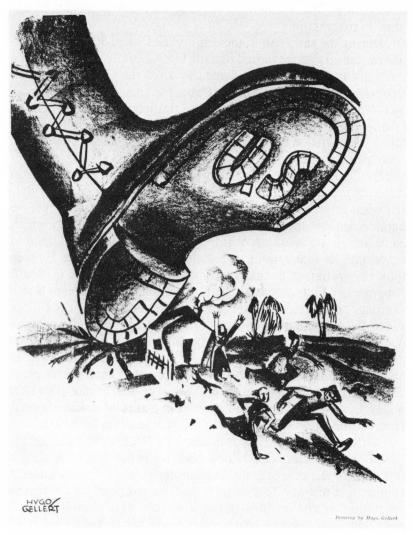

Drawing by Hugo Gellert

"Goodwill." A critical view of U.S. policy in Nicaragua in the 1920s. (*New Masses*, Library of Congress)

nomic diplomacy. Many historians have correctly noted that the roots of Franklin Roosevelt's Good Neighbor policy can be seen in the 1920s.

Foreign policy in the 1920s, with its emphasis on economic diplomacy, public/private power sharing, voluntarism, continental self-sufficiency, and disarmament and its rejection of direct military commitments, might seem strange and quaint to the contemporary observer. Yet, in the past two decades, American leaders have reconsidered and tested many of these same options in addressing international problems of the present. As a result of a long and costly Cold War struggle, in which military commitment and resort to the use of arms became a watchword of U.S. policy, many Americans now recognize the limits of the nation's vast military power. A seemingly futile nuclear arms race has rekindled interest in disarmament as a viable diplomatic option. The increasing interdependence of the world economy has reemphasized the importance of economic diplomacy and underscored the necessity of public/private power sharing in solving many international economic as well as political problems. The oil crisis of the 1970s has renewed some interest in continental self-sufficiency. Even the concept of voluntarism, which was anathema to post-World War II leaders, is again spoken of as a viable, although limited, strategy in the recent era of détente.

The current reconsideration of diplomatic strategies associated with the 1920s does not mean that U.S. foreign policy in that decade can be termed a success. American leaders in the post-World War I decade overvalued the usefulness of voluntary agreements and underestimated the value of military commitments. Attempts to bring about meaningful disarmament in the 1920s were in many cases naive and illusory. The reliance on public/private power sharing worked well in some instances, most notably the Dawes Plan, but was poorly coordinated in other cases, such as in the Young Plan negotiations. America's strategy of continental self-sufficiency, in both a military and an economic sense, was narrowly conceived in the 1920s in light of the technological breakthroughs with possible military applications and the emerging interdependent world economy. The nation's high tariffs and its refusal to cancel the war debts ran counter to the larger policies of economic diplomacy designed to ensure world peace and stability through an ever-expanding commercial network. In retrospect, the 1920s were a transitional decade in American foreign policy in which new strategies in diplomacy were attempted. Some were innovative and relatively successful, and others proved to be shortsighted and ineffective.

Sources and Suggested Readings

Adler, Selig. *The Uncertain Giant, 1921–1941: American Foreign Policy between the Wars*. New York, 1965.

Buckley, Thomas H. *The United States and the Washington Conference, 1921–1922*. Knoxville, TN, 1970.

Cohen, Warren I. *Empire without Tears: America's Foreign Relations, 1921–1933*. New York, 1987.

Costigliola, Frank. *Awkward Dominion: American Political, Economic, and Cultural Relations with Europe, 1919–1933*. Ithaca, NY, 1984.

DeBenedetti, Charles. *The Origins of the Modern American Peace Movement, 1915–1929*. Millwood, NY, 1978.

———. *The Peace Reform in American History*. Bloomington, IN, 1980.

DeConde, Alexander. *Herbert Hoover's Latin American Policy*. Stanford, CA, 1951.

Dulles, Foster Rhea. *America's Rise to World Power, 1898–1954*. New York, 1954.

Ellis, L. Ethan. *Republican Foreign Policy, 1921–1933*. New Brunswick, NJ, 1968.

Ferrell, Robert H. *Peace in Their Time: The Origins of the Kellogg-Briand Pact*. New Haven, CT, 1952.

Grieb, Kenneth J. *The Latin American Policy of Warren G. Harding*. Fort Worth, TX, 1977.

Hoff-Wilson, Joan. *American Business and Foreign Policy, 1920–1933*. Lexington, KY, 1971.

Hogan, Michael J. *Informal Entente: The Private Structure of Cooperation in Anglo-American Economic Diplomacy, 1918–1928*. Columbia, MO, 1977.

Iriye, Akira. *After Imperialism: The Search for a New Order in the Far East, 1921–1931*. Columbia, MO, 1977.

Jones, Kenneth Paul, ed. *U.S. Diplomats in Europe, 1919–1941*. Santa Barbara, CA, 1981.

Leffler, Melvyn P. *The Elusive Quest: America's Pursuit of European Stability and French Security, 1919–1933*. Chapel Hill, NC, 1979.

Parrini, Carl. *Heir to Empire: United States Economic Diplomacy, 1916–1923*. Pittsburgh, 1969.

Schuker, Stephen A. *The End of French Predominance in Europe: The Financial Crisis of 1924 and the Adoption of the Dawes Plan*. Chapel Hill, NC, 1976.

Trachtenberg, Marc. *Reparations in World Politics: France and European Economic Diplomacy, 1916–1923*. New York, 1980.

Tulchin, Joseph S. *The Aftermath of War: World War I and U.S. Policy toward Latin America*. New York, 1971.

Williams, William Appleman. *The Tragedy of American Diplomacy*. New York, 1972.

Wood, Bryce. *The Making of the Good Neighbor Policy*. New York, 1961.

The Diplomacy of the Depression

Jane Karoline Vieth

From behind their broad ocean moats, many Americans in the 1920s and 1930s viewed international events with a certain aloofness, demanding that American foreign policy guarantee their political detachment from international squabbles. Consequently, throughout the 1920s they turned inward and rejected President Woodrow Wilson's dream of international cooperation and collective security through membership in the League of Nations.

The dogged public and congressional desire to abstain from foreign political involvements forced even a staunch internationalist and big-navy man such as Franklin D. Roosevelt to trim his sails. His Wilsonian credentials were impeccable. As Wilson's devoted assistant secretary of the navy, Roosevelt shared the president's international perspective. Well traveled and experienced in foreign problems, he vigorously campaigned for an expanded navy, which he kept aggressively vigilant. By 1916, Roosevelt was calling for America's entrance into World War I and for the creation of an even greater military force than his superiors desired. When the United States did enter the war in 1917, he relished the important duties required of the Navy Department.

Roosevelt was an observer at the Versailles Peace Conference in 1919 and became an enthusiastic supporter of President Wilson's dream of American membership in the League of Nations. The League's ultimate rejection by the Senate in 1920, however, convinced Roosevelt that public opinion was shifting substantially. Once favorable, it was growing weary of Wilsonianism.

Despite the Republicans' political ascendancy throughout the decade, Roosevelt worked tirelessly to promote his own political fortunes. In 1920 he was chosen as a compromise running mate for the Democratic party's presidential candidate, Ohio's colorless governor, James M. Cox. Throughout the 1920s, FDR gingerly continued to support America's entry into the League of Nations and to offer leadership by writing magazine articles on foreign policy. He also loyally supported Al Smith's unsuccessful presidential ambitions and campaigned for his reelection as governor of New York. In 1928, Roosevelt again gained national recognition by successfully nominating Smith for the presidency. Although Smith lost the election, FDR emerged victorious as the new governor of New York and as a natural contender for some future presidential race. By the end of the decade he had cleverly achieved his personal goal. He had become a national figure and the beneficiary of the Wilsonian legacy.

Once Roosevelt decided to run for the presidency in 1932, he courted the support of isolationist elements within the Democratic party by aligning himself with the current nationalist mood and disavowing his Wilsonian past. Now he opposed American membership in the League and even refused to urge cooperation with it or to applaud its work. FDR also reversed himself on war debts and argued that the Allies and other European nations should pay back the American money borrowed to finance the war and relief and reconstruction efforts. After all, he reasoned, Europe's large expenditures for armaments illustrated that it could afford to meet its financial obligations. Such was the necessary political price for gaining his party's nomination. "A chameleon on plaid," grumbled his Republican opponent, Herbert Hoover.

During the 1932 national campaign, Roosevelt's strategy was to avoid the subject of foreign policy as much as possible, especially since his old Wilsonianism was unpopular and because he had few differences with Hoover. Anxious not to risk any of his political popularity, FDR even substantially moderated his earlier position in support of reciprocal trade agreements. By the end of the campaign, he was arguing for high protective tariffs. Actually, he made no major campaign speech exclusively on foreign policy, but his temporizing masked his true views. He continued to believe that the world was economically interdependent, that peace and prosperity were interrelated, and that a sound foreign policy required a national consensus, but he also worried that domestic problems would hinder his ability to achieve his foreign policy objectives. Nevertheless, Roosevelt was determined to try.

After the tremendous election victory in which he swept forty-two out of the forty-eight states, the new president established an administration that was personal, centralized, and haphazard. Steeped in the aristocratic tradition of noblesse oblige, Roosevelt had an exalted sense of his own position and unlimited confidence in his own influence and abilities. He fully regarded himself as the equal of royalty and preferred personal conferences with foreign statesmen to indirect negotiations through official channels and subordinates. He supplemented his personal conduct in diplomacy by keeping in close contact with foreign representatives in Washington, by transacting business in a slipshod fashion over the telephone with his own representatives in capitals abroad, and by sending personal emissaries on diplomatic missions. He was not a systematic thinker but rather an on-the-spot improviser, pragmatic, even capricious. Frequently he accepted contradictory advice. Go "weave the two together," Roosevelt told a surprised adviser who presented him with two conflicting versions of a tariff proposal. Despite all that has been written about him, he remains an extremely enigmatic man, a reserved and self-sufficient figure, one not easily influenced, who quite independently made up his own mind and followed his own advice. "Never let your left hand know what your right hand is doing," he once told his close friend, Henry Morgenthau. "Which hand am I, Mr. President?" he asked. "My right hand, but I keep my left hand under the table," Roosevelt answered.

He failed to take congressional leadership into his confidence on foreign policy issues, and he often went over the heads of Congress by appealing directly to the good sense of the country in his "homey" public addresses and fireside chats. Roosevelt's major speeches were all based on his own outlines, and his assistants were essentially executors, not formulators, who played a minor role in foreign policy design. His chief collaborators in foreign policy were Secretary of State Cordell Hull and Secretary of the Treasury Morgenthau, an avid New Dealer and a Dutchess County neighbor. "To Henry," Roosevelt's inscription on one of his photographs reads, "from one of two of a kind." Roosevelt's dependence on Morgenthau created friction between him and Hull and exacerbated FDR's already chaotic and uncoordinated, but still effective and well-informed, administration.

As disorganized an administrator as his chief, Hull complained about Roosevelt in his gently lisping manner as "that man across the street who never tells me anything." He was the conservative influence, discreet, inflexible, a man of high integrity and practical political experience. Roosevelt respected him, valued his opinions, and kept him as well informed as his personal habits permitted. One adventuresome and pliable, the other cautious and restrained, they complemented each other well. Behind the secretary's air of benevolent Southern gentlemanliness lurked an avenging

evangelical dogmatism on the subject of economic internationalism. He believed that "the king of evils" was the protective tariff,
"the breeder of economic war." "We must eliminate these trade baa-
yuhs, heah, theah, and ev'ywheah," mimicked his critics. Hull's
presence in the administration indicated Roosevelt's long-range
foreign policy objectives and the president's determination to return to the internationalism of his Wilsonian days, but all in his
own good time.

Except for his own political appointees such as Under Secretary Sumner Welles, a patrician from Boston and an experienced
diplomat who headed the Latin American section at the age of
twenty-eight, FDR particularly disliked the State Department and
distrusted career officers as a class. He sarcastically referred to them
as professional perfectionists. In a letter to Hull the president once
wrote, "I am reminded of a remark made to me by an old career
service man. 'You can get to be a Minister if (a) you are loyal to the
service, (b) you do nothing to offend people, (c) if you are not in-
toxicated at public functions.' " He also believed there was "a lot
of dead wood in the top three grades that should never have got
there."

By creating overlapping areas of authority in foreign policy, by
setting various cabinet officials, personal envoys, and government
agencies against each other, and by keeping them all jockeying with
one another for influence and power, Roosevelt masked his intentions until he was ready to act. He set Morgenthau against Hull,
Hull against Welles, Hull against his assistant secretary of state,
New Dealer Raymond Moley, and personal emissaries such as
Norman Davis against career diplomats, and he pitted a host of
other bureaucrats and congressional groups against each other. By
having the State Department espouse two mutually exclusive views
at the same time, such as Hull's internationalism and Moley's self-
protective program of independent economic nationalism—
"intranationa-lism"—FDR undercut the department's ability to
pursue a consistent course in international affairs and ensured his
control of American foreign policy, just exactly as he wanted.

The president's major concern, as he told his inaugural audience in 1933, was to put "first things first." "Our international trade
relations, though vastly important, are secondary . . . to the establishment of a sound national economy." Yet, despite his tough inaugural address on avoiding foreign entanglements, there were
vestiges of his old Wilsonianism. During FDR's first six weeks in

office, he tried to prop up the disarmament conference in Geneva, supported Hull's reciprocal trade agreement program, and called for lowering barriers to world trade. By the fall of 1933, Roosevelt even extended official recognition to the Soviet Union, something that had been withheld since the Bolshevik Revolution of 1917. He did so by encouraging a consensus among businessmen and religious leaders who believed that recognition would increase the trade and prosperity in both countries and reduce the threat of Japanese aggression against Russia by enhancing Soviet prestige.

Actually, Roosevelt thought intranationalism was viable only in the short run and not as a long-range policy. He hoped that the nationalistic monetary and economic policies urged by advisers such as Moley would work quickly enough to permit him to support currency stabilization and tariff agreements at the London World Economic Conference. But, after FDR torpedoed the conference in July 1933 with the famous "bombshell" message in which he reaffirmed the primacy of domestic recovery over Hull's arguments for international financial cooperation, he began to back away from decisive action in foreign affairs. Nevertheless, he still wanted the United States to play a role in reducing international tensions.

During the first two years of his administration, Roosevelt had a relatively free hand in fashioning American foreign policy. This was a period of general indifference throughout the country and of a widespread preoccupation with the problems created by the Great Depression. Roosevelt acted decisively in domestic affairs by extending government assistance to private bankers, cutting federal spending to balance the budget, taking the country off the gold standard, ending Prohibition, and stepping up economic recovery and unemployment relief by creating the New Deal's alphabet agencies: the National Recovery Administration (NRA), the Agricultural Adjustment Administration (AAA), and the Civilian Conservation Corps (CCC). Often indecisive in foreign affairs, however, FDR rambled back and forth, following a policy of internationalism and then of intranationalism and anti-imperialism, of self-determination, and of traditional power politics as events seemed to dictate. But, from late 1934 through 1935, events in Europe had frightened Americans and made them wary of foreign involvements and fearful of a general war. The tension caused by Germany's rearmament, the crisis unfolding between Italy and Ethiopia, France's doubling of the existing period of military service for conscripts, Japan's attempt to gain hegemony over China, and the League of

Nations' consideration of sanctions against aggressive states prompted FDR to write that "these are without a doubt the most hair-trigger times the world has gone through" in his lifetime.

Americans responded to these events by espousing isolationism, a policy that began to dominate national thinking and cost Roosevelt his flexibility in foreign affairs. FDR always skirted controversial solutions that might undermine his political popularity and wreck his New Deal. He was also particularly sensitive to criticism that he favored radical departures in economic policy; consequently, he was eager to minimize charges that he supported major changes in America's traditional foreign policy. Such caution led him to steer a course of least resistance in international affairs, one of political expediency, economic nationalism, and political isolationism. Not only was he unwilling to take aggressive, unpopular stands, but he also seemed indifferent to the problems inherent in pursuing conflicting domestic and foreign policy objectives. To have resolved such contradictions would have been inconsistent with the philosophy of the early New Deal—one of short-term, quick, pragmatic solutions rather than of long-range, systematic planning.

Privately, he was a loyal internationalist and believed in collective action to maintain peace; publicly, he frequently sounded and sometimes acted very much like an isolationist. In 1935 he wrote to Colonel Edward M. House, Wilson's trusted adviser, that he had several proposals by which American influence could help reduce the armaments race. His reason for rejecting these schemes was always the same: "I fear any suggestions . . . would meet with [a] chilly, half-contemptuous reception." However, he frequently spoke of keeping America uncommitted. In his major campaign address in 1936, he mouthed the slogans of neutrality: "Despite what happens in continents overseas, the United States of America shall and must remain, as long ago the Father of our Country prayed that it might remain, unentangled and free."

In Congress key progressive Republican senators, such as William E. Borah of Idaho, Gerald P. Nye of North Dakota, Robert M. La Follette, Jr., of Wisconsin, California's crusty Hiram W. Johnson, and the powerful chairman of the Foreign Relations Committee, Key Pittman, staunchly defended a foreign policy of isolationism and opposed even symbolic American involvement in international affairs. Although few in number, they were extremely influential; Roosevelt believed that he dare not alienate them on foreign policy issues since they warmly supported his New Deal legislation. It was they who urged a reluctant FDR in 1934 to support the Johnson Act, which forbade loans to any foreign government in default on its war debts. Roosevelt thereby cemented a valuable political relationship with these progressive Republican isolationists.

A further reason for FDR's caution in foreign affairs was provided by the sensational revelations of the Nye Committee in 1934. The hero of the drama was Nye, a stern young senator, whose committee investigated the influence of the armaments industry and the banking interests on American entry into World War I. It condemned these "merchants of death" for their lies and trickery. The timing was perfect. The committee's findings contributed to a general revulsion against intervening in Europe's squabbles.

Even a mild proposal that the United States not interfere with League sanctions against an aggressor nation was defeated because Johnson mobilized the Senate isolationists against it. So, too, was FDR's plan in 1935 for American entry into the World Court, the one internationalist gesture most likely to succeed. "To hell with Europe and the rest of those nations," announced one senatorial opponent. Roosevelt deeply resented this congressional defeat: "As to the thirty-six Senators who placed themselves on record against the principle of a World Court, I am inclined to think that if they ever get to Heaven, they will be doing a great deal of apologizing for a very long time—that is, if God is against war—and I think He is." The president and his advisers interpreted their defeat as a major crossroads in American foreign policy. It had aroused, they believed, a strong and vocal isolationist opposition, not just in Congress but in the country as a whole, which would temporarily hamstring the president's conduct of foreign affairs. "We shall go through a period of non-cooperation in everything . . . for the next year or two," Roosevelt predicted.

By the summer of 1935 congressional isolationists responded to the growing threats to peace by demanding neutrality legislation that would define America's conduct toward a European war. They wanted an embargo on all armaments trade during wartime. Both Roosevelt and Hull approved the embargo scheme, but they wanted broad discretionary power to distinguish between victim and aggressor and the right to embargo arms only to the latter. Such executive authority, they reasoned, would provide a strong deterrent to aggression.

Congress resolutely opposed their request since it meant taking sides in a war and therefore implied American involvement. A compromise was drafted by Senators Pittman and Borah and accepted over the president's protest. It requested Roosevelt to declare a mandatory embargo on implements of war to all belligerents. The first Neutrality Act was signed in August 1935 and was applied against both Italy and Ethiopia after the Italian invasion of Ethiopia in the fall. The major weakness of the act, which Roosevelt and Hull previously had recognized, was that it embargoed only arms and munitions but not raw materials such as steel, coal, and oil, Italy's most vital imports. In attempting to undermine this unintentional aid, Roosevelt announced a "moral embargo," a voluntary agreement to cut back on the commodities sent to Italy. Predictably, however, Haile Selassie's soldiers were defeated in December 1935 by the Italian war machine, which was unintentionally aided by the inflexible provisions of the Neutrality Act.

By 1935, Roosevelt had almost given up any hope of conducting his own foreign policy. His attempts to gain congressional approval for his "moral embargo" on war materials and for executive discretion were repeatedly dashed by the congressional isolationists. Time was running out; the Neutrality Act was about to expire. After six weeks of debate, Roosevelt and Hull grudgingly faced defeat and accepted the second Neutrality Act in February 1936. Essentially, it was a continuation of the previous act, but it also prohibited loans to belligerents and required the president to embargo arms to any belligerent. It embodied the isolationists' major argument, the Nye thesis, that embargoes on arms and trade would prevent American involvement in war. Its application to the Spanish Civil War, however, ironically aided the spread of fascism by cutting off supplies to the democratically elected Spanish Republican government.

In the 1936 presidential election, Roosevelt devised a strategy of wooing isolationists and pacifists by reminding them of his administration's efforts on behalf of peace. "Peace, like charity," he told his audience, "begins at home and that's why we have begun at home. . . . But peace in the western world is not all we seek." He recited the administration's various attempts to maintain peace and concluded that all of this had come to naught. Therefore, he would now seek to "isolate America from war. . . . I have seen war. . . . I hate war." Once the election was behind him, Roosevelt believed that he could turn his attention to searching for peace, and his first major attempt at peacemaking was his decision to attend the Buenos Aires Conference in December 1936. He hoped to solidify the Good Neighbor policy, which had been initiated by his predecessor President Hoover on the principles of equality and partnership with the other American republics, the elimination of artificial economic barriers, and the union of the Americas against outside threats. He told his cabinet before leaving that, if he were successful in achieving an understanding of peace and disarmament at the conference, then perhaps a similar agreement could be reached in the Pacific and elsewhere. The Buenos Aires agreements had the effect of transforming the Monroe Doctrine from a unilateral declaration into a multilateral agreement.

Even as Roosevelt attended the Buenos Aires Conference, he continued to mull over ways to help Europe maintain peace, but it seemed completely hopeless. Hitler had seized the Rhineland in violation of the Versailles treaty, the Spanish Civil War raged on, Japan and Germany had signed the Anti-Comintern Pact against the Soviet Union, and the aimless drift of the democracies, Britain

"Thanksgiving 1936." Uncle Sam reflects on the sentiment of American isolationism. (Library of Congress)

and France, dictated a policy of watchful waiting. Despite his desire to avoid controversy on foreign policy, Roosevelt had to face the May 1 expiration date on the 1936 neutrality law and a new Congress that was even more suspicious of his intentions because of his tremendous landslide in the election. Two new provisions were part of the 1937 Neutrality Act. One prohibited Americans from traveling on belligerents' ships, while the other established the "cash-and-carry" plan, under whose terms nations at war could buy American supplies and arms provided that they paid cash and carried them away on their own ships. The president was given the authority to name the commodities to which cash-and-carry applied, although it was not nearly as much authority as Roosevelt would have liked. (This plan was limited to two years and was never applied under the act.) So overwhelming was America's desire for peace that the act was immensely popular.

The most serious congressional assault on the president's control of foreign policy was the Ludlow Amendment. Its debate in Congress was immediately prompted by the December 12, 1937, Japanese bombing of the USS *Panay*, which was anchored in the Yangtze River and prominently flying the American flag. Roosevelt was indignant and discussed with his cabinet and the military high command the possibility of economic or military retaliation. He drew back, however, when he realized that there was no public outcry for such action and that, in fact, peace sentiment had been strengthened.

The *Panay* incident showed the precariousness of peace and stimulated congressional action on the Ludlow Amendment. Intended to be an amendment to the Constitution, it would provide that the government, except in the case of an attack on American soil, could declare war only when a majority voted to do so in a national referendum. Severe White House pressure prevented the passage of this amendment, which would have deprived the president of control over foreign policy, one of his chief constitutional prerogatives. It was finally defeated in the House of Representatives in January 1938 by a vote of 209 to 188. The 188 votes illustrated Roosevelt's tenuous control over foreign policy, the intensity of congressional distrust and isolationist sentiment, and the national aversion to war.

Throughout the spring and summer of 1937 the president continued to pursue his dream of a world conference modeled on that held in Buenos Aires. Roosevelt sent Norman Davis, a respected internationalist and an adviser to both Wilson and Hoover, to the Continent to discuss presidential plans informally with European leaders, and he invited Neville Chamberlain to the United States. Davis reported that most of the British and French politicians endorsed Roosevelt's ideas, but Chamberlain, the new British prime minister, was less sympathetic. Although he wanted the democracies and the dictatorships to work out a solution to their problems, Chamberlain did not like Roosevelt's suggestion for a comprehensive plan undertaken by many nations. He believed that foreign affairs were so fluid that any plans made would quickly become obsolete. Twice, Roosevelt invited Chamberlain to visit him and discuss the international threats, and twice the prime minister refused.

Apparently, Chamberlain's rejection of Roosevelt's invitation prompted the president to accept the advice of Davis and Secretary of State Hull. They had been urging him to give a speech stressing international cooperation and to do so in an isolationist stronghold. Roosevelt liked the dramatic gesture, as it would give him an opportunity to criticize the aggressor nations publicly and to educate Americans to the threat of international lawlessness. On October 5, 1937, the president created an international sensation in Chicago by launching into a stern lecture on foreign affairs and doing so as no other president had dared for sixteen years. In an obvious but indirect reference to Japan's undeclared war against China, Roosevelt condemned the "present reign of terror and international lawlessness" and stated that unjustified interference in the affairs of other countries "has now reached a stage where the very foundations of civilization are seriously threatened." If chaos continues, "let no one imagine that America will escape." Then, in a dramatic departure from the suggested State Department outline, came the Rooseveltian climax: "When an epidemic of physical disease starts to spread, the community approves and joins in a quarantine of the patients in order to protect the health of the community against the spread of the disease. . . . War is a contagion, whether it be declared or undeclared." He ended on a positive note, saying that "America hates war. America hopes for peace. Therefore, America actively engages in the search for peace."

The crowd cheered its approval, and most of the country responded favorably to Roosevelt's address, but not the outraged opposition. Some isolationist congressmen even threatened him with impeachment. Indignant at the lack of support from his own party leaders, the president complained that "it's a terrible thing to look over your shoulder when you are trying to lead and to find no one there." Afterward, he shunned any further explanation of his speech. Perhaps he realized that a "quarantine" seemed to imply some kind of action without war, something beyond the usual political or military steps, and he knew that he had nothing more to offer and could not fulfill the expectations aroused by his speech. Regardless, the quarantine speech showed that he was still pursuing a variety of schemes for preserving the peace and that this was simply one more in a series, as the Buenos Aires Conference had been.

On the day after the speech the president asked Under Secretary Welles to outline a new peace program—the October Plan—to provide for American participation in collective action. Roosevelt intended to hold a dramatic meeting and appeal for a solution to international problems. Acting on Hull's cautious advice, he first sent a confidential outline of his proposal to Chamberlain, who rejected it, arguing that it might jeopardize Britain's efforts to appease Italy and Germany. Disappointed at the prime minister's rebuff, Roosevelt nevertheless sent Chamberlain an obliging note, saying that he agreed to defer the proposal and await the outcome of Britain's appeasement policy. The president's proposal became one of history's "might have beens." Despite his rejection of the note, Chamberlain repeatedly tried, with mixed results, to secure Roosevelt's approval for his appeasement policy during the spring and summer of 1938. The wily FDR refused, however, to be taken in by Chamberlain's "game," as he called it.

The president's reaction to Germany's annexation of Austria also showed his refusal to make a commitment to Chamberlain's policy. When the British passively accepted the Anschluss, Roosevelt declined to do anything that might undermine their appeasement initiatives. In response to the crisis the U.S. government merely sent Hitler a meek note of protest. One State Department official succinctly summed up the American position: "We certainly can't be thought, whatever our sympathies may be, to assume any responsibility, legal or moral, in Europe at the moment."

During the winter and spring of 1938, Roosevelt's hopes for a revision of the neutrality legislation and its application to Spain were repeatedly dashed. He momentarily considered lifting the Spanish embargo but decided against it, in part out of fear of domestic repercussions and of alienating Catholics who supported it, and in part because London and Paris intended to continue their

policy of nonintervention regardless. Roosevelt further reasoned
that lifting the embargo would probably not have helped the Spanish Loyalists (Republican forces). Ultimately, in February 1939,
after the collapse of the Loyalist regime and the fall of Madrid, the
American government recognized General Francisco Franco's new
Fascist government, as did London and Paris.

Despite Spain, Roosevelt gave an "unofficial blessing" to a
congressional push to allow greater presidential discretion in applying an embargo, but, when Congress refused to act, he drew
back. Repeatedly, domestic political considerations restrained him
from pressing too hard for revision. In the spring of 1938 he was

"GOOSE-STEPPING, NEVILLE?" An American view of the appeasement policy of
British prime minister Neville Chamberlain. (Wilmington *Morning News*, 1938,
Library of Congress)

preoccupied with a recovery program designed to end the seven-month recession and to help the four million unemployed Americans, many near starving, find jobs. In a fireside chat radio broadcast the president reminded his audience that several nations had rejected democracy "not because the people disliked democracy but because they had grown tired of unemployment and insecurity." Thus, the priority given to economic and domestic considerations, the still-seething political backlash over his attempt to enlarge the Supreme Court and to "pack" it with New Deal sympathizers, the fresh charges of "dictator" that sprang up over his ill-fated proposal to reorganize the executive agencies, and the continued opposition of conservative Democrats who disapproved of his New Deal legislation made FDR unwilling to risk spending his declining political capital on a fight for neutrality revision which, even if successful, he believed would probably have been ineffective.

The crisis over Czechoslovakia was the next European problem that the president faced. His response was the same: "No risks, no commitments." It was a policy of "pinpricks and righteous protests." Although Secretary Hull stated publicly that the American government was following these critical events with "close and anxious attention," Roosevelt refused either to defend appeasement or to urge military resistance to Hitler's demands. As the crisis thickened and war seemed imminent, the president on several occasions appealed to the European powers not to break off negotiations over Czechoslovakia, but always he concluded with the traditional statement of American foreign policy: "The United States has no political entanglements."

In September 1938, Hitler invited Chamberlain to Munich to meet with him to discuss the Czech crisis. French premier Edouard Daladier was also present as an uncomfortable witness, as was Italy's Benito Mussolini, the conference's self-styled mediator. The Czech representatives waited quietly at a hotel throughout the thirteen-hour meeting in which four foreigners carved up their republic. After numerous arguments and conversations dominated by Mussolini, the only one of the four who could speak the others' languages, an agreement was reached at 2 A.M. Czechoslovakia was to be left defenseless and to cede its border fortresses and the Sudetenland to Germany. Roosevelt sent Chamberlain a terse, two-word message: "Good man." Although FDR has been given much of the credit for persuading Hitler to call the Munich Conference, his appeals actually were probably rather inconsequential. Hitler must have seen them as mere gestures, nothing more.

Munich marked a watershed in American foreign policy. A pair of shrewd observers, *New York Herald Tribune* columnists Joseph Alsop and Robert Kintner, wrote that "before Munich this country's role in world politics was chiefly that of a chorus, somewhat overgiven to gloomy gesture and hortatory speech." After Munich, however, Roosevelt grew increasingly alarmed over European affairs since Hitler had proved once again that Germany could expand without encountering anything more than verbal protests from the democracies. Because of their increasing skepticism over America's policy of isolationism and their dislike of Chamberlain's appeasement policy, Roosevelt, Hull, and Welles began to reexamine foreign policy assumptions. To the trio, U.S. interests dictated a firm, specific course. War must be prevented; if that proved impossible, then victory for the democracies must be ensured.

In his State of the Union address in January 1939, the president signaled a change in policy by calling for "methods short of war" and suggesting that these might curb aggression. At the very least, he wanted the neutrality law repealed, particularly its mandatory embargo section, so that he could make American arms available to friendly nations. Despite his appeals, Congress remained unmoved. Many politicians believed that Roosevelt would not run for a third term and viewed him as a lame-duck president. This, combined with the Republicans' gains in the 1938 congressional elections and their alliance with suspicious and rebellious anti-New Deal Democrats, explains his weakened political position. Furthermore, his confidential remarks to members of the Senate in which he was quoted as saying that "our frontier is on the Rhine"—a quote passed on to Washington columnists Alsop and Kintner and one that Roosevelt denied making—further alarmed suspicious senators already worried that he would drag the United States into a war. Reluctantly, FDR concluded that once again neutrality revision would have to be postponed.

Roosevelt's anxiety over the threat to peace in Europe was justified. Despite Hitler's promise at Munich not to acquire any more territory, in March 1939 he devoured the rest of the Czech nation and began a "war of nerves" against Poland by demanding that it cede the Free State of Danzig to Germany and permit the building of a German road across the Polish Corridor that divided East Prussia from the rest of Germany. Both Britain and France reversed their appeasement policy and guaranteed aid to Poland and later to Greece and Romania. The president denied recognition to Hitler's Czechoslovakian conquests and refused to acknowledge Mussolini's acquisition of Albania on April 7. Mussolini's latest venture created the impression that he would join with Hitler in a mutual enterprise. Roosevelt also sent the "Saturday Surprise" message to Hitler and Mussolini, asking them to guarantee thirty-one nations against attack. If they did so, the United States would join in international discussions of armaments and trade. The president's unconventional intervention had provoked tremendous popular response in the United States. Events in Europe were arousing Americans to the threat to peace.

Beginning in mid-April, Roosevelt quietly returned to the issue of neutrality revision. He met with lukewarm senators and representatives and explained that repealing the arms embargo was the best way to keep the peace and defend American interests. Hull helped him. According to Alsop and Kintner, the delightfully quotable secretary of state told the legislators that the coming struggle was hardly "another goddam piddling dispute over a boundary line." Not to repeal this "wretched little bobtailed sawed-off domestic statute," he said, was "just plain chuckle-headed." However, these arguments failed to persuade the isolationists who remained unalterably opposed to revision. Thus, Congress adjourned in early August without acting on neutrality legislation.

Roosevelt was angered by the opposition and privately told Morgenthau: "I will bet you an old hat . . . that when [Hitler] wakes up and finds out what has happened, there will be great rejoicing in the Italian and German camps. I think we ought to introduce a bill for statues of [Senators] Austin, Vandenberg, Lodge, and Taft . . . to be erected in Berlin and put the swastika on them." Actually, Roosevelt and Hull overestimated the extent to which Hitler cared for, or could be deterred by, an arms embargo. He had little regard for the United States and saw it as a "mongrel society," hopelessly weak and incapable of interfering with his plans. His desire to go to war with Poland depended not on American neutrality legislation but on British, French, and German negotiations with Moscow and the necessity of neutralizing Hitler's eastern border. The status of the neutrality law, despite Roosevelt's belief, therefore had almost no impact on the course of events in Europe or on Hitler's thinking.

By August 1939 all signs pointed toward a German-Polish crisis over Danzig, and, on August 22, Hitler achieved one of his major foreign policy objectives when Moscow agreed to sign a Nazi-Soviet nonaggression pact. Now he would not have to fight a long two-front war since Soviet neutrality would be guaranteed when he invaded Poland. Roosevelt continued his last-minute efforts for peace, suggesting a settlement through direct negotiation and offering to be the mediator. His appeals were for domestic effect; he wanted to "put the bee on Germany," he said, which nobody had done in 1914. On September 1 the long-awaited crisis exploded as Nazi bombers and several divisions invaded Poland. Two days later, France and Britain declared war on Germany. World War II had begun, and still the United States remained shackled by its neutrality legislation. It was not fully repealed until October 1941, only two months before the Japanese bombing of Pearl Harbor and America's entrance into the war.

The nature of Roosevelt's leadership in foreign policy throughout the 1930s and its relationship to the outbreak of World War II are topics of complex and heated continuing historical debate. Many official documents became available in the immediate postwar decade of the 1950s. Their accessibility to scholars has stimulated research, writing, and further discussion. Controversy rages over what FDR's intentions in foreign policy were and whether the president was deceitful or candid with Congress and the American public about his intentions.

One view of Roosevelt's leadership is critical of his conduct of foreign policy and argues that he pursued a number of insidious schemes to steer the country deliberately into war. Despite his awareness that the American public had consistently demonstrated its desire for peace, particularly in the 1940 election, isolationist and revisionist historians such as Charles A. Beard contend that, sometime around the outbreak of the war in Europe in 1939, the president decided that the United States must enter the conflict and deceitfully worked to bring this about as quickly as possible.

By contrast, another historical position, represented by William L. Langer and S. Everett Gleason, supports the view that by September 1940 most Americans were eager to approve of virtually any form of aid to the Allies. Actually, Roosevelt worked consistently to keep the country out of the war and was quite worried about America's ability to avoid the conflict. He underestimated popular support for his foreign policy, however, and was reluctant to be candid with the public because he feared congressional opposition, which he was prone to exaggerate. Far from acting decisively and quickly, as isolationist and revisionist critics such as Beard have charged, the president's keen sense of timing enabled him to wait patiently for the right moment. His acute political instincts made him realize that no leader could get too far ahead of his followers.

Another more recent historical view stresses America's contribution to Germany's appeasement throughout the 1930s. Critical historians have charged that the president failed to implement bold policies and to take decisive action, and that he was responsible for numerous tragic diplomatic blunders that culminated in the Munich Agreement. In fact, Roosevelt behaved little better than Chamberlain. Even at Munich, these critics have argued, FDR failed to grasp that more than the survival of Czechoslovakia was at stake.

Still another view, developed by historian Robert Dallek, states that Roosevelt acquiesced in the popular American preference for a passive foreign policy. He did so because he realistically concluded that at home he lacked the strong political consensus so essential to decisive and effective action abroad. He did not try to trick his country into war. On the contrary, Dallek has contended, the most striking aspect about Roosevelt was not his arbitrariness in pushing America into the conflict but rather his restraint. Thus, the scholarly controversy concerning Roosevelt's diplomacy and World War II is filled with contradictions, which no doubt will contribute even further to the ongoing debate.

To summarize, in the early months of Roosevelt's first administration, he pursued a variety of schemes as circumstances dictated, from his old Wilsonianism to the economic nationalism of the New Deal, but his long-range plans called for internationalism, collective action, and reciprocal trade agreements. By 1935 his political flexibility was undercut by domestic isolationist sentiment. Consequently, he reluctantly acquiesced to the popular feeling and waited for events to educate the American public. During his second administration, however, the situation in Europe and the Far East convinced him that he must find some way to avert war, and he began the risky venture of trying to educate the public to the threats to its security. Cautious and prudent, Roosevelt was determined to build a consensus for his foreign policy and to maintain his political leadership.

Sources and Suggested Readings

Adams, R. J. *British Politics and Foreign Policy in the Age of Appeasement, 1935–1939.* Stanford, CA, 1993.

Alsop, Joseph, and Kintner, Robert. *American White Paper.* New York, 1940.

Beard, Charles A. *American Foreign Policy in the Making, 1932–1940: A Study in Responsibilities.* New Haven, CT, 1946.

Blum, John Morton. *From the Morgenthau Diaries.* Vol. 1, *Years of Crisis, 1928–1938.* Boston, 1959.

Burns, James MacGregor. *Roosevelt: The Lion and the Fox.* New York, 1956.

Dallek, Robert. *Franklin D. Roosevelt and American Foreign Policy, 1932–1945.* New York, 1979.

Hull, Cordell. *The Memoirs of Cordell Hull.* 2 vols. New York, 1948.

Langer, William L., and Gleason, S. Everett. *The Challenge to Isolation: The World Crisis of 1937–1940 and American Foreign Policy.* New York, 1952.

Leuchtenburg, William E. *Franklin D. Roosevelt and the New Deal, 1932–1940.* New York, 1963.

Moffat, J. C. *The Moffat Papers.* Cambridge, MA, 1956.

Moley, Raymond. *After Seven Years.* New York, 1939.

Offner, Arnold A. *American Appeasement: United States Foreign Policy and Germany, 1933–1938.* New York, 1969.

Rock, William R. *Chamberlain and Roosevelt: British Foreign Policy and the United States.* Columbus, OH, 1988.

Roosevelt, Elliott, and Lash, Joseph P., eds. *F.D.R.: His Personal Letters, 1928–1945.* 2 vols. New York, 1950.

Rosenman, Samuel I. *Working with Roosevelt.* New York, 1952.

―――, ed. *The Public Papers and Addresses of Franklin D. Roosevelt, 1928–1945.* 13 vols. New York, 1938–1950.

Schlesinger, Arthur M., Jr. *The Age of Roosevelt.* Vol. 2, *The Coming of the New Deal.* Boston, 1965.

U.S. Department of State. *Foreign Relations of the United States, 1938.* Washington, DC, 1956.

The United States Enters World War II

Jonathan G. Utley

On Monday, December 8, 1941, President Franklin D. Roosevelt asked Congress to recognize that a state of war had existed following Japan's "unprovoked and dastardly attack" against American forces at Pearl Harbor. War had come to America. Why had it come? What series of events brought the United States into the war? The American people did not seek this war. There was none of the bravado of 1898 when Americans went off to trounce the hated Spaniard, nor was there the optimism of 1917 when the nation set forth to make the world safe for democracy. This time the mood was one of grim determination. Thus, it is not the people to whom we must look for an explanation of why the nation went to war but to their leaders, to President Roosevelt, Secretary of State Cordell Hull, and the rest of the Washington foreign policy establishment that led the country along a path ending in war.

Sometimes national leaders see a war coming, decide they should enter it, and resolutely direct their nation toward that end. At other times a nation stumbles into war because its leaders do not foresee a conflict and proceed blindly down a path that they think will guide them to peace. With World War II and its leaders, both explanations apply. To see how, it is necessary first to survey what happened and then to explore why the U.S. government acted as it did.

In the 1930s two great military powers threatened to alter the world order. Increasingly militaristic and extremist, imperial Japan looked toward the establishment of a New Order in East Asia. In Europe, Adolf Hitler's Nazi Germany sought to establish a thousand-year Reich, uniting all the German-speaking peoples in Europe and dominating the rest of the Continent.

To this end, Germany annexed Austria in March 1938. Later in the year Hitler demanded that Czechoslovakia hand over the Sudetenland with its large German-speaking population. The Czechs wanted to fight and turned to their French and British allies for support, but neither of those nations was psychologically or militarily prepared for war. Instead, they sought to buy peace through appeasing Hitler with the Sudetenland.

Throughout these events Roosevelt kept an official silence. He did not trust Hitler and did not think that appeasement would work, but he too remembered the horrors of World War I. Like most Americans, the president was prepared to go to almost any length to avoid another war. Besides, given the isolationist mood of the people, there was little he could do.

Appeasement did not work. In the spring of 1939, Hitler took over the remainder of Czechoslovakia, and in September his armies blasted their way through Poland in less than one month. For Britain and France the loss of Poland was too much, and they declared war on Germany. That began the European phase of World War II.

With the outbreak of the war, Roosevelt invoked the Neutrality Act, a law prohibiting Americans from making loans or selling war matériel to any of the belligerents. The president, whose sympathies were with the Allies, quickly persuaded Congress to revise the law so that any nation could buy whatever it wanted in the United States so long as it paid cash and carried it away in its own ships. Roosevelt claimed that his "cash-and-carry" program was totally neutral, but almost everyone understood that it favored the British, who had both the cash and the ships and whose navy could keep Germany from taking advantage of the program.

During the winter of 1939–40, Britain and France used cash-and-carry to help prepare for the German spring offensive, but it was too little, too late. German armies attacked Norway and Denmark in early April and moved against the Netherlands and Belgium one month later. In both cases the German blitzkrieg was spectacularly successful. In less than five weeks British armies were pushed off the Continent and France was conquered. By the end of June 1940, Hitler had made himself the master of western Europe, while a bloodied but not yet beaten Britain waited for the German invasion of the British Isles.

Shocked by these German victories, the United States began to act. Roosevelt ordered a major preparedness program. Planes, tanks, and ships had to be built. Gasoline, copper, rubber, and all the other matériel needed for a modern industrial war had to be stockpiled. Congress appropriated vast sums for defense and even instituted the first peacetime draft in the nation's history. In an effort to help Britain guard its ships from German submarines, Roosevelt "traded" fifty overage destroyers for ninety-nine-year leases on a chain of British naval bases stretching from Newfoundland to British Guiana. Most Americans approved of these actions because they would help the nation to defend the Western Hemisphere should Germany try to cross the Atlantic. On the other hand, the American people were not prepared to cross the Atlantic themselves and confront German armies.

By the time Germany had crushed France, Japanese and Chinese armies had been fighting for three years. This Asian war began as an isolated incident in northern China but soon grew into a full-scale struggle for control of that country. China lost battle after battle but did not surrender. Instead, the Chinese traded land for time, retreating farther and farther into the interior. Soon, Japan found itself mired in a war it could not win but from which it could not extricate itself without humiliation.

During the first three years of the Sino-Japanese War the Roosevelt administration did little to help China or hinder Japan. It had given China a modest loan, protested many of Japan's actions, and implied that some form of commercial pressure might be applied against Japan if it did not mend its ways. In reality, however, no pressure was applied, Japan did not mend its ways, and the war dragged on with no end in sight. The German conquest of Europe changed all that.

Japan hoped to dominate East and Southeast Asia politically, militarily, and economically. What held it back was its inability to conquer China and overcome the British and U.S. presence in the region. Britain was the most formidable power because of its major investments in China, its colonies of Hong Kong and Malaya, and its large naval base at Singapore. But, by the fall of 1940, Britain was fighting for its life in Europe and was powerless to stop Japan in Asia.

Moreover, the German conquest of the Netherlands and France had left their Asian colonies vulnerable. Japan was interested in the French colony of Indochina because the northern part controlled the flow of supplies into China, while the southern half was an excellent base for launching an invasion against Singapore and the oil-rich Netherlands East Indies. That was a tempting target for a nation dependent upon the Western powers for its oil.

This situation was painfully apparent to Roosevelt and Hull even as the German offensive began. Consequently, when Japan showed a particular interest in the Netherlands East Indies, the secretary of state responded with a blunt warning that Japan should not cast a covetous eye on Southeast Asia. To emphasize American determination, Roosevelt and Hull ordered the U.S. fleet to remain in Hawaiian waters, where it was on maneuvers, rather than return to the fleet's home base in southern California two thousand miles farther away from Japan.

These warnings did not stop Japan. The magnitude of the German victories in Europe and the vulnerability of Southeast Asia led Tokyo further down the road of conquest. In September 1940, Japan joined a military alliance with Germany and Italy and occupied the northern half of French Indochina. The Roosevelt administration responded by embargoing all exports of scrap iron and steel to Japan. Such an embargo would not bring Japan to its knees, but Hull hoped it might bring it to its senses and stop its expansion into Southeast Asia. Had they wanted to, Roosevelt and Hull could have imposed far-reaching economic sanctions, even cutting off oil exports to Japan. Concerned that economic sanctions would provoke that country to attack the Netherlands East Indies, neither the president nor his secretary of state was willing to go that far, and trade with Japan continued in most items, especially oil.

Meanwhile, the United States moved closer to an alliance with Britain. When the British ran out of money for their cash-and-carry purchases, Roosevelt persuaded Congress to approve his Lend-Lease program. In his own sly way the president compared the program to lending your garden hose to a neighbor whose house was on fire. It was nothing of the kind. It placed the full economic and industrial resources of the United States behind Britain and marked the abandonment of even the pretense of American neutrality.

It did no good, however, to produce goods for Britain if they could not get past the German submarine wolf packs that prowled the Atlantic Ocean. In the first six months of 1941, Britain lost 3.5 million tons of shipping, with over 700 ships sunk and another 1,400 damaged. If those rates continued, Britain would be starved into defeat. Roosevelt had to do something.

Since the earliest days of the war the president had used the U.S. Navy to patrol waters around the Americas. These "neutrality patrols" were designed to locate German ships and broadcast their location to the British. During 1940 he had gradually increased the size and aggressiveness of the naval forces in the Atlantic. By February 1941, when Roosevelt formally created the Atlantic Fleet, it was a powerful force of 159 ships, including 2 aircraft carriers, 3 battleships, 8 cruisers, and 79 destroyers. Noting the direction the president was taking, Chief of Naval Operations Admiral Harold R. Stark commented that it was now a matter of when, not whether, the United States would enter the war against Germany. In March, Roosevelt inched still closer to war by ordering the Atlantic Fleet to prepare for combat.

Although plans for convoying were ready by the start of 1941, Roosevelt hesitated to implement them. Once U.S. warships began escorting American and British ships across the Atlantic, it would be impossible for a German submarine commander to distinguish between an American destroyer and a British one. Inevitably, there would be casualties, and those casualties would lead to war. Rather than order convoying, Roosevelt aggressively extended his neutrality patrolling by ordering the navy to search for German submarines as far east as the 25th meridian, a line overlapping the German war zone surrounding the British Isles. With American destroyers looking for German submarines in this zone, it was only a matter of time until there was trouble. Surprisingly, it did not come until September when the USS *Greer* clashed with a submarine. Although neither side drew blood in this engagement and the *Greer* was clearly the aggressor, Roosevelt went on nationwide radio to denounce the German submarines as the "rattlesnakes of the Atlantic" and promised that American ships would not wait for them to strike again. He ordered the U.S. Navy to begin convoying and to shoot at German warships on sight.

The war in the North Atlantic quickly escalated. In mid-October the *Kearny* entered a ferocious battle with a wolf pack of German submarines and received a torpedo in the side for its trouble. Through superior seamanship and good luck, the battered destroyer limped to safety with its dead and wounded. "America has been attacked," Roosevelt declared. "The U.S.S. *Kearny* is not just a Navy ship. She belongs to every man, woman, and child in this nation." Still, he did not ask for a declaration of war; he knew that Congress would not vote for it. Even when over one hundred sailors died on the USS *Reuben James* at the end of October, the American people held back. The old fear of war that permeated the land was still too strong. Most Americans were willing to go along with the president when it came to Lend-Lease, neutrality patrolling, and even convoying or shooting on sight, but they were not willing to cross the Atlantic and engage in the war.

Meanwhile, Japanese-American relations were deteriorating at an alarming rate. To keep this spiral from descending into war, Secretary of State Hull and Japanese ambassador Kichisaburo Nomura held many lengthy meetings during the spring of 1941 in a vain effort to find a basis for an agreement. By June, as the Hull-Nomura talks dragged on, the European war took a startling turn, once again upsetting the Asian balance of power.

In a surprise move, Hitler unleashed his armies against the Soviet Union on June 22, 1941. As the German divisions pushed back the Red Army, Japan saw its chance. With Russia preoccupied in Europe, it could safely send its armies into the resource-rich areas of Southeast Asia. Ignoring the long series of American warnings, Japanese troops in late July moved into southern French Indochina and began preparations for an assault on British Malaya, Singapore, the Netherlands East Indies, and perhaps the U.S.-controlled Philippine Islands as well.

The Roosevelt administration reacted forcefully. It cut off all trade with Japan, including oil, and began a major buildup of American armed forces in the Philippines. Peace was slipping away in the Pacific. Denied oil, Japan could not allow negotiations to drag on indefinitely. Unless an agreement was reached with the United States, it would have to capitulate to the American demands or seize the oil in the East Indies. Japanese expansion had provoked American economic warfare, thereby forcing Tokyo to choose between abandoning its Asian ambitions or going to war against the United States.

In both Washington and Tokyo there were civilian and military leaders who recognized the seriousness of the situation and sought ways to avoid war. Their efforts failed, and Japan chose to go to war. It needed to reach the oil wells of the Dutch East Indies but feared doing so because of the U.S. Pacific Fleet sitting menacingly at Pearl Harbor. Roosevelt and Hull had placed it there for the very purpose of deterring Japanese southern expansion. But, when Japan decided it had to go south no matter what the consequences would be, the fleet ceased to be a deterrent and became a target.

Thus, in a brilliant and daring maneuver, Japanese naval air units attacked and devastated the Pacific Fleet on the morning of December 7, 1941. At the same time, other Japanese forces pushed south into British Malaya and the Philippines. Germany honored its alliance with Japan and declared war on the United States, which responded in kind. The United States had entered World War II.

This narrative of events does not explain why American policy took the shape it did. Why did national leaders consider Germany a threat? Why did the Roosevelt administration challenge Japan's expansion into Southeast Asia when it refused to confront Japan in China? To what extent was American policy the product of idealistic principles, national self-interest, power realities, and stereotypical portrayals of the other side? To answer these questions the attitudes of the men who guided U.S. foreign policy must be examined.

In the twentieth century the United States emerged as the great industrial power of the world. Blessed with abundant raw materials, cheap labor, and dynamic corporate leadership, it became a wealthy nation whose goods and investments spread around the globe. America's dollars, coupled with its business and engineering skills, developed the resources of less developed states (known as developing nations today and what were referred to as "backward peoples" a half century ago).

It was a good world for the United States, and American leaders naturally sought to preserve it. They recognized and accepted the need for change but insisted that the change be orderly and peaceful. Thus, between the two world wars, there was much talk of a society governed by international law and respect for the sanctity of treaties. Such principles appealed to Americans, who enjoyed the status quo, but offered no hope to nations such as Japan and Germany, which each sought to improve its position in the world. Americans denounced German or Japanese aggression as unlawful or evil, forgetting that their own country had climbed to its lofty position through the conquest of land belonging to Spain, Mexico, Hawaii, and a variety of North American Indian nations and ignoring a tendency toward gunboat diplomacy in Latin America and Asia. Although the German and Japanese attempts to revise the world order by force was only another in a long history of struggles for "a place in the sun," it was no less disturbing to the Roosevelt administration.

The most obvious aspect of the German-Japanese revisionism was that it used military conquest to achieve its end. Roosevelt and Hull were most disturbed, however, about what these nations sought to do with the territory they had conquered. In the 1930s both Germany and Japan had become autarchic powers—that is, they sought economic self-sufficiency by having the raw materials and the markets they needed within their own borders or spheres of influence.

For Japan that meant undisputed control over East and Southeast Asia, from the iron ore of Manchuria to the oil in the Netherlands East Indies. For Germany it meant domination of the labor, raw materials, and industrial plants of Europe. Such control would be exclusive; neither Germany nor Japan would leave any room for American interests in their spheres of influence.

By contrast, U.S. leaders believed in a liberal commercial world order in which all nations would have equal opportunity to invest or trade in any country. Rather than exclusive spheres, they talked of a fair field without favor for all nations, an "open door" to free competition. Not surprisingly, this liberal commercial philosophy favored the United States with its great masses of capital and business and technical skill. Americans also were convinced that their way of liberal commercialism benefited all the people of the world. Development in China, for example, helped the Chinese as much as it did the American company engaged in the project. Thus, they viewed the challenge of Germany and Japan not only as a threat to American interests but also as a threat to world progress.

Militarily, the United States was not prepared to preserve a liberal commercial world order. Naval arms limitation treaties created a balance of power that prevented it from operating in the western Pacific and Japan from operating in the eastern Pacific. In the Atlantic the United States relied upon the presence of the mighty British navy to stop any hostile force from interfering in the Western Hemisphere.

Keeping these factors in mind, we can begin to see why Roosevelt responded as he did to German expansion. Both the president and the rest of his foreign policy staff made a clear distinction between what was undesirable and what was intolerable. The seizure of the Sudetenland by the Germans and their subsequent conquest of the remainder of Czechoslovakia were undesirable, but their control of Czechoslovakia did not significantly disrupt the liberal commercial world order and certainly did nothing to threaten the supremacy of the British fleet in the Atlantic. The same could be said of the German conquest of Poland. The fall of France in June 1940, however, was a totally different matter. Virtually all of western Europe had come under Germany's economic control and had been removed from the liberal commercial world order. Moreover, the future of Britain and its navy was very much in doubt.

By October the first test had been passed. The Royal Air Force had denied the Luftwaffe the air supremacy that Hitler needed to launch an invasion of the British Isles, but the issue was still in doubt. Although Prime Minister Winston Churchill assured Roosevelt that his country would never surrender, no American president could be certain that the British people and economy could indefinitely withstand the strains of war. A new British leader might offer to buy peace with Germany in exchange for neutralization of the fleet. For the United States it was hardly better to have the British fleet neutral than captured because in either case the Atlantic became a highway for German expansion rather than an obstacle to it. To keep Britain fighting, Germany would have to be pushed back, and Britain could not do that by itself. In other words, making sure that Britain did not lose meant that Germany must be defeated, and that would require American involvement in the war.

German conquest posed not only a military threat to the United States but an economic one as well. Even as Hitler seized Czechoslovakia, Roosevelt showed his anxiety. He told a group of reporters that if such aggression went unchecked, it would choke off free trade in the world and thus overburden the economies of the democratic states. One year later, as the 1940 German spring offensive began, the president repeated his warning. Washington foreign policy managers worried that once Germany controlled Europe, it might use its economic leverage to demand political or military concessions from other nations. For example, Hitler might insist upon a submarine base in Argentina in exchange for allowing Argentine beef to be sold in Europe. If the United States tried to block these German designs by buying Argentine beef and the exports of every other nation in Latin America, it would place an unbearable strain on its economy.

Besides the danger that Germany could use its economic leverage to gain military advantages, its autarchic control of Europe threatened to destroy the progress and prosperity that the world had enjoyed for over a century. It was an argument stated eloquently by William A. Clayton, a wealthy cotton exporter who had joined the Roosevelt administration and sought to awaken the business community to the perils that Germany posed. Speaking early in 1941, he explained that "to understand what is happening in the world today, one must go back to the Industrial Revolution which had its early beginnings in England a little over a century and a half ago." The Industrial Revolution brought in the age of the machine, which freed the world from excessive toil and fear of want while it opened up great progress in intellectual, spiritual, and cultural growth. Clayton warned, however, that such progress could come only through the "basic, unchangeable laws of the machine . . . production and more production and the free movement thereof through the world." He denounced Hitler's autarchic system for denying this law by trying to put Europe under a centralized authority. With tentacles reaching into the Western Hemisphere, the Führer's economic system sought to drive American trade from the world, thereby causing "severe strain on our traditional way of life."

The fall of France in June 1940 therefore established an intolerable situation. For both economic and military reasons it would be necessary to force Germany back to its original borders, or at least back to the situation in 1939. That could not be done without active American participation in the war. Whether Roosevelt was willing to accept this as early as June 1940 is not clear; the president kept such observations to himself. What is clear is that during the year following the fall of France, Roosevelt moved cautiously in opposing Germany. Some Roosevelt watchers attributed this hesitancy to the president's fear of losing popular support. Others argue that he was waiting until he had his military and diplomatic house in order; it took time for the nation's military establishment to prepare for war, and it was not until August 1941 that Roosevelt and Churchill met to discuss war aims. Whatever the reasons for his caution, by August FDR was ready to act and seized upon the *Greer* incident to confront Germany.

Developments in Asia followed much the same path as in Europe, although Japan never posed the same military threat as Germany. The early Japanese expansion was undesirable to American leaders but not intolerable. From July 1937 to the spring of 1940 most of this expansion was confined to China. While the Roosevelt administration was sympathetic toward the Chinese, their country was not strategically important to the United States, nor was its loss to the liberal commercial world order of any great consequence. The costs of war with Japan to preserve the Open Door in China would far outweigh any possible economic benefits that might be gained. The United States had never been willing to fight for China, except possibly fighting the Chinese, and it was not willing to do so now.

Only when Japan moved beyond China into Southeast Asia did the United States see important interests threatened and begin to offer strong resistance to Japanese expansion. One reason for this was economic. If China by itself was not a major loss to the liberal commercial world order, China and all of Southeast Asia would be. In the short run the United States could survive without the rubber, tin, and manganese that came from that region, but in the long run Washington policymakers believed that neither the United States nor the rest of the world could prosper with such a large part of the globe monopolized by Japan. Just as in Europe, where the United States could live with the loss of Czechoslovakia and Poland but not all of the Continent, so too the United States could tolerate the loss of China but not all of East and Southeast Asia as well.

A second reason was strategic. As Japan moved farther south it threatened areas important to Britain: the naval base at Singapore, the colony of Malaya, and the Commonwealth countries of Australia and New Zealand. Even a small Japanese advance into Southeast Asia would force Britain to divert desperately needed military forces from the European war in order to protect its own interests. If Japan launched an all-out attack against the British and captured Singapore (as it did in 1942), they would be denied access to the men and matériel of their Asian colonies and allies. Moreover, if Germany should push into the Middle East and capture the Suez Canal, it could link up with Japan through the Indian Ocean and draw upon the resources of Asia to fuel its war machine. There was also the nagging problem of the Philippines. Militarily indefensible and economically insignificant, the islands stood as hostage to a fortune that could drag the United States into an Asian war if Japan moved south.

British strategic planners hoped to persuade Americans to protect Southeast Asia. As important as that region was, however, U.S. policymakers were most concerned about Europe because they believed that once Germany was defeated, the Americans and British could easily turn back Japan, while a war with Japan would leave the German threat still to be faced. Thus, it was important to concentrate on the European theater and avoid war with Japan.

Avoiding war with Japan was not such an easy task. Secretary Hull worked diligently to find the basis for a lasting peace, but it was a futile effort. Tokyo was too committed to its autarchic New Order in East Asia to give it up, and the United States was too deeply devoted to the liberal commercial world order to tolerate Japan's New Order. Eventually these two systems would clash. Hull did not see any alternative and did not think that peace could come to Asia through a face-saving withdrawal of Japanese troops from China. That would only help the Japanese militarists extricate themselves from an embarrassing war and assure their continued control of Japan.

Like everyone else in Washington, Hull believed that the Japanese leaders were determined to dominate all of East and Southeast Asia, and, until Japan underwent a regeneration and purged itself of its extremist leaders, there was no hope for peace and therefore no reason to seek a short-term agreement with Tokyo. The events of July and August 1941 undercut the secretary's assumptions. Japan's decision to move south and the resulting American trade embargo meant that if the United States hoped to avoid a war with Japan, it had to abandon the search for a lasting peace and begin negotiating a short-term, limited understanding, or what the diplomats call a modus vivendi.

Japanese prime minister Konoye Fumimaro realized this as well and urgently sought a meeting with Roosevelt during August and September. He hoped that the two leaders could strip through the technicalities which seemed to be the diplomats' stock in trade and reach an agreement that, if it did not assure peace for all time, would postpone a war.

Roosevelt was interested—he always liked proposals that stressed personal diplomacy—but Hull and the State Department were strongly opposed. It was a trick, Hull warned the president. If the Japanese leaders were ready to live in peace, there was no need for a summit conference. If they were not, no amount of talk between the two national leaders would alter that fact. Therefore, during the critical months of September and October 1941, Hull spent his time looking for a comprehensive agreement that would restore peace in East Asia. Not until the middle of November during the eleventh hour of the negotiations did he consider a modus vivendi.

The agreement approved by State, War, and Navy department officials offered Japan moderate amounts of American oil if it would withdraw its forces from southern Indochina, limit the number of troops in northern Indochina to twenty-five thousand, and make no further advances in the South Pacific. The agreement was to last three months. Hull had to decide whether to offer Japan this modus vivendi or to admit that there was no diplomatic solution, issue a statement for the record, and turn the matter over to the army and navy. There were good arguments for both courses.

A variety of strategic factors favored an agreement with Tokyo, even one that would last only two or three months. The U.S.

Army was building up its strength in the Philippines and believed that once it was fortified with new B-17 bombers, Japan would not dare move into Southeast Asia. Three months, army officers argued, would radically alter the balance of power in Asia. Moreover, by the spring of 1942 more American warships would be in service, and the bitter Russian winter might have stopped the German armies. In that situation, Japan might be more hesitant to expand south, and war might be averted indefinitely.

On the other hand, the American strategy for containing Japan in the Pacific assumed that Tokyo would continue to have one million soldiers bogged down in China. Army officers believed that Japan did not have the resources to fight both in China and against the well-defended Philippines. Yet, when Hull broached the modus vivendi to the Chinese government, it reacted with much vehemence, declaring that its people would consider it appeasement and might be so demoralized that they would be unable to continue the war against Japan.

There seemed to be no desirable choice before the Roosevelt administration. If by yielding to Chinese protests it abandoned the modus vivendi proposal, diplomacy would end and war would surely come. American intercepts of secret Japanese messages revealed that unless an agreement was reached immediately, "things were automatically going to happen." But, if the administration went ahead with the proposal, China might collapse, with disastrous results for American interests in Asia.

To a remarkable degree the decision rested with Secretary Hull. While Roosevelt closely directed the policy toward Europe, Hull dominated the negotiations with Japan. For eight months he had sought an agreement. Early on November 26 he ended the search by recommending that the modus vivendi not be offered. In reaching this decision, he was greatly influenced by the possibility of the collapse of China, but there was more to it than a dispassionate weighing of the pros and cons. It was a decision made under great stress and after many months of lengthy and exhausting negotiations. Hull's determination to "kick the whole thing over" and to "wash his hands" of it reflected his fatigue and frustration at not being able to fashion a lasting agreement.

Important matters of state, especially those of war and peace, are supposed to be made by clear-minded leaders who, after weighing the evidence carefully, select the best option. But such decision makers are people, too, subject to stress and fatigue. When tired and under great pressure, they tend to avoid the complicated solutions and look for the simpler ones. Perhaps if Hull had not been so worn down by the months of negotiations, he could have summoned the energy to stand up to the Chinese leaders, assure them that they were not being abandoned, and insist that they continue the war while the United States tried to buy three months of peace, but he could not bring himself to do that. Instead, he phoned Secretary of War Henry L. Stimson and told him that it was now in the hands of the army and navy. Diplomacy had ended.

The War and Navy departments sent out warnings to their bases throughout the Pacific, notifying American commanders that since diplomatic negotiations had ended, they could expect war with Japan at any time. When the attack came ten days later, U.S. forces in the Hawaiian Islands and the Philippines were not prepared. From that day to this, Americans have wondered how the Japanese navy could steam so far across the Pacific undetected and wreak such destruction upon the U.S. fleet at Pearl Harbor.

Implicit in many such questions was a racism which assumed that an Asian people were not capable of doing such damage to a Western nation without the complicity of someone within the United States. Unwilling to credit Japan's success to superior planning, American error, and just plain good luck, a variety of critics has accused Roosevelt and members of his administration of deliberately leading Japan to attack Pearl Harbor as a way of bringing the United States into the war. This "back door" thesis maintains that Roosevelt really wanted war with Germany, but, unable to provoke it in the Atlantic, he turned to the Pacific and Germany's ally, Japan.

Dozens of government and historical investigations have found no firm evidence to substantiate this point of view. What is clear is that Roosevelt and his administration knew Japan was about to attack. They even guessed some of the locations (the Isthmus of Kra, as Japan prepared to move toward the British naval base at Singapore, for example). What is in dispute is whether the president and his staff knew that the attack was coming against Pearl Harbor and did nothing about it. Roosevelt's critics charge that he withheld vital information from Pearl Harbor in order to keep the U.S. fleet in a state of unpreparedness and thus draw Japan into an attack. His defenders argue that the so-called vital information was actually fragments of intelligence, the meaning of which became clear only with hindsight. They maintain that the reason why so little of this information was shared with American commanders in the field was partially because of confusion over who already had access to it and partially out of fear of compromising the top-secret ways in which intelligence was gathered. Very few historians who have studied this issue accept the conspiratorial interpretation of the Pearl Harbor attack. Since it is impossible to provide positive proof that a conspiracy did not exist and since Americans are intrigued by conspiracies, the debate will certainly continue.

The debate over a conspiracy must not distract us from the more important question of how we got to the point where an attack would take place. If we concentrate not on December 7, 1941, but on the years from 1937 to 1941, we can learn much about the American nation and its role in world affairs. It was not out of an idealistic sympathy for the Chinese, French, Poles, or British that the United States moved toward war, nor was it the result of an emotional attachment to the ideal of international law and the sanctity of treaties. Instead, Roosevelt, Hull, and the others in Washington who crafted policy moved the nation deliberately, but gradually, against the Axis because it sought to partition the world into autarchic spheres of influence, thereby destroying the liberal commercial world order on which the American people had built a good life.

Sources and Suggested Readings

Anderson, Irvine H., Jr. *The Standard-Vacuum Oil Company and United States East Asian Policy, 1933–1941*. Princeton, NJ, 1975.

Borg, Dorothy. *The United States and the Far Eastern Crisis of 1933–1938*. Cambridge, MA, 1964.

————, and Okamoto, Shumpei, eds. *Pearl Harbor as History: Japanese-American Relations, 1931–1941*. New York, 1973.

Compton, James V. *The Swastika and the Eagle: Hitler, the United States, and the Origins of World War II*. Boston, 1967.

Dallek, Robert. *Franklin D. Roosevelt and American Foreign Policy, 1932–1945*. New York, 1979.

Divine, Robert A. *Roosevelt and World War II*. Baltimore, 1969.

Feis, Herbert. *The Road to Pearl Harbor: The Coming of the War between the United States and Japan*. Princeton, NJ, 1950.

Haglund, David G. *Latin America and the Transformation of U.S. Strategic Thought, 1936–1940*. Albuquerque, NM, 1984.

Heinrichs, Waldo. *Threshold of War: Franklin D. Roosevelt and American Entry into World War II*. New York, 1988.

Iriye, Akira. *Power and Culture: The Japanese-American War, 1941–1945*. Cambridge, MA, 1981.

Langer, William L., and Gleason, S. Everett. *The Challenge of Isolation: The World Crisis of 1937–1940 and American Foreign Policy.* New York, 1952.

———. *The Undeclared War, 1940–1941.* New York, 1953.

Layton, Edwin T. *"And I Was There": Pearl Harbor and Midway—Breaking the Secrets.* New York, 1985.

Leutze, James R. *Bargaining for Supremacy: Anglo-American Naval Collaboration, 1937–1941.* Chapel Hill, NC, 1977.

Prange, Gordon W. *At Dawn We Slept: The Untold Story of Pearl Harbor.* New York, 1981.

———. *Pearl Harbor: The Verdict of History.* New York, 1985.

Reynolds, David. *The Creation of the Anglo-American Alliance: A Study in Competitive Cooperation.* Chapel Hill, NC, 1982.

Utley, Jonathan G. *Going to War with Japan, 1937–1941.* Knoxville, TN, 1985.

Wilson, Theodore A. *The First Summit: Roosevelt and Churchill at Placentia Bay, 1941.* Boston, 1969.

World War II and
the Coming of the Cold War

Robert L. Messer

World War II and the ensuing Cold War shaped modern American diplomacy. Ideas about national security and military preparedness were never the same after the "day of infamy" at Pearl Harbor. The wartime generation's conclusions about the futility of appeasing aggression and the necessity of maintaining an active, leading role in the postwar world became the basis for the Cold War consensus that dominated American foreign policy for more than four decades. The experiences and lessons of World War II formed the guiding principles of U.S. policy during the postwar era that we call the Cold War. These two global conflicts are inextricably linked. Any description of one would be incomplete without reference to the other.

Unlike World War II, the Cold War between the United States and the Soviet Union had no formal declaration of hostilities to mark its beginning. Historians disagree not only about how or why the Cold War began but also when. However, most attempts to explain the origins of the Cold War start with the fact of the American-Soviet alliance during World War II and then describe its deterioration. Mutual hostility and distrust predate World War II, but the breakup of the wartime alliance and the struggle for economic, ideological, and military supremacy in the postwar world define the Cold War.

How did these two allies, victors over the Axis aggressors, come to see one another as enemies? A partial answer to this complex question lies in the nature of their wartime partnership. British prime minister Winston Churchill christened the Allied coalition "the Grand Alliance." Others, including Adolf Hitler, considered this unlikely union of imperial Britain, democratic America, and Communist Russia an inherently unstable alignment of forces so alien that the strains of coalition warfare would surely pull it apart. However strange or unnatural, the combination of these three Great

Powers was indeed grand. Only their combined resources of population, productive capacity, and armed might could have defeated the Axis alliance of Germany, Italy, Japan, and their satellite states. In the aftermath of that colossal military undertaking, these three victorious powers, acting together, had the capacity to exercise unprecedented control over a world ravaged and radically altered by the destruction of history's greatest war, a world wounded by the deaths of some fifty-five million people, and a world of chaos and ruin. Rebuilding a new international structure upon the rubble of World War II demanded the sort of combined, all-out effort expended in winning the war. That the victorious allies proved incapable of performing this formidable task is a reflection of the differences in the meaning of the conflict for each of the Big Three. Each fought a different war; each looked forward to a different peace.

Generalissimo Joseph Stalin did not even give his war the same name. In the West the conflict was first called the War for the United Nations and then the Second World War, but in the USSR it was officially named the Great Patriotic War of the Soviet Union. Stalin's war began on June 22, 1941, when Hitler launched a massive three-pronged invasion of Russia. For the next three years this war was fought largely on Soviet soil. In it the Soviet victors suffered by far the greatest losses of any of the combatants in World War II, including the losers. In a bloody struggle made even more brutal by inhuman conditions of weather, guerrilla warfare, and the scorched-earth tactics of both sides, an estimated twenty million Russians perished, more than five times the total German losses and twenty-five times the combined total of British and American war dead.

In Stalin's view the Western allies did not effectively enter his war until mid-1944. The Anglo-American invasion of France came less than one year before Germany's total collapse and more than one year after the decisive battles of Stalingrad and Kursk. Long before D-Day at Normandy the Red Army had defeated the bulk of German armed strength, inflicting 80 percent of all German casualties. In its scale, timing, and strategic significance, Stalin's war on the Russian or Eastern Front was very different from that waged in the West by the British and Americans.

Perhaps most important, Stalin's war differed fundamentally in its purpose. As its name implies, it was a war strictly of and for the Soviet Union. At first it was a battle for survival. By mid-1943, with the German armies in retreat, it became a war for revenge, both to justify the enormous losses suffered in the conflict and to make certain that such an onslaught never again could threaten the survival of the USSR and the Soviet form of government. In Stalin's war the Soviet Union was not just a major victor; it was the only victor. Because he believed he had earned it, Stalin expected the lion's share of the spoils of this war. At the very least he expected to recover the lands lost as a result of the German invasion and to maintain a controlling influence over any other territory wrested from the conquered enemy.

To Stalin that enemy was not just Hitler or Germany. It was prewar Europe and everything it stood for in the experience of that generation of Soviet leaders. Stalin and those around him remembered vividly the West's armed intervention in the Russian civil war of 1918–1920 and the years of diplomatic isolation and ideological hostility. The prewar appeasement of Hitler by the British, French, and Americans seemed to him to have been motivated primarily by Western anticommunism. The war against Hitler and his Italian and east European allies only seemed to confirm Stalin's earlier experience in dealing with the rest of the Continent. Anti-Soviet, Fascist Europe was the enemy that had to be defeated, punished, and permanently subdued. When Stalin insisted upon having only "friendly" governments on Russia's borders, he declared his refusal even to risk reestablishment of the prewar cordon sanitaire of non-Communist, anti-Soviet regimes.

Despite his hatred of Soviet communism, dating back to the Bolsheviks' separate peace with Germany in World War I, Churchill's approach to his war was not unlike Stalin's. Churchill, too, had imperial ambitions. Rather than expanding his area of control, however, he sought only to hang on to as much of the prewar British empire as possible. To do this while defeating Hitler and at the same time avoiding the debilitating carnage of the First World War, Churchill had to rely upon the enormous manpower that only Stalin could provide. As the prime minister put it immediately after the outbreak of the Soviet-German war, "If Hitler invaded Hell, I would make at least a favorable reference to the Devil in the House of Commons." Harboring no illusions about the satanic qualities of Stalin and his dictatorial regime, Churchill nonetheless saw Hitler's Nazi Germany as the greater or more menacing evil in the world and publicly pledged British support for Soviet resistance.

A strategy of relying upon Stalin to help defeat Hitler had its price. Providing that the price of victory could be kept within acceptable limits, Churchill saw little choice but to pay it. The British leader's fatalistic acceptance of a Soviet "sphere of action" in eastern Europe was made explicit in October 1944 when he and Stalin concluded their secret "percentage deal." In return for a controlling interest in the affairs of Greece and equal shares in Yugoslavia and Hungary, Churchill, in effect, conceded the rest of eastern Europe to Stalin.

Conspicuously absent from this bargain was Poland, which for Churchill remained a special case. His war had begun in September 1939, in response to Hitler's invasion of Poland from the west, followed soon after by the Soviet occupation of the eastern portion of the country. This earlier Soviet participation in the partition of Poland, the revelation of the Katyn Forest massacre of ten thousand Polish officers captured by the Russians, and Stalin's later refusal to intervene in the abortive Warsaw uprising in order to save the non-Communist underground forces from annihilation at the hands of the retreating Germans all combined to make a mockery of the subsequent Soviet "liberation." The British, who had gone to war for Poland, hardly could be expected to endorse its subjugation by a second conqueror. For Churchill, Poland remained the "test case" of the Anglo-Soviet alliance.

That belated, mutually expedient alliance could not erase the memory of a period when Churchill and Stalin had been on opposite sides in the war over Poland. After the Nazi-Soviet non-aggression pact of August 1939 and the ensuing defeat of France, Britain had stood alone against Hitler. During its time of trial, Stalin not only collaborated in the destruction of Poland but also continued to ship vital raw materials to Germany until the very moment of Hitler's treacherous attack. Repeated British and American warnings of that betrayal went unheeded. Although historians disagree as to what extent, the rapid German advance deep into the Soviet heartland and the heavy price paid by the Russian people in losing and regaining that land were at least partly due to Stalin's miscalculations regarding Hitler's intentions. Thus, it can be argued that Stalin's later claims for compensation in return for his nation's great sacrifices in the war were based on losses for which he was to some degree responsible. Certainly, from Churchill's perspective, Stalin's case for special treatment was reminiscent of the boy on trial for murdering his parents who asked for mercy on the grounds that he was an orphan.

In concluding his pact with Hitler, Stalin had attempted to buy time and some additional territory in anticipation of eventual war with Germany, but he did so at the expense of Britain and its allies. Thus, aside from the lack of sufficient manpower and equipment, Churchill was in no great hurry to mount an early cross-Channel invasion onto the beaches of France just to please his new "friend" Stalin. If Churchill had had his way, there might never have been such an invasion. He would have preferred penetrating what he optimistically called the "soft underbelly" of Europe with an invasion from the Mediterranean, intersecting the Continent south to north and cutting off the Russians from Germany and the rest of Europe. This dubious military-political maneuver, however, was vetoed by the third and, in many ways, most important of the Big Three leaders.

President Franklin D. Roosevelt was the last member to join the wartime Big Three, but his involvement in both Churchill's and Stalin's wars began long before December 1941. From a prewar policy of isolationist self-interest and indirect support for appeasement, Roosevelt had moved warily toward an increasingly open and active policy of intervention to forestall an Axis victory.

Although the country remained officially neutral and fervently antiwar, from the beginning of the conflict in 1939 both Roosevelt and the overwhelming majority of Americans were morally committed to the forces opposing Hitler. Gradually that moral commitment was backed by a growing economic one as the United States took on the role of the "arsenal of democracy." War matériel from that arsenal went to the increasingly impoverished British under Lend-Lease, a unique aid program that authorized the president to "lend" ships, planes, tanks, guns—virtually anything needed to fight a war—to any country whose defense he deemed vital to American security. If not yet to the point of willingness to enter the war directly, by late 1941 Roosevelt had succeeded in convincing most Americans that Churchill's war was also their war.

An important part of that domestic sales effort was a joint declaration of Anglo-American war aims published after Roosevelt and Churchill's first summit meeting off Argentia, Newfoundland, in August 1941. In this eight-point communiqué, which the American press immediately dubbed the Atlantic Charter, the two leaders pledged to fight for "common principles," including the right of self-determination of all peoples "forcibly deprived" of it; free trade among all nations, "with due respect for their existing obligations"; and a mutual opposition to territorial "aggrandizement" or undemocratic territorial changes.

The qualifications were inserted to satisfy Churchill that these lofty goals would not interfere with the existing British imperial system of colonies and trade preferences. A few weeks after Pearl Harbor the rest of the twenty-six-member anti-Axis alliance was called upon to endorse these same war aims in the United Nations Declaration. In affixing his signature to this document, the Soviet representative fashioned an even larger loophole by adding the stipulation that "the practical application of these principles will necessarily adapt itself to the circumstances, needs, and historic peculiarities of particular countries." But Roosevelt's American audience took public declarations such as the Atlantic Charter as guarantees that this time there would be no secret deals in violation of the nation's democratic principles. This sort of rhetoric also assured Americans that Britain was worthy of their support.

In the case of Stalin's war, Roosevelt encountered more resistance to any such American commitment. Memories of the Nazi-Soviet Pact, the Winter War against tiny Finland, the opposition of religious and ethnic groups, and the widespread antipathy toward communism in general and Stalin's dictatorship in particular posed special problems in convincing Congress and the public that the USSR, too, was a fitting recipient of the products of democracy's arsenal. Untroubled by the contradiction of waging a war for democracy in league with a totalitarian dictator, Roosevelt echoed both Churchill's priorities and his metaphor in explaining his private attitude toward Stalin as an ally: "I can't take communism . . . but to cross this bridge I would hold hands with the Devil."

Obviously, Churchill and Roosevelt looked upon their liaison with Stalin as a Faustian bargain and not a marriage made in Heaven. But their concerns were of this world, a world threatened by Hitler more than by Stalin. Their first concern was how to win the more urgent war against the Axis powers. The way that conflict was fought and won gave rise to the Cold War that followed.

At the beginning it was by no means clear that Soviet help would be decisive in defeating Hitler. Indeed, most Western military experts expected the Red Army to collapse in a matter of weeks. But Roosevelt was willing to gamble American money and supplies on the chance that such an investment would prolong the war on the

Eastern Front, at least until the creation of an Anglo-American second front in the West.

The failure of that second front to materialize until late in the war was, in the words of Roosevelt biographer James MacGregor Burns, "perhaps the most determining single factor" in the origins of the Cold War. The first cracks in the wartime alliance began over the issue of the second front and formed the gap between promise and reality that widened steadily during 1942 and 1943. Forced by British reluctance and shortages of troops and matériel into repeated delays in launching a cross-Channel invasion, Roosevelt tried to bridge that widened gap in the American-Soviet alliance with Lend-Lease supplies. He was buying time and avoiding horrendous American casualties with dollars while Stalin was buying territory with his most expendable resource, the lives of millions of Russian soldiers.

How significant was Lend-Lease to the Soviet war effort? As with so much else about the alliance, the answer is relative. From the American perspective the numbers speak for themselves. From late 1941 to the end of the war, the United States shipped to the USSR over 18,000 planes, 10,000 tanks, 700 ships, 200,000 trucks, 5 million pairs of boots, millions of tons of food, and much more. The total cost of this aid was over $10 billion. Soviet historians point out that this impressive volume was less than 10 percent of the total Soviet war production and less than the amount provided to Britain. Moreover, most of these supplies arrived after the decisive phase of the war on the Eastern Front. It is clear, however, that Lend-Lease aid was an important qualitative contribution to the Red Army's fighting capabilities and formed a major link in American-Soviet relations during the war.

Determined to give the Russians every possible assistance, Roosevelt rejected suggestions that he use this aid as leverage to ensure Stalin's good behavior. His aid policy was based not upon any naive trust in the dictator's good intentions but upon his personal appreciation for the military burden that Stalin was bearing on behalf of the Western allies. Roosevelt knew firsthand, as he told General Douglas MacArthur in 1942, that "the Russian armies are killing more Axis personnel and destroying more Axis matériel than all the other twenty-five United Nations put together." The president also came to realize that this imbalance would continue not only for that year but also throughout the next and well into 1944.

First in 1942 and again in 1943, Roosevelt and Churchill had promised Stalin a second front in Europe, only to find that they could not make good on this pledge. Instead of a direct assault on Germany in a cross-Channel invasion of the Continent, the Western allies busied themselves on the periphery of the Axis empire, first with an invasion of North Africa in late 1942 and the next summer by invading Sicily and Italy. Neither of these actions constituted a real second front. Rather they forced the postponement of a cross-Channel invasion and allowed Hitler to divert troops from the west to throw against the Soviet forces in the east. In perhaps the unkindest cut of all, the North African and Mediterranean operations diverted supplies and shipping originally promised to the Soviet Union under Lend-Lease.

The reasons for the delay in the second front were sound enough from the British and American point of view: insufficient trained personnel, equipment and shipping shortages, and lack of air superiority. To Stalin, however, these excuses could not erase the fact that promises had been made and broken. The Western allies' concern that any attempt to breach Hitler's "Atlantic Wall" should have a reasonable chance for success and a reasonable cost in lives could only seem unreasonable to a leader whose nation was engaged in a desperate struggle for survival. What to Roosevelt and Churchill, politicians answerable to public opinion, were unacceptable losses were to Stalin the unavoidable price of victory. The three Allied leaders faced differing realities. Churchill and Roosevelt had a choice of how, when, and where to attack; Stalin had none.

Roosevelt realized the seriousness of Stalin's position and worried that the Soviet Union might be forced out of the war. Raising hopes of an imminent second front, publicly declaring the Western allies' commitment to settle for nothing less than "unconditional surrender," and sending Stalin as much Lend-Lease aid as could be spared were all part of his effort to keep the USSR in the war.

Like Churchill, Roosevelt needed Stalin to win in Europe, but the president also sought Stalin's support in other areas. The Allies were committed to a "Europe first" strategy, reflecting their agreement that Germany posed the greater and more urgent threat. Nonetheless, Roosevelt had to think ahead to winning the war against Japan. Following the defeat of Nazi Germany, the huge Red Army could relieve the Americans of the daunting task of expelling the Japanese from the mainland of Asia. The nearly two million battle-hardened Japanese troops in China, Manchuria, and Korea were a formidable force against which the Chinese under Jiang Jieshi (Chiang Kai-shek) had proved totally ineffective.

Roosevelt also sought Stalin's cooperation in the postwar peace. The president's plans for peace, following the defeat of Japan, envisioned a system of collective security designed to avoid the pitfalls of Woodrow Wilson's League of Nations. This revised version of the League, comprising the anti-Axis "United Nations," would be run by an executive council made up of all the world's major powers, including the Soviet Union and the United States, whose absence from the League had helped to render it ineffective. To succeed, this new system would have to rely upon the enforcement or police power of the victorious major Allied powers. To gain Churchill and Stalin's cooperation in such a system, Roosevelt would have to make concessions to their war aims involving spheres of influence and violations of democratic principles. He considered such concessions as temporary expedients, made in response to Soviet security concerns and what he termed "Victorian" British ideas about the necessity of formal colonies. The need for such interim arrangements would decline once the new world organization was in full and effective operation.

That new international peace-keeping organization, however, could not begin to operate without the approval of the American people and Congress. Just one-third plus one of the Senate could veto this entire postwar system and with it destroy Roosevelt's hopes for a lasting peace. That all-important support at home could be jeopardized by premature revelation of any secret power politics that contradicted American ideals and public war aims. The ghost of Wilson and the fate of his League haunted Roosevelt as he prepared for the peace. He was, as Warren Kimball puts it, a "juggler" balancing public, private, military, diplomatic, and political policies.

Roosevelt's debut on the stage of Big Three summit diplomacy came in November 1943 when he, Stalin, and Churchill met for the first time at Tehran, Iran. There the three leaders set a final, and this time firm, date for the invasion of France. Roosevelt gained Stalin's verbal commitment to enter the war against Japan after the defeat of Germany. He also put forth his plans for the peace.

Explaining the postwar role of the "Four Policemen," the president proposed that Britain and Russia police western and eastern Europe, respectively; the United States would be responsible for North and South America and the Pacific, presumably including

Japan. Rather wistfully adding China to the big-power club, Roosevelt expressed his hope that China would keep the peace on the mainland of Asia. Although Churchill remained concerned about the future of the British empire in such a system and Stalin expressed some doubts about China's capacity and Europe's willingness to be policed, the three leaders agreed upon the broad outlines of the American proposal.

On other more politically sensitive agenda items, such as the postwar borders of Poland, Roosevelt had to be more cautious. He privately raised no objection to Churchill and Stalin's agreement that Poland be moved to the west at the expense of Germany, with the Soviet Union regaining much of the territory in eastern Poland occupied in 1939 under the Nazi-Soviet Pact. Referring to the more than six million Polish Americans in the United States and his upcoming reelection campaign, Roosevelt pointed out that as a "practical man" he could not yet publicly support such territorial changes. This sort of private acquiescence in a British and Soviet division of spoils in Europe, while publicly disavowing any such secret agreements, was characteristic of Roosevelt's dual, often contradictory,

THE ALLIED BIG THREE AT YALTA, FEBRUARY 1945. Fatigue and the ravages of declining health are clearly visible on the face of President Roosevelt as he sits with his wartime partners. (National Archives)

wartime diplomacy. One year later he again privately acquiesced in the Churchill-Stalin percentage deal dividing political control of eastern Europe, only reminding his allies that any final arrangements should be concluded when the three of them next met.

With the second front in Europe at last a reality and with the 1944 presidential race safely behind him, Roosevelt set out for what was to be his last meeting with Churchill and Stalin. This most important wartime Big Three summit was held in February 1945 at Yalta on the Crimean peninsula. The conference site is indicative of the relative bargaining position of the participants. The ill, in fact dying, Roosevelt was obliged to undertake an exhausting and dangerous trip to meet Stalin on Soviet soil. The president was willing to go this last mile in order to nail down the exact terms and timing of the USSR's entry into the war against Japan and to secure final agreement on just how the new peace-keeping international organization would operate. He succeeded in both these objectives.

In return for two extra votes in the General Assembly, Stalin agreed to the American formula for the United Nations Organization. He also signed a secret protocol on the Far East, pledging to declare war on Japan three months after the defeat of Germany. The price for this much-needed help against Japan was essentially restoration of the czarist spheres of influence in Manchuria and North China, including rights to naval bases and railroads.

On other conference issues involving eastern Europe, the military situation at the time gave Stalin a commanding bargaining position. The Red Army had occupied most of eastern Europe and at that moment had advanced to within sixty miles of Berlin. The British and Americans were still recovering from the last German counteroffensive at the Battle of the Bulge and had not yet reached the Rhine. Under such unfavorable circumstances, putting some limits on what the Russians had already gained on the battlefield was as much as Roosevelt and Churchill could hope to gain from the negotiations at Yalta.

The result was a private recognition of the Soviets' domination of the area already under their military occupation and a public Declaration on Liberated Europe which reiterated the Atlantic Charter's goals of self-determination and "free and unfettered elections," without providing an effective means to realize this goal. All that Roosevelt came away with was Stalin's verbal assurance that some sort of pretense of democratic procedure would be carried out as soon as possible.

Upon his return from the conference, Roosevelt once again encouraged his domestic audience to focus upon the public myth rather than the private reality of Yalta. Responding to a carefully orchestrated White House public relations campaign, the press immediately hailed the unenforceable Declaration on Liberated Europe as the "Crimean Charter," a triumph of American democratic war aims over selfish national interest and power politics. Roosevelt encouraged this illusion of diplomatic success in an attempt to garner support at home for a matter that he considered more important: congressional approval of his peace plans. The temporary, politically useful gap between myth and reality was apparently something that he was willing to live with, but, within weeks after returning from Yalta, Roosevelt was dead of a brain hemorrhage. His successor had a very different perspective on the war and on the American-Soviet alliance.

Harry S. Truman's war was not the same one that Roosevelt had waged in partnership with Churchill and Stalin. Truman's war in many ways more closely resembled the war experienced by most other Americans. His was one in which the U.S. military and economic contributions had been decisive. Unaware of the significance of the second front issue in Allied diplomacy, Truman assumed that the D-Day landings in Normandy had been the decisive moment in the defeat of Nazi Germany. Although certainly aware through press accounts of the heavy fighting on the Eastern Front during 1941–1944, Truman, like many of his countrymen, assumed that Lend-Lease had been the key to Soviet survival. Unlike Roosevelt, who felt indebted to the Soviets because they had borne the brunt of the fighting against Germany, Truman privately denigrated their contribution to the war. As he put it shortly after the war: "Without these [Lend-Lease] supplies furnished by the United States, Russia would have been ignominiously defeated." In Truman's mind the Russians owed us; we did not owe them. This attitude influenced his views regarding the continuation of Lend-Lease after Germany's surrender and the denial of a Soviet request for a $6-billion postwar loan.

Whereas Roosevelt had moved during the war toward what Robert Dallek has termed a "regional internationalist" plan for a world peace-keeping system, Truman was much more a nationalist in his approach to the war and the peace. Truman's views early in the war reflected the isolationist self-interest common among his midwestern constituents. Immediately after the German invasion of the USSR in mid-1941, the then obscure junior senator from Missouri offered his opinion on the proper policy toward the war on the Eastern Front: "If we see that Germany is winning the war we ought to help Russia, and if Russia is winning we ought to help Germany, and in that way let them kill as many as possible." Truman hastened to add that he did not want Hitler to win under any circumstances, but his basic position was very near that of other senators who saw no point in America helping "to make Europe safe for communism" and who publicly questioned whether a victory for Stalin was really any better than a German one. A loyal Democrat, Truman eventually fell into line and supported Lend-Lease for the USSR, but his initial public reaction to the issue, before Roosevelt had made known his position, revealed Truman's more parochial view of national self-interest and his identification of Hitler and Stalin.

By the time he took over as president in 1945, Truman no longer sought to kill off the Russians. Like most Americans he had come to accept Stalin as an ally against Hitler. He was willing to get along with the Soviets after the war. Truman's view of the basis of that postwar relationship, however, differed substantially from Roosevelt's. He told his ambassador to Moscow, W. Averell Harriman, immediately after assuming the presidency, that "the Soviet Union needed us more than we needed them" and that while he did not think we would be able to get 100 percent of what we wanted in dealing with them, he fully expected to get at least 85 percent. This presumption of an American preponderance of power in the postwar world resulted in a reversal of many of Roosevelt's wartime priorities.

At Yalta, Roosevelt traded what he did not have—temporary control of eastern Europe—for Soviet participation in the worldwide American peace-keeping system. In his first meeting with a high-ranking Soviet official, Truman bluntly gave Stalin's emissary the choice of either fulfilling the American expectations about free elections in the liberated areas or dropping out of the United Nations Organization. Even on relatively minor procedural issues, such as whether France and China would participate in drafting preliminary peace treaties with Germany's east European satellites, Truman instructed his negotiators to tell the Soviets "to go to Hell" if they refused to accept the Anglo-American position. Woefully unprepared and uninformed about Roosevelt's highly personal and secret wartime diplomacy, Truman tended to take public documents such as the Atlantic Charter and the Yalta Declaration on Liberated Europe at face value, and he expected Stalin to, as he put it, "live up to" those agreements.

This changed perception of the war and the wartime alliance following Roosevelt's death was immediately evident when Truman, within days of taking office, delivered what he called at the time "the old one-two to the jaw" of the Soviet foreign minister, Vyacheslav Molotov, on the subject of the Yalta Polish agreement. Even Roosevelt had been disappointed by Stalin's performance in Poland following the Yalta meeting. Nonetheless, to the end of his life Roosevelt had urged upon Churchill the necessity to minimize such divisive issues. Truman's verbal fisticuffs alarmed Molotov, but this sudden shift in presidential manner did not change Soviet policy in Poland.

THE BIG THREE CONFERENCE AT BERLIN (POTSDAM), JULY 1945. Seated (left to right): British prime minister Clement Attlee, President Harry S. Truman, Generalissimo Joseph Stalin. Standing (left to right): White House chief of staff Admiral William D. Leahy, British foreign secretary Ernest Bevin, Secretary of State James F. Byrnes, Soviet foreign minister V. M. Molotov. (Library of Congress)

After this initial bluster, Truman moderated his tone and sent Roosevelt's confidant Harry Hopkins to Moscow to work out an agreement that led to American recognition of the Warsaw government, after only cosmetic changes in its composition. During this same period, Truman first abruptly cut off and then restored Soviet Lend-Lease shipments. As Truman struggled to get a grip upon his unfamiliar role as diplomat, Stalin was receiving conflicting signals from the new American president. Their first and only face-to-face meeting helped clarify for both men the image of the other.

Truman, Churchill, and Stalin met in July 1945 at Potsdam on the outskirts of the ruined city of Berlin. Truman's first and last Big Three summit conference was aptly code-named "Terminal." The war against Germany had ended more than two months before. Stalin would not enter the war against Japan until August, two days after the Americans dropped the first of two atomic bombs on that nation and less than a week before Japan's surrender. Nonetheless, Potsdam signaled the end of the wartime alliance.

The new president dreaded his initial encounter with "Mr. Britain" and "Mr. Russia." He put off the meeting as long as he could, in part because he wanted to know the results of the American attempt to build an atomic bomb but also because of his personal sense of insecurity and self-doubt. Privately, he repeatedly expressed his anxiety over having to fill Roosevelt's shoes. Once begun, the longest and least productive of the wartime conferences was plagued with difficulties. At its outset Stalin apparently suffered a mild heart attack. Truman suspected a stalling tactic. Then, in the middle of the talks, Churchill was unexpectedly voted out of office and had to be replaced by the new prime minister, Clement Attlee.

Even before Churchill's stunning electoral defeat, Britain had been relegated to following the American lead in dealing with the Russians. The war had reduced the once-powerful British empire to the role of America's junior partner. Despite his subordinate status, Churchill had used the time between Roosevelt's death and the next Big Three meeting to impress upon Truman, in their frequent correspondence, the need for a united front against the Soviets. In contrast to Yalta, where Roosevelt often had sided with Stalin against Churchill, at Potsdam it was almost invariably Truman and the British aligned against Stalin. The American-Soviet formula on German reparations, agreed to at Yalta by Roosevelt and Stalin but temporarily blocked there by Churchill, was changed at Potsdam.

The new American plan gave the Western allies effective control over how much the Soviets could expect to get out of Germany.

The single, most important event during the Potsdam Conference occurred outside the negotiations just as the Big Three were about to begin their talks. A radio message from the War Department couched in the terms of a birth announcement informed Truman that the $2-billion gamble called the Manhattan Project had paid off beyond all expectations. The United States now possessed the world's first atomic bomb. In the words of the man who briefed him on the successful first test of the bomb, the news "tremendously pepped up" the president and gave him an entirely new sense of confidence in his approach to the conference. In Truman's words at the time, the bomb was both "the most terrible thing ever discovered" and "the greatest thing in history."

The news of the bomb dramatically altered American strategic thinking about the necessity of Soviet entry into the war against Japan. The president's military advisers now told him that, in view of this revolutionary new weapon, "the Russians were no longer needed" to defeat Japan. Indeed, Truman's foreign policy advisers suddenly viewed any Soviet declaration of war as an attempt to "get in . . . on the kill." Truman concluded that one way or another Japan would soon "fold up," either as a result of Soviet entry or after the Americans used the atomic bomb. The terrible prospect of invading Japan had suddenly given way to the exhilarating vision of a quick, cheap American victory.

Aware of Japan's effort to seek peace through Moscow's mediation, Truman concluded that Soviet entry into the war would mean, in his words, "Fini Japs." The question for him was no longer if or even when the war would end, but how and on whose terms. His highest priority remained ending the fighting by the quickest, surest method. The Manhattan Project scientists had given him a means that Roosevelt only could have hoped for. Truman did not hesitate to use it. In ordering the atomic attacks on two Japanese cities, his primary objective was to force Tokyo's immediate surrender. A secondary consideration was that this surrender be on American terms, minimizing Soviet involvement and thereby containing Soviet influence in postwar Japan, the Pacific, and the Asian mainland. What the Soviets later called "atomic diplomacy" was conspicuously absent in the actual negotiations at Potsdam. Although not yet demonstrated to Stalin and the world, the bomb nonetheless had a significant impact upon the American-Soviet alliance.

Stalin's spies had infiltrated the American atomic bomb project early on. He knew of its existence, and he knew that Roosevelt had deliberately kept that information secret from his ally. While Roosevelt had reserved the option of using the bomb militarily and diplomatically if and when it came into being, the entire project remained for him only a future possibility, or what he called an "iffy" question. It was not something he could base his wartime policy upon. How he might have handled the reality of the bomb at Potsdam is beyond knowing, but it seems unlikely that he would have played the sort of cat-and-mouse game Truman did. Truman went through an elaborate charade in order to be able to claim later that he had informed the Soviet leader of this important new development. Stalin feigned indifference and incomprehension about what Truman offhandedly referred to only as "a powerful new weapon." Knowing what the president was trying to say without saying it, Stalin reportedly remarked to his aides after the encounter that "they just want to raise the ante"; he immediately ordered a speedup in the two-year-old Soviet bomb project. Truman, an avid poker player, certainly felt that he had been dealt a winning hand at Potsdam. As he put it, the bomb was his "ace in the hole" in dealing with Stalin.

By the end of the Potsdam Conference the Grand Alliance was rapidly coming apart, but the disaffection of allies at the end of a war is not the same thing as the outbreak of a cold war. Although incensed by what he termed "Bolsheviki land grabs" such as the Polish border changes, Truman still believed that he could work with the Soviet leader. As he wrote in his diary at Potsdam, "I can deal with Stalin. He is honest and smart as Hell."

After the stunning demonstration of the bomb's power at Hiroshima and Nagasaki, Truman soon realized that Stalin refused to play by the American rules. His anticipation that the bomb as America's "sacred trust" would be the "winning weapon" in war and peace proved only half right. Continued Soviet consolidation of its control of eastern Europe, the exposure of a Soviet atomic spy ring in Canada, and Moscow's refusal to be impressed by the American atomic monopoly in negotiating a series of outstanding disputes all prompted Truman to abandon his earlier optimism about being able to deal with the man whom he later called that "little son of a bitch."

Why the Cold War with the Soviet Union happened is an immensely more complicated question than when it began. The changes of perception and expectations that gave rise to the Cold

War happened in the minds of different people at different times for various reasons. Focusing on the perceptions and expectations of the Allied leaders does not explain the larger process. There are events that even totalitarian dictators and "imperial" presidents cannot control. Nonetheless, the diversities among these leaders shed light on how the Cold War developed out of the wartime Grand Alliance.

Historian John Lewis Gaddis has pointed out that during the war Roosevelt attempted to contain Soviet postwar power by integrating it into an international system of big power cooperation. Truman abandoned that approach in favor of Churchill's containment by segregation. Whether either policy was better or more realistic is unprovable since Roosevelt did not live to continue his integrationist approach into the postwar period. Given the legacy of mutual distrust, the fundamental ideological disparities, and the vast differences of experience, it is doubtful that Roosevelt could have succeeded completely. Unlike Truman, however, he probably would have tried harder and longer, thereby at least clarifying an issue that continues to be debated among historians of American foreign policy.

The breakup of the Soviet Union in 1991 and the West's "victory" in the Cold War may help to clarify the origins of that conflict. To date, historians have only begun to analyze the evidence about the Soviet side of the process derived from newly opened archives in the former Soviet Union. Although important on many specific points, this post-Cold War scholarship has not fundamentally altered the history of how the wartime allies became postwar enemies. In his recent study, completed as the Soviet Union self-destructed and the Cold War ended, Melvyn Leffler persuasively demonstrates that American policy after World War II was predicated upon a strategy of maintaining a "preponderance of power," economic and military, throughout the world. Such a strategy necessarily brought the United States into conflict with Soviet-backed or simply left-wing movements in a variety of places where forces of radical change had been unleashed by World War II. Decolonization, nationalism, modernization, and development in Asia, Africa, Latin America, and the Middle East, as well as the reconstruction and restoration of a world ravaged by war, were all part of the context in which Washington's leaders made decisions and foreign policy. The result has been aptly called the "creation" of modern American diplomacy.

Sources and Suggested Readings

Alperovitz, Gar. *Atomic Diplomacy: Hiroshima and Potsdam*. Rev. ed. New York, 1985.

Burns, James MacGregor. *Roosevelt: The Soldier of Freedom*. New York, 1970.

Clemens, Diane Shaver. *Yalta*. New York, 1970.

Dallek, Robert. *Franklin D. Roosevelt and American Foreign Policy, 1932–1945*. New York, 1979.

Eubank, Keith. *Summit at Teheran*. New York, 1985.

Ferrell, Robert H., ed. *Off the Record: The Private Papers of Harry S. Truman*. New York, 1980.

Gaddis, John Lewis. *Strategies of Containment: A Critical Appraisal of Postwar American National Security Policy*. New York, 1982.

Harbutt, Fraser. *The Iron Curtain: Churchill, America, and the Origins of the Cold War*. New York, 1986.

Herken, Gregg. *The Winning Weapon: The Atomic Bomb in the Cold War, 1945–1950*. New York, 1980.

Kimball, Warren F. *The Juggler: Franklin D. Roosevelt as Wartime Statesman*. Princeton, NJ, 1991.

Larson, Deborah Welch. *Origins of Containment: A Psychological Explanation*. Princeton, NJ, 1985.

Leffler, Melvyn. *A Preponderance of Power: National Security, the Truman Administration, and the Cold War*. Stanford, CA, 1992.

Maddox, Robert J. *From War to Cold War: The Education of Harry S. Truman*. Boulder, CO, 1988.

Mastny, Vojtech. *Russia's Road to the Cold War: Diplomacy, Strategy, and the Politics of Communism, 1941–1945*. New York, 1979.

McCullough, David. *Truman*. New York, 1992.

Mee, Charles L., Jr. *Meeting at Potsdam*. New York, 1975.

Messer, Robert L. *The End of an Alliance: James F. Byrnes, Roosevelt, Truman, and the Origins of the Cold War*. Chapel Hill, NC, 1982.

Paterson, Thomas G. *On Every Front: The Making of the Cold War*. New York, 1979.

Resis, Albert. *Stalin, the Politburo, and the Onset of the Cold War, 1945–1946*. Pittsburgh, 1988.

Sherwin, Martin J. *A World Destroyed: The Atomic Bomb and the Grand Alliance*. New York, 1977.

Thomas, Hugh. *Armed Truce: The Beginnings of the Cold War, 1945–1946*. New York, 1987.

Volkogonov, Dmitri. *Stalin: Triumph and Tragedy*. New York, 1991.

Wilson, Theodore A. *The First Summit: Roosevelt and Churchill at Placentia Bay, 1941*. Boston, 1969.

Yergin, Daniel. *Shattered Peace: The Origins of the Cold War and the National Security State*. Boston, 1977.

Containment and American Foreign Policy, 1945–1963

Mark H. Lytle

In October 1944, with France recently liberated and the Allies nearing victory, Winston Churchill had journeyed to Moscow to see Joseph Stalin. Getting down to work only at ten in the evening (Stalin liked to do business late at night), the two men discussed how the Great Powers might prevent conflicts once the war was won. Churchill jotted down on a sheet of paper a number of east European nations. Beside each one he put a percentage indicating the amount of influence that Great Britain or the Soviet Union might have: Romania, 90 percent for the Soviets; Greece, 90 percent for the British, along with the Americans; Bulgaria, 75 percent for the Soviets; Hungary and Yugoslavia, 50 percent each. Stalin read the list impassively, checked each item with a red pencil, and then handed it back to Churchill.

The British prime minister, somewhat embarrassed that the two had so casually divided the Balkan region, suggested destroying the paper. A stone-faced Stalin told him to keep it. As far as more public discussions went, Churchill thought it "better to express these things in diplomatic terms and not to use the phrase 'dividing into spheres' because the Americans might be shocked. But as long as he and Marshal Stalin understood each other, he could explain matters to the President"—that is, to Franklin D. Roosevelt.

Churchill had come of age during the glory days of the British empire. A world divided into spheres of influence made sense to him. And since Britain's power had waned after World War I, new spheres offered one means of preserving some of the empire's fading glory. It offered, too, in the case of the Balkans, a way to prevent old rivalries from dragging Europe into yet another war. Most American leaders were, as Churchill recognized, less comfortable with spheres of influence—even those who recognized that the United States maintained a sphere of its own. The Monroe Doctrine and its (Theodore) Roosevelt Corollary justified dominance in the Western Hemisphere. And, in thinking about the peace, Franklin Roosevelt had himself considered a postwar world managed by the Four Policemen—the United States, Russia, Britain, and China. Obviously, the president recognized that the Soviet Union could not be denied its own sphere.

Roosevelt also knew that such big-power settlements went against his country's long-cherished ideals. Since the early Republic, Americans had championed, in principle at least, the right of small nations to determine their own fates. The U.S. sphere in the Western Hemisphere had been established in part as a reaction against European expansion. Further, struggles over spheres of influence had led in 1914 to the collapse of Europe's balance of power and a bloody world war. Progressive American diplomats believed that the war demonstrated the bankruptcy of the old world system. As their leading spokesman, Woodrow Wilson advocated a new system of treaties and an international organization to guarantee the peace. The failure of the League of Nations between the world wars had not extinguished their faith. In the 1941 Atlantic Charter, issued even before the United States entered World War II, Roosevelt had echoed many of their hopes for a peace based on free trade, self-determination, and international cooperation. During the conflict he had publicly condemned spheres of influence as a bankrupt legacy of the old diplomacy. That conviction inspired his decision to support the United Nations.

Through the new world body, Roosevelt had hoped to strike a balance between the idealism of Wilsonian internationalism and the more practical reality that the major powers would continue to guarantee their own security. Spheres of influence inevitably would continue to exist. What was not clear was just how far each sphere would extend. Harry S. Truman, his successor, was a different man; and the world Truman faced was, if anything, more uncertain than the one that Roosevelt had tried to rearrange. The central problem for Truman was how to fathom just what postwar ambitions Stalin might entertain. What, after all, were the Kremlin's real intentions? Lacking Roosevelt's easy confidence that he could manage the dictator, the new president approached the Soviets with considerably more suspicion. "Stalin is an SOB, but of course he thinks I'm one, too," Truman commented after their meeting at Potsdam in July 1945.

The question of how to deal with the Soviet Union's postwar ambitions arose from both immediate circumstances and historical roots. After the October Revolution of 1917, most Americans viewed V. I. Lenin's Bolsheviks with a mixture of fear, suspicion, and loathing. In their grasp for power the Communists had often used violence, terror, and crime to achieve their ends. As Marxists they rejected both religion and the notion of private property, two institutions central to the American dream. Stalin's brutal purges during the late 1930s created a horrifying image of the Soviet Union: a totalitarian state ruled by terror. Its propagandists had made no secret of the fact that they intended to export revolution throughout the world, including to the United States. In 1939 the cynical non-aggression pact with Germany had freed Stalin to stab Poland in the back and make war on his Finnish neighbors. Would the defeat of Germany and Japan allow him to renew Soviet expansion? If it did, would the United Nations be any more successful than the League of Nations had been in limiting aggression?

The events leading to World War II provided one lesson in what the failure to respond forcefully to aggression could mean. When British prime minister Neville Chamberlain attempted to satisfy Adolf Hitler's demands in Munich in 1938, it only emboldened the Nazis to expand further. After the war, Secretary of the Navy James Forrestal applied the Munich analogy to the new situation in Europe. Giving in to Moscow's claims would only seem like an attempt "to buy their understanding and sympathy. We tried that once with Hitler. . . . There are no returns on appeasement." To many of Truman's advisers, the Soviet dictator seemed to be as bent on conquest as Hitler.

Stalin's wartime territorial and political demands fueled those suspicions. Although his determination to adjust Poland's borders was easy to understand (the new boundaries there would strengthen Soviet national security), Stalin also had asked Turkey to join him in assuming control of the Dardanelles, the narrow straits linking Soviet ports on the Black Sea with the Mediterranean. During the war, both Roosevelt and Churchill had been willing to consider such a change, especially since Turkey had leaned toward the Axis. In the uncertain postwar atmosphere, however, Stalin's intentions seemed more ominous—he had suggested that the Soviet Union become trustee of Libya, Italy's former colony in North Africa. As one British diplomat at Potsdam aptly put it, the great debate was "whether Russia [is] peaceful and wants to join the Western Club but is suspicious of us, or whether she is out to dominate the world and is hoodwinking us." Truman and his advisers, like the diplomat, tended to opt for the same answer: "It always seems safer to go on the worst assumption."

Americans' suspicions were not eased when they looked to eastern Europe, where Soviet occupation forces dominated internal affairs, or to Greece, where local Communists led the fighting to overturn the monarchy. Asia, too, seemed a target for Communist ambitions. Soviet occupation soldiers in Manchuria were turning over captured Japanese arms to the Chinese Communist forces of Mao Zedong (Mao Tse-tung), and Soviet troops controlled the northern half of Korea. In Vietnam leftist nationalists were fighting against the return of colonial rule. This combination of menace and disorder soon erupted into the Soviet-American rivalry known as the Cold War. To fight it, President Truman and his advisers sought to find a policy that would prevent Communist expansion beyond the areas occupied by the Soviets at the war's end.

Iran, lying along the Soviet Union's southern border, seemed a likely target for such expansion. During World War II, Iran was the only country where each of the Big Three had stationed troops. While the British and Americans withdrew their forces in the fall of 1945, Russian occupation troops remained. By November those soldiers had virtually sealed off the north from the government in Tehran and from American and British diplomats. Further, they had actively abetted the organizing efforts of the pro-Soviet local Communists and of Azerbaijani separatists who sought to establish regional autonomy. George Kennan, the American chargé d'affaires in Moscow, saw this as part of a larger strategy: "Azerbaijan appears to conform to the nationality pattern observed in Bessarabia, Ruthenia, and Eastern Poland and currently evident with respect to Sinkiang and Turkish Armenia. As in other areas, Soviet fissionist technique seems based on racial affinities transcending the Soviet border." He concluded that in this way the Soviets could claim to honor their agreement to respect the Iranian government's sovereignty while separating Azerbaijan.

Hence, American officials were not surprised when Azerbaijani separatists on November 12 declared their autonomy. What did surprise them was the extent of Moscow's support for the rebellion. Soviet troops armed the rebels and blocked any effort of Iranian police or army forces to intervene. To Joseph Alsop, a leading Washington columnist with ties to the Roosevelt family, this crisis had ominous implications. He admitted that it was difficult for Americans "to lie awake nights worrying about a bleak and distant nation with a backward population and a frowzily corrupt government," but that was just what he thought they should do. Alsop saw Iran in light of a domino theory, widely held in the State Department. After Azerbaijan, the Soviets would seize control of the government in Tehran and then cancel the enormously valuable Anglo-Iranian Oil Company concession, thus delivering the British economy a crippling blow. With a foothold in the Persian Gulf, they would pressure Iran's neighbors in Iraq and Saudi Arabia. Not only would British prestige in the Middle and Far East suffer a mortal blow, but Soviet success in Azerbaijan also meant that "the United Nations would be done to death," and with it any remnants of Roosevelt's plans for a stable peace.

By January 1946 the United Nations had become the forum in which Iran sought to reverse Soviet gains in Azerbaijan. Despite open threats from Moscow, the Iranians saw an appeal to the United Nations as a way to press the Kremlin to withdraw its troops. At the same time they undertook more secret negotiations with the Soviets. Secretary of State James Byrnes saw the crisis as an opportunity for a showdown. Eager to send Moscow a message that the United States would stand firm wherever aggression threatened, he was equally determined to silence the domestic critics who accused him of being too soft in the face of Soviet demands. Thus, when he learned for certain that Moscow had violated its agreement to remove its troops from northern Iran by March 2, he smacked his fist into his hand and exclaimed to his staff, "Now we'll give it to them with both barrels!"

Eventually he personally argued Iran's cause at the United Nations, but the crisis ended with an agreement negotiated in Moscow between the Iranian and Soviet governments. In return for an oil concession (which Tehran never ratified), the Soviet Union removed its troops by May. Even though many commentators praised Byrnes for winning a victory for the United Nations, the crisis showed that the international body could not prevent the Soviets from extending their postwar sphere of influence. Most American policymakers believed that the United States needed a more effective way to limit Soviet ambitions.

That need seemed compelling because the Iranian crisis was only one of several issues that had arisen by early 1946. Stalin had announced in February that the Soviet Union would take unilateral steps to preserve its national security. In a world dominated by capitalism, he warned, future wars were inevitable. The Russian people had to ensure against "any eventuality" by undertaking a new five-year plan for economic development. Although some Americans saw Stalin's speech as a means to rally support for his domestic programs, others saw their worst fears confirmed. *Time* magazine, an early voice for a get-tough policy, called the speech "the most warlike pronouncement uttered by any top-rank statesman since V-J day." In March, Churchill warned that the Soviets had dropped an "Iron Curtain" between their satellite nations in Eastern Europe and the free world.

As policymakers groped for an effective way to deal with these developments, the State Department received a diplomatic cable, extraordinary for both its length (eight thousand words) and its impact in Washington. The author was George Kennan, the chargé d'affaires in Moscow and long a student of Soviet conduct, who argued that Kremlin leaders, including Stalin, were so paranoid that it was impossible to reach any useful accommodation with them. This temperament could best be explained by "the traditional and instinctive Russian sense of insecurity." But that insecurity, when combined with the Marxist ideology that viewed capitalism as evil, created a potent force for expansion. Soviet power, Kennan explained, "moves inexorably along a prescribed path, like a toy automobile wound up and headed in a given direction, stopping only when it meets some unanswerable force."

The response that Kennan recommended was "containment": the United States must apply "unalterable counterforce at every point where [the Soviets] show signs of encroaching upon the interests of a peaceful and stable world." The idea of containment was not particularly novel; indeed, the State Department had conceived of an aid program to Iran during the war as a way to contain the Soviet threat there. What Kennan did, however, was to provide leaders in Washington with a framework for analyzing and responding to Soviet actions. His approach was part historical, locating the roots of Moscow's ambitions in both the traditions of czarist diplomacy and the logic of Marxist-Leninist ideology. Kennan also added a psychosocial dimension in attributing Soviet reactions to a national character shaped by insecurity and to a paranoia that reacted aggressively when threatened.

More important to Washington policymakers, Kennan's concept of containment offered a strategic plan for blocking Soviet expansion in the short run and eliminating the Communist menace in the long run. Secretary of the Navy Forrestal was so impressed with Kennan's Long Telegram, as it came to be known, that he sent copies to high officials in the administration as well as to American diplomats abroad. Truman soon thereafter applied the doctrine of containment on a global scale. Democrats and Republicans, liberals and conservatives—a bipartisan coalition—accepted Kennan's argument that by applying firm diplomatic, economic, and military counterpressure when a threat arose, the United States could contain Soviet aggression. Eventually, if firmness frustrated its external ambitions, the Kremlin might be forced by the failings of its system to reform its domestic institutions. Most American leaders believed that only with religious tolerance, free speech, a free press, and democratic elections in the Soviet Union would a reasonable accommodation between East and West be possible.

The containment doctrine provided the United States with a rationale for an internationalist policy to protect its own national security. That policy, based on Kennan's analysis and the precedent set in areas such as Iran, would be highly interventionist. But Kennan himself was quite vague on the form that intervention should take. In containing the Soviet threat, should the United States be most active in Europe or Asia or in the areas (such as Iran) near the Soviet border? He did not say, although, along with most American diplomats, he saw Europe as the key to his country's security. And by what means would that security best be ensured: diplomacy, economic measures, or military force? Kennan by temperament and training preferred diplomacy and trade to force. Yet, as the Cold War became hotter and nuclear weapons production increased, Washington policymakers made military measures the primary mode of containment. Kennan later admitted that in order to gain a hearing for his Long Telegram, he had overstated the Soviet menace, but that militarization of containment grossly distorted his intentions. Indeed, by 1950, Kennan became so disillusioned with the degree to which defense spending, military alliances, and foreign military aid came to dominate government policy that he resigned from the State Department.

By presenting the case from the American viewpoint, the rationale for containment thus far seems incontrovertible, but the historical evidence is not so clear. Even though policymakers accepted Kennan's analysis, Stalin's true intentions were then, and have remained since, an open question. Historians have had until recently little information about the inner workings of the Soviet state. Nonetheless, a case can be made that Kennan, or at least those who adopted his ideas, exaggerated the scope of Moscow's postwar ambitions. After the war the Soviet Union was threatened as much by disorder from within as by danger from without. While that country was trying to rebuild, it saw the United States rapidly expanding its global influence. American occupation forces in Europe and Asia ringed the Soviet Union, while American corporations owned or controlled vast oil fields in the Middle East and, along with the French and British, were a strong presence in Southeast Asia. In Latin America, the United States had its own well-established sphere of influence. At the new United Nations, countries friendly to Washington far outnumbered those with links to Moscow. And, of course, the United States alone at this time possessed the atomic bomb. Stalin had reason to fear that the anti-Communists in the American government would seek to exploit the weakness of his war-ravaged nation.

The Russians, too, had mastered their own lessons of history. Napoleon had invaded their nation in 1812; twice in the nineteenth century the big powers of Europe had forced Russia to give up territory. Germany had violated their homeland twice during the twentieth century. Given such precedents, Stalin might well have wished to protect the Soviet Union by controlling the countries surrounding him. Indeed, for a dictator accustomed to absolute power within his own territory, such an outlook was almost habit. As one Yugoslav Communist leader remarked of Stalin, "Everything beyond the control of his police was a potential enemy." To make matters worse, the United States cut its wartime economic aid and resisted Soviet claims on reparations from the Germans. In many ways, Stalin had as much reason to fear his former allies as they had to fear him. What the Americans viewed as Soviet expansion may have appeared in Moscow as containment in reverse.

Few officials in Washington entertained the idea that these Soviet actions might be defensive in nature. If they had, the Iranian crisis might have suggested the limits to Moscow's ambitions. In the face of Anglo-American diplomatic opposition, the Soviets backed down. But American diplomats came to quite another conclusion: rather than ease tensions, success in Iran only confirmed for them their worst assumptions about the Soviet Union. They saw the Iranian crisis as a reason to raise their guard higher.

An opportunity to apply containment more broadly came in early 1947. As Europe reeled under severe winter storms and a depressed postwar economy, Great Britain announced that it could no longer support the governments of Greece and Turkey. Without British aid, the local Communists seemed destined to win critical victories. In Washington, President Truman decided that the United States should contain this threat. He went before Congress in March, determined to raise $400 million for military and economic aid to the embattled Greek and Turkish governments. To overcome resistance to his interventionist policy, he decided to "scare hell out of the country." The world was now divided into two hostile camps, the president warned. To preserve the American way of life, the United States now must step forward and help "free people" threatened by "totalitarian regimes." (This rationale for aid to Greece and Turkey became known as the Truman Doctrine.) Critics were quick to point out that the president had placed no limits on the American commitment. His proposal was not only to contain Communists in Greece and Turkey but also to resist Soviet expansion everywhere. Republican senator Robert Taft of Ohio, once a leader of congressional isolationists, thought that it was a mistake to talk about a bipolar world divided between Communist and anti-Communist camps. Congress, however, supported the new Cold War crusade and voted overwhelmingly to grant aid to Greece and Turkey.

The Truman Doctrine marked a new level of American commitment to the Cold War. Just what responsibility the Soviets had for unrest in Greece and Turkey remained unclear, but the president had linked communism with rebel movements across the globe, which committed the administration to a relatively open-ended struggle. In the battle between communism and freedom, Truman gained expanded powers to act when unrest threatened. Occasionally, Congress would regret giving the executive branch so much power, but by 1947 anticommunism had become the dominant theme in government policy, both foreign and domestic.

Even though the Truman Doctrine marked a bold departure for American foreign policy, it did not address the area of primary concern to Washington: Western Europe. Countries there had yet to recover from the devastation of the war. Across the region national treasuries were empty, factories were closed, city streets stood dark, homes lacked heat, and people were starving. State Department diplomats warned that without aid to revive the European economy, Communists would seize power in Germany, Italy, and France. In June 1947, Secretary of State George C. Marshall stepped before a Harvard commencement audience to announce a recovery plan. He invited all European nations, East or West, to request assistance to rebuild their economies. Unlike Truman, Marshall did not emphasize the Communist menace. Nevertheless, his massive aid plan was designed to eliminate conditions that produced the discontent often exploited by the Communists. Humanitarian aid also had its practical benefits. Generous credits that increased European demand for American goods would ensure markets and prosperity for the United States. The secretary did not rule out participation by the Soviet Union or its East European satellites, but he gambled that fears of American economic domination would lead the Soviets and their allies to reject his offer.

At first neo-isolationists in Congress opposed the aid proposals, claiming that the United States could not afford such generosity. But when Communists expelled the non-Communists from Czechoslovakia's government, the Cold War seemed to spread. Congress then approved the so-called Marshall Plan. And as the secretary anticipated, the Soviets blocked the efforts of Czechoslovakia and Poland to participate. The blame of dividing Europe fell, as Marshall guessed that it would, on the Soviet Union, not the United States. Here was a case in which an economic and diplomatic approach to containment won a great Cold War victory.

Stalin responded to the more aggressive American approach by seeking to consolidate Soviet political and military domination of Eastern Europe. In 1947 he moved against the moderate government in Hungary, run since 1945 by leaders chosen under relatively free elections, and brutally imposed a Communist regime dependent on Moscow. In February 1948, Communists toppled the duly elected government of Czechoslovakia, where shortly thereafter the popular foreign minister, Jan Masaryk, fell from a window to his death. Suicide was the official explanation, but many people suspected murder. In response to the Marshall Plan, Moscow initiated a series of trade agreements tightly linking the Soviet and East European economies. It also established the Cominform, or Communist Information Bureau, to exert greater political control over Communist parties abroad.

Stalin's aggressive steps provoked the Truman administration into taking a more militaristic approach to containment. By 1949 the United States and Canada had joined with Britain, France, Belgium, the Netherlands, Luxembourg, and five other countries to establish the North Atlantic Treaty Organization (NATO) as a mutual defense pact. For the first time since George Washington had warned in his Farewell Address of 1796 against entangling alliances with European nations, the United States during peacetime had committed itself to defend Western Europe. A crisis over Germany had precipitated that departure from tradition. In the process of forming NATO the Western powers had decided to transform their postwar occupation zones into an independent West German state. The Western-controlled sectors of Berlin, however, lay over one hundred miles to the east, well within the Soviet Zone. On June 24, 1948, the Soviets reacted by blockading all land access to Berlin. Truman did not hesitate: "We are going to stay, period!"—but he did say no when General Lucius Clay proposed to shoot his way through the blockade. Instead, the United States began a massive airlift of supplies to Berlin that lasted almost a year. In May 1949, Stalin lifted the blockade, conceding that he could not prevent the creation of West Germany.

By 1948, therefore, the Cold War framed all aspects of American foreign policy. Truman, a Democrat, had won election that year in large part because he successfully forged a bipartisan consensus to contain communism, but after 1949 the Republicans successfully seized control of the anti-Communist issue. They persuaded a majority of voters that they, more than the Democrats, could contain communism at home and abroad. Two events added to the erosion of Truman's leadership. First, American scientists reported in August that rains monitored in the Pacific contained traces of hot nuclear waste. Only one conclusion seemed possible: the Soviet Union was testing its own atomic bomb. When Truman announced the news, Congress was debating whether to spend $1.5 billion for military aid to the newly formed NATO alliance. The House stopped debating and voted the bill through, while the president directed that research into a newer, more powerful fusion, or hydrogen bomb, should continue. Senator Arthur Vandenberg, a Michigan Republican with wide experience in international affairs, summed up the reaction of many to the end of the American nuclear monopoly: "This is now a different world."

Second, in December came more bad news. The long-embattled Nationalist government of Jiang Jieshi (Chiang Kai-shek) fled mainland China to the offshore island of Taiwan (formerly Formosa). Jiang's defeat at the hands of Communist forces led by Mao Zedong came as no surprise to the State Department. Officials there had long regarded Jiang and his Nationalists as hopelessly corrupt and inefficient. Despite major American efforts during and after the war to save his regime and stabilize China, poverty and civil unrest spread. By February 1949 almost half of Jiang's demoralized troops had defected to the Communists, so the December defeat was hardly unexpected. But Republicans, who until 1949 had supported the president's foreign policy, now broke ranks. For some time a group of wealthy conservatives and Republican senators had resented the administration's preoccupation with Europe. *Time* and *Life* publisher Henry Luce used his magazines to campaign for a greater concern for Asian affairs, and especially for more aid to defeat Mao. Luce and his associates, known as the China lobby, were supported in part with funds from the Chinese embassy. When Jiang's government collapsed, his American backers charged that the Democrats had let the Communists win. When Secretary of State Dean Acheson published State Department documents showing that nothing short of direct American intervention could have saved Jiang's unpopular regime, the China lobby charged that Acheson's White Paper was nothing more than a "whitewash."

Soon afterward, Senator Joseph McCarthy began his hunt for "traitors" in the State Department. By 1950 anticommunism had created a climate of fear where legitimate concerns mixed with irrational hysteria. An undistinguished Republican first-termer from Wisconsin, McCarthy saw in that fear an issue with which to build his own political fortunes. To an audience in Wheeling, West Virginia, in February he waved a sheaf of papers in the air and announced that he had a list of 205—or perhaps 81, 57, or "a lot" of—Communists in the State Department. (No one, including the senator, could remember the number, which he continually changed.) In the following months McCarthy claimed that he had penetrated the "iron curtain" of the State Department to discover "card-carrying Communists," the "top Russian espionage agent" in the United States, "egg-sucking phony liberals," and "Communists and queers" who wrote "perfumed notes."

McCarthy may even have sincerely opposed communism. But in another sense, he was the bitter fruit that Truman and the Democrats reaped from their own attempts to exploit the anti-Communist mood, in part to justify containment abroad. The senator, more than the president, had tapped the fears and hatreds of a broad coalition of Catholic leaders, conservatives, and neo-isolationists who harbored suspicions of all things foreign, liberal, internationalist, European, or intellectual. They saw McCarthy and his fellow witch-hunters as the protectors of a vaguely defined but deeply felt spirit of Americanism. The international concerns of the foreign policy establishment, especially for European affairs, made the State Department an inviting target for these witch-hunters.

Although irritated by its extremist critics, the Truman administration itself was adopting a more assertive foreign policy, one that went beyond Kennan's notion of containment. This new policy was developed by the National Security Council (NSC), an agency created by Congress in 1947 to help the executive branch respond more effectively to Cold War crises. The Army, Navy, and Air Force were united under a single Department of Defense. All overseas intelligence gathering and espionage activities became the responsibility of the Central Intelligence Agency (CIA). To the NSC fell the job of advising the president about foreign and military affairs. From the beginning, it had lobbied for an active policy not only to contain the Soviets but also to win the Cold War. In April 1950 it sent Truman a document, NSC-68, which would serve as the framework for American containment policy over the next twenty years.

NSC-68 argued that rather than merely hold the Soviets at bay, the United States should "strive for victory." To that end it called for an immediate increase in defense spending from $13 billion to $50 billion per year, which would require a large tax increase. Most of the funds would go to rebuild conventional forces, but the NSC urged that the hydrogen bomb be developed to offset the new Soviet nuclear capacity. At the same time the American people had to be mobilized to make the necessary sacrifices, while the United States worked (NSC-68 never explained how) to make "the Russian people our Allies" in undermining their totalitarian government.

Efforts to carry out NSC-68 at first aroused widespread opposition. Kennan argued that the Soviets had no immediate plan for domination outside the Communist bloc. Thus, NSC-68 was too simplistic and militaristic. Fiscal conservatives, both Democratic and Republican, resisted any proposal for higher taxes. Truman's own secretary of defense, Louis Johnson, claimed that the new military budget would bankrupt the country. But all such reservations were swept away on June 25 when "Korea came along and saved us," as Secretary of State Acheson later remarked.

In 1950, Korea was probably the last place where Americans might have imagined themselves fighting a war to contain communism. When Acheson discussed policy in Asia at the National Press Club in Washington in January, he did not even mention the country. On June 24, however, he learned that North Korea had launched a full-scale invasion of South Korea. Truman and his advisers wanted to respond firmly enough to deter aggression without provoking a larger war with the Soviet Union or China. American troops would fight the North Koreans, but the United States would not declare war; thus, the fighting in Korea would be a "police action" supervised by the United Nations. The president's forceful response won immediate approval across America, and Congress quickly voted the huge increase in defense funds needed to carry out the recommendations of NSC-68.

Although UN troops scored some early successes, a Chinese invasion to save North Korea turned the war into a deadly stalemate. Rising frustration on the home front provoked a heated debate over policy. At first, public anger focused on the controversy between Truman and General Douglas MacArthur, the celebrated victor in the war in the Pacific and now the commander of the UN forces. MacArthur's unauthorized political comments embarrassed the president and contradicted administration efforts to limit the war. Truman finally determined, with the support of the Joint Chiefs of Staff, to fire MacArthur in 1951. Few presidential decisions have ever been so unpopular. Truman especially outraged archconservatives for whom the general was a hero of mythic proportions.

The furor over the firing of MacArthur and the frustration with the ongoing military stalemate obscured for most Americans the real debate over Korea. MacArthur, like the China lobby, believed that Asia held the key to his own country's power and security. Hence, he saw a larger war there as a way to ensure future American interests. Truman, Acheson, and other architects of the containment policy disagreed. To them, Korea was a sideshow, while Europe remained the key to the Cold War. Former World War II hero General Omar Bradley summed up their criticism of MacArthur's strategy for all-out conflict when he described Korea as "the wrong war, at the wrong place, at the wrong time, and with the wrong enemy."

In the 1952 election the Republicans made anticommunism one of their most effective issues. At home and abroad, they charged, the Democrats had failed to contain communism. Their campaign strategy was summed up in the formula K1C2: Korea, corruption, and communism. By March, Truman's popularity had sunk so low that he lost the New Hampshire presidential primary to Senator Estes Kefauver of Tennessee. With that defeat, he announced that he would not run for reelection. The outcome in 1952 was never much in doubt. The Democrats had no candidate as popular as Dwight D. Eisenhower.

Even before taking office, Eisenhower moved to end the stalemate in Korea. But to secure the Republican claim on the anti-Communist issue, he would need more than a negotiated truce: his administration would have to give containment a "New Look." To this end he appointed as his secretary of state John Foster Dulles, who approached his job with a somber enthusiasm. Coming from a family of missionaries and diplomats, he viewed the Soviet-American struggle in almost religious terms: a fight of good against evil, in which the differences between the two superpowers were irreconcilable. Admirers praised his global vision, while detractors saw him as "the woolliest type of pontificating American." Certainly, Dulles did not lack confidence. "With my understanding of the intricate relationship between the peoples of the world," he told Eisenhower, "and your sensitiveness to the political considerations, we will make the most successful team in history." In the end, the differing temperaments of the two men led to a policy that seesawed from confrontation to conciliation. Both were cautious, but Eisenhower was consistently less hostile toward the Soviets. Dulles, on the other hand, often raised cautionary roadblocks when the Kremlin suggested compromise. Still, for all their differences, both men remained firmly committed to containing communism. "Freedom is pitted against slavery," Eisenhower declared, "light against darkness."

The new administration intended to turn Truman's containment strategy into a more dynamic offensive. Dulles wanted the United States to aid in liberating the "captive peoples" of Eastern Europe and other Communist nations, while Eisenhower was equally determined to cut military spending in order to keep the budget balanced. The president, a former five-star general who knew how the military services and their allies in defense industries competed for government money, was irked at the "fantastic programs" that the Pentagon kept proposing. Thus, Eisenhower and Dulles hit upon a more economical strategy. Rather than rely on conventional forces, they would use the threat of massive nuclear retaliation to intimidate the Soviets into behaving less aggressively. Dulles insisted that Americans should not shrink from the threat of nuclear war: "If you are scared to go to the brink, you are lost." And as Secretary of the Treasury George Humphrey put it, a nuclear strategy was much cheaper: "a bigger bang for the buck." Henceforth, "brinksmanship" would give U.S. foreign policy its New Look, although behind the more militant rhetoric lay an ongoing commitment to containment.

Moving beyond talk of brinksmanship to concrete action did not prove easy. While Eisenhower and Dulles could accept Kennan's definition of the ends of containment policy, they, like him, had no definite sense of the appropriate means. Where in the world should the United States concentrate its efforts? And what role should its allies play? When, for example, Dulles announced American intentions to "unleash" Jiang to attack mainland China (the People's Republic) from his outpost on Taiwan, PRC foreign minister Zhou Enlai (Chou En-lai) threatened to liberate Taiwan from the Nationalists. At that, Eisenhower ordered the Seventh Fleet into the area to protect, rather than unleash, Jiang. By 1955, Dulles had staked the defense of Taiwan on tiny coastal islands, especially Quemoy and Matsu. If the Communists attacked, he bluntly stated, "we'll have to use atomic weapons."

French Indochina (Vietnam) also revealed the limits of the New Look. Between 1950 and 1954 the United States provided $1 billion in military aid to the French in their struggle to destroy a nationalist movement led by Ho Chi Minh. Eisenhower worried that if Vietnam fell to communism, other nations of Southeast Asia would soon follow. "You have a row of dominoes set up," the president warned. "You knock over the first one. . . . You could have the beginning of a disintegration that would have the most profound influences." So when the French moved to end their involvement in Vietnam, Dulles refused to accept the terms agreed upon at the international peace conference at Geneva.

During the negotiations cosponsored by the British and the Soviet Union, Ho had agreed to withdraw his forces north of the 17th parallel, temporarily dividing the nation into North and South Vietnam. Because of Ho's widespread popularity, he assumed an easy victory in the elections that were scheduled to be held within two years. Dulles, however, viewed any Communist victory as unacceptable, even if the election was democratic. He persuaded Eisenhower to support a South Vietnamese government under Ngo Dinh Diem, who, Dulles insisted, was not bound by the Geneva Accords to hold any election. The United States then became further involved by sending a military mission to train an army to keep Diem in power. In that way, the determination to contain communism opened the door to much deeper involvement in the future.

Dulles and Eisenhower also pursued their activist foreign policy through the use of covert operations, conducted most often by the CIA. Created in 1947 to coordinate foreign intelligence gathering, the agency also directed covert operations designed to undermine Communists or their sympathizers. The CIA backed the overthrow of a nationalist government in Iran in 1953 and a democratically elected government in Guatemala in 1954. Success in Iran and Guatemala created among American policymakers a misplaced faith that covert operations could achieve dramatic results at low cost. But in overthrowing popular governments or defending unpopular ones, the United States gained a reputation in many Third World countries as a foe of national liberation, popular democracy, and social reform.

To Dulles and Eisenhower, these crises could be traced back to the Soviet dictatorship. Although nationalist governments around the globe were leading countries such as India to declare themselves neutral or nonaligned, Dulles continually warned them that they could not sit on the fence: they must choose either the "free world" or the Communist bloc. Throughout the 1950s the secretary of state crisscrossed the globe setting up mutual defense pacts patterned on NATO, as another means to achieve containment. Yet, in all this activity, it was becoming harder to decide what the motives of the Soviets themselves might be.

An unprecedented opportunity to reconsider containment and defuse the Cold War arose in March 1953, when Stalin died. In the uncertain period following his death and before Nikita Khrushchev gained control, the Soviet Union was governed by "collective leadership." Khrushchev was a party stalwart with a formidable intellect and peasant origins in the farm country of the Ukraine. In some ways he resembled another Farm Belt politician, Harry Truman. Both were unsophisticated yet shrewd, earthy in their sense of humor, energetic, short-tempered, and largely inexperienced in international affairs. American diplomats found Khrushchev puzzling: at times he could be genial and conciliatory, then suddenly he might become demanding and boastful.

At home Khrushchev established a more moderate regime, gradually shifting the economy toward production of consumer goods. Abroad he called for détente: an easing of tensions and reduced forces in Europe in order to make the West Europeans less dependent on the United States. If successful, such a policy would erode containment in what most Americans thought was the Cold War's most vital arena. In Washington the Eisenhower administration was not sure how to receive the new overtures. The spirit of McCarthyism still reigned, so that compromise with the Soviets involved great political risks, and Secretary Dulles was temperamentally suspicious of all "Godless" Communists. It was actually Winston Churchill who suggested that the Soviet Union might be serious about negotiating. Further overtures from Moscow finally brought the Americans, British, French, and Soviets together in a summit conference at Geneva in 1955. Little came of the summit other than a cordial "spirit of Geneva," which promised a cooling-off period in the arms race.

The spirit of Geneva soon evaporated. In 1956 nationalist unrest once again created doubts about Cold War boundaries. Among the Soviet Union's East European allies, Khrushchev's more liberal policies encouraged nationalists to push for greater independence. Riots erupted in Poland, while in Hungary students took to the streets demanding that a coalition government replace the puppet regime established in 1947 by Stalin. When the rioting spread, Moscow accepted the new Hungarian government and began to pull out Soviet tanks. But when Hungary announced that it was withdrawing from the Warsaw Pact, Khrushchev balked. On October 31 he sent tanks rolling back into Budapest to crush the uprising. The State Department issued formal protests but did nothing to help liberate the "captive nations." Despite all their tough talk, the New Look given by Eisenhower and Dulles to foreign policy seemed very much like Truman's version of containment. Both administrations recognized that they would not intervene in the Soviets' sphere of influence.

As the areas of Cold War tension shifted to the Third World, each superpower found it difficult to interpret the other's motives. The Soviets exploited nationalist revolutions where the opportunity arose: more successfully in Cuba, less so in Egypt. At such times Khrushchev spoke belligerently. "We will bury you," he admonished the United States, although it was not clear whether he meant through peaceful competition or military confrontation. In a speech to the United Nations the Soviet premier even took off his shoe and pounded it angrily on the table.

Nevertheless, Europe remained the primary arena of the Cold War and containment. That focus became clear in November 1958 when Khrushchev issued to the Western powers an ultimatum on divided Germany. He insisted that they withdraw all of their troops from West Berlin within six months, declare Berlin a free city, and negotiate access to it with the East Germans, a government that the Western powers had refused to recognize. When Eisenhower flatly rejected the ultimatum, Khrushchev backed away from his hard-line stance. Sobered by this confrontation, Eisenhower determined that he would devote the remaining eighteen months of his presidency to improving Soviet-American relations. A shift in policy from containment to détente was made easier when the ever-cautious Dulles died of cancer. In September 1959, at the president's invitation, Khrushchev visited the United States. Although their meetings at Camp David produced no significant results, the two leaders agreed to hold another summit meeting in Europe. Eisenhower's plans for a visit to Moscow were abruptly canceled on May 17, 1960, as the Paris summit conference collapsed over the disclosure of American spy flights over the Soviet Union. Only weeks earlier the Russians had shot down a high-altitude U-2 plane over Soviet territory. At first, Eisenhower claimed that the plane had strayed off course while researching weather conditions, but Khrushchev sprung his trap: the CIA pilot, Francis Gary Powers, had been captured alive. The president then admitted that he had personally authorized the U-2 overflights for reasons of national security. That episode ended Eisenhower's hopes that his personal diplomacy might create a new framework for Soviet-American relations.

Those efforts were constrained further by increased popular concerns triggered by several Soviet technical achievements. The success of the atomic bomb project during World War II had persuaded many Americans that superior science and technology would give the United States a decisive military advantage. Until 1949 the atomic monopoly had offset the enormous manpower advantages of the Soviet army. The United States also had superior strategic airpower and had laid the groundwork for an advanced missile program, but the Soviet Union had deadlocked the nuclear race when it developed a hydrogen bomb by 1954. Then in 1957 came a crushing blow: stunned Americans learned that the Soviets had sent into orbit the first space satellite, *Sputnik*. Its reflected light was even visible in American skies. By September 1959, when Khrushchev visited Washington, his country's scientists had crash-landed a much larger payload on the moon. If the Russians could target the moon, then surely they could launch nuclear missiles against the United States. In contrast, the American space program had suffered so many delays and mishaps that rockets exploding on launch were nicknamed "flopniks" and "kaputniks."

Eisenhower knew from intelligence sources, but could not admit publicly, that the so-called missile gap was not real. Its dramatic failures belied the fact that the U.S. missile development program was far more mature than its Soviet counterpart. While willing to spend more money, Eisenhower refused to heed the calls for a "crash" defense program at any cost. He left office with a warning that too much military spending would lead to "an unwarranted influence, whether sought or unsought," by the "military-industrial complex" at the expense of democratic institutions. In looking back over his two terms he could take some comfort in the knowledge that his conduct of foreign policy had kept the country out of war. On the other hand, he had not been able to place Soviet-American relations in a more stable framework.

Hence, the election of 1960 became somewhat of a referendum on containment. The issue, as in 1952, was not over the ends of containment, on which both candidates agreed, but on whether the Democrats and John F. Kennedy—or the Republicans led by Richard M. Nixon—could more effectively fight communism abroad and revive the economy at home. Nixon, like Eisenhower, knew that the issue of the missile gap was phony and that Kennedy, having been briefed by American intelligence, knew so as well. Yet, during the campaign, the Massachusetts senator kept insisting that the United States had fallen behind in the competition with world communism. This decline could be reversed only through a "supreme national effort," which he would pursue "with vigor" to "get the country moving again" toward a "New Frontier."

In his inaugural address in January 1961, Kennedy stirred his listeners with his call "to pay any price, bear any burden" to contain communism and any other threat to the American way of life. That rhetoric would prove a devil's deal for him and for other proponents of containment. It had taken the Democrats ten years to recover from the charges that they had lost China and bogged down the United States in a futile war in Korea. If he expected to win again in 1964, Kennedy could afford no such foreign policy disasters. Indeed, he would have to reverse some of the supposed losses of the last few years, as in the missile race or Fidel Castro's seizure of power in Cuba.

Kennedy believed that Eisenhower had not realized how much the Cold War had shifted from the traditional battlefronts of Europe to the developing nations in Asia, Africa, and Latin America. A successful containment policy required a more flexible range of military and economic options. The Alliance for Progress, announced in the spring of 1961, indicated one course that the new president would follow. Kennedy promised to allocate $20 billion in foreign aid to Latin America over the next ten years. Through the Peace Corps the United States would send idealistic young men and women to Third World nations to provide technical, educational, and public health services. Under the Alliance, the majority of Peace Corps volunteers was assigned to Latin America.

In addition to these peaceful initiatives, Kennedy wanted more military options. The Pentagon established schools to train the police and paramilitary forces of Third World nations in guerrilla warfare and began to develop special forces such as the Green Berets, who were drilled in jungle warfare. Kennedy believed, too, that after *Sputnik* and the successful launch of a manned space flight in 1959, the Soviets had made space the "final frontier" of the Cold War. The United States would contain the threat in space by sending a man to the moon by the end of the decade.

The Peace Corps, the moonshot, the Alliance for Progress, and other Kennedy initiatives to redirect the Cold War in Africa, Asia, and Latin America all excited considerable popular enthusiasm. They also left the president's critics skeptical, for, in the final reckoning, the Cold War remained a conflict between the United States and the Soviet Union. To contain the latter, Kennedy would have to confront the ambitions of Nikita Khrushchev, and in June 1961 he had his first chance to take the measure of the Soviet leader. At a summit meeting held in Vienna, the Khrushchev who met Kennedy was brash and belligerent: Germany must be reunited, he demanded; further, the Berlin problem must be settled within six months. After two long days, Kennedy left Vienna worried that Khrushchev had perceived him as weak and inexperienced. By August events in Berlin confirmed his fears. The Soviets threw up a heavily guarded wall dividing their zone from the West, but they did not seal off West Berlin's access to West Germany. Despite American protests, the wall stayed up.

Continuing tensions with the Soviet Union also led the new administration to rethink its approach to nuclear warfare. Under the Dulles doctrine of massive retaliation, almost any incident might trigger a launch of the full arsenal of nuclear missiles. Kennedy and his secretary of defense, Robert McNamara, sought to establish a "flexible response doctrine" that would limit the level of a first nuclear strike and therefore leave room for negotiation. In that case, however, conventional forces in Europe would have to be built up so that they could better deter aggression. McNamara proposed equipping them with smaller tactical nuclear weapons. But what if the Soviets were tempted to launch a first-strike attack to knock out American missiles? McNamara's flexible response policy required that enough missiles survive in order to retaliate. If the Soviets knew that the United States could survive a first strike, then they would be less likely to launch a surprise attack. McNamara, therefore, began a program to bury missile sites underground and develop submarine-launched missiles. The new flexible response policy resulted in a 15 percent increase in the 1961 military budget, compared with only 2 percent increases during the last two Eisenhower years.

Thus, in his determination to show that a Democrat could be as tough on the Kremlin as any Republican, Kennedy sowed the seeds of future crises that would destroy the consensus over containment. For example, the effort to preserve South Vietnam's unpopular government soon would come to look to much of the world, and to ever-growing numbers of Americans, not as containment but as some form of U.S. imperialism. Kennedy's buildup of military defenses helped confirm Khrushchev's decision to place offensive missiles in Cuba. The nuclear showdown there of October 1962 gave a sobering idea of what containment might cost. In the long run the Cuban missile crisis would lead the Soviets to greatly expand their nuclear arms program. And as they reached nuclear parity by the 1970s, détente began to seem more practical than containment.

George Kennan had opposed the Kennedy policies undertaken in the name of containment. He attributed the Cuban missile crisis to errors, opposed the war in Vietnam, and rejected nuclear deterrence. In 1958 he had said of the atomic bomb that "there can be no coherent relations between such a weapon and the normal objects of national policy." Kennan was even more offended by the way in which special-interest groups had appropriated containment to pursue much more narrow ends: the military to increase defense budgets, or politicians to promote partisan interests. He had always preferred the subtle discourse of diplomatic professionals to the bombastic rhetoric of politicians and generals.

More important, while he had not been clear about this in 1946, Kennan always had a much more limited concept of containment than the universalistic military doctrine that evolved from the Truman administration through Eisenhower to Kennedy and Lyndon Johnson. "When I talked about containment," he told a news commentator in 1975, "what I had in mind was an effort on our part to stiffen the hope, the confidence, of European nations in themselves, and to persuade them that they didn't need to yield to one great power or another, that they could resume life. We could help them do it. . . . I didn't think the Russians wanted to attack anyone." Since containment came to have little to do with the policy that he had conceived, Kennan did not regret its collapse in the wake of the Vietnam War and President Nixon's trips to Beijing and Moscow in 1972. "In a world so troubled as ours today," he wrote in 1976, "the favorable opportunities have to be cherished and nurtured, not sacrificed to prejudice, vanity, or political ambition."

Containment had turned into a strategic strait-jacket. Successive administrations had come to see in almost all crises the hidden hand of Communist expansion. Presidents from Truman to Johnson seldom sought or accepted opportunities for negotiations. Instead, they allowed the Cold War to take its menacing course as each side stockpiled ever more lethal weapons, as isolated political events in remote Third World countries posed a risk of nuclear war, and as Americans seeking responsible discussion of foreign policy issues were branded as traitors, dupes, or subversives. Only in the sense that containment provoked no major world wars (only several bloody Asian ones) could it be counted a success.

Sources and Suggested Readings

Beschloss, Michael. *The Crisis Years: Kennedy and Khrushchev, 1960–1963*. New York, 1991.

Brands, H. W., Jr. *Cold Warriors: Eisenhower's Generation and American Foreign Policy*. New York, 1988.

Callahan, David. *Dangerous Capabilities: Paul Nitze and the Cold War*. New York, 1990.

Gaddis, John Lewis. *Strategies of Containment: A Critical Appraisal of Postwar American National Security Policy*. New York, 1982.

————. *The Long Peace: Inquiries into the History of the Cold War.* New York, 1987.

Hixson, Walter L. *George F. Kennan, Cold War Iconoclast.* New York, 1989.

Hogan, Michael. *The Marshall Plan: America, Britain, and the Reconstruction of Europe, 1947–1952.* New York, 1989.

Immerman, Richard. *The CIA in Guatemala.* New York, 1982.

Kennan, George. *Memoirs, 1925–1950.* Boston, 1967.

————. *The Nuclear Delusion: Soviet-American Relations in the Atomic Age.* New York, 1983.

LaFeber, Walter. *America, Russia, and the Cold War.* 7th ed. New York, 1993.

Lytle, Mark H. *The Origins of the Iranian-American Alliance, 1941–1953.* New York, 1987.

McDougall, Walter. *Heavens and the Earth: A Political History of the Space Age.* New York, 1985.

Melanson, Richard, and Mayers, David, eds. *Reevaluating Eisenhower: American Foreign Policy in the 1950s.* New York, 1987.

Paterson, Thomas G. *On Every Front: The Making of the Cold War.* New York, 1979.

Whitfield, Stephen. *The Culture of the Cold War.* Baltimore, 1991.

Yergin, Daniel. *Shattered Peace: The Origins of the Cold War and the National Security State.* 2d ed. New York, 1989.

The Cold War in Asia

Marc Gallicchio

Despite the many crises that flared up during the Cold War, Europe managed to survive the struggle between the United States and the Soviet Union without suffering the destruction caused by yet another war. Several factors account for the absence of direct conflict in Europe, but most important was the partitioning of the Continent into spheres of influence that accorded well with the vital interests of the United States and the Soviet Union. Both adversaries understood that further expansion in Europe or any overt effort to breach their rival's sphere would lead to conflict on a scale greater than the last war. In these circumstances, neither Washington nor Moscow deemed the further acquisition of influence or territory worth the risk of losing those areas already securely within its sphere.

This Long Peace, to borrow a term coined by the historian John Lewis Gaddis, did not extend to East Asia, or to other regions of the globe. In Asia, American and Soviet interests were less clearly defined, both countries having been more concerned with Europe before World War II. Japan's sudden collapse in 1945 also contributed to this uncertainty and encouraged a degree of opportunism and risk-taking not found in Europe. Even more unsettling, however, was the momentum that Japan's early victories had given to the cause of nationalism throughout Asia. The presence of independent-minded militantly nationalistic movements, many of them Communist-led, added another element of complexity to the international setting that frequently confounded the calculations of policymakers in Washington and Moscow. The fall of the Japanese empire, the rise of Asian nationalism, and the emergence of the Soviet Union as an Asian power presented American policymakers with a perplexing array of problems as they attempted to define their own nation's interests in the region. How important was ideology in determining the foreign policies of these nationalist movements? Did a Chinese Communist victory strengthen the Soviet

Union? Would a Vietnamese Communist government act as a satellite of Moscow or Beijing? And did Communist victories in either of these places or in Korea jeopardize important U.S. interests? These questions confronted Americans as they tested the limits of their new power in Asia.

America's involvement in East Asia had grown in the first decades of the twentieth century, but U.S. officials did not consider the region vital to its economic or defense interests during that time. Japan's invasion of China in 1937 posed a serious challenge to the international system created during the interwar period, but it was only in 1941, after the government in Tokyo allied itself with Germany and threatened both the Soviet Far East and British possessions in Southeast Asia, that the United States risked war in the Pacific by cutting off the supply of oil to Japan and adopting an uncompromising position in negotiations. Having crossed the threshold of war with Japan primarily to defend the nations then fighting Germany in Europe, President Franklin D. Roosevelt and the heads of the armed services, the Joint Chiefs of Staff (JCS), adopted a strategy for waging war consistent with their belief that Germany posed the greatest danger to the United States. This "Europe first" strategy made the campaign against Japan's empire the second priority and relegated the war in China to a distant third place as far as the distribution of resources and manpower was concerned.

Although conditions in China made prospects for offensive operations against Japan unlikely, Roosevelt and the JCS recognized that the Nationalist government led by Jiang Jieshi (Chiang Kai-shek) could contribute to an Allied victory and to the maintenance of peace after the war. Nationalist (Guomindang) armies kept a large number of Japanese troops tied down on the mainland, and for a time it appeared that American bombers would be able to strike at Japanese cities and coastal shipping from bases in southeastern China. An alliance with China also promised to give the United States influence with the Asian country thought most likely to fill the vacuum created by Japan's defeat. To shore up this relationship and salve Jiang's bitterness over Washington's inattentiveness, Roosevelt sent a steady stream of envoys to the wartime capital in Chungking. In place of American armies, he offered China Great Power status, a seat on the UN Security Council, and, in the Cairo Declaration (1943), the promise that its lost provinces in Manchuria would be restored after Japan's defeat.

These pledges of postwar assistance did little for China's immediate concerns. By late 1944 it seemed possible that Japan's final offensive would drive the Nationalists out of the war. In taking stock of the situation, Roosevelt looked to Moscow for assistance in ridding the Asian mainland of Japanese forces. In February 1945 he met with Soviet leader Joseph Stalin and Britain's prime minister Winston Churchill at Yalta in the Crimea. Although the Big Three conferred on issues relating to the postwar map of Europe, Churchill deferred to Roosevelt and Stalin on East Asian matters. The talks between the president and the Soviet leader proceeded smoothly, ending in a formal agreement to be kept secret even from Jiang until Stalin consented to its release. To begin, Stalin renewed his pledge, first made at the Tehran summit conference (November 1943), to enter the war against Japan within three months of Germany's surrender. In exchange, he requested the return of czarist concessions lost to Japan earlier in the century. Roosevelt agreed. The subsequent Far Eastern protocol called for Soviet-Chinese joint ownership of the Eastern and South Manchurian railways, a Soviet-leased naval base at Port Arthur, the control of the port at Dairen in Manchuria, and the return of South Sakhalin Island. The agreement also provided for Soviet acquisition of the Kurile Islands, although Japan had obtained these through peaceful negotiations in the nineteenth century.

With the exception of the Kuriles, the Far Eastern protocol gave to the Soviet Union little that it could not take by force. In return, Roosevelt received a pledge of timely assistance against Japan. The agreement infringed on China's sovereignty in Manchuria and thus conflicted with FDR's earlier promise to Jiang, but it also contained a pledge that the Kremlin would recognize and deal only with the Nationalist government. Stalin's agreement, if he honored it, meant that when the war ended, the Chinese Communist Party (CCP), Jiang's rival for power, would be isolated internationally and deprived of external support. Some historians have mistakenly interpreted this part of the Yalta accords as Roosevelt's attempt to contain the Chinese Communists, but such was not the case. The president's policy is best understood if one recognizes the limited nature of his goals on the Asian mainland.

FDR's principal objective was to build a foundation for cooperation with the Soviet Union that would last into the postwar era. To this end he granted freely those concessions that Stalin thought necessary for the country's security. The Soviet leader might try to seize more territory after the war, but in doing so he would lose international approval for the substantial gains made at Yalta. Roosevelt gambled that Stalin would not take that risk, but with American forces scattered throughout the Pacific and with the first stage of the invasion of Japan scheduled for November 1945, he saw few alternatives.

Given these choices, the president found it easy to pay for Soviet cooperation in Chinese territory. Roosevelt had once hoped for a Chinese-American partnership in Asia, but the Guomindang's corruption, inefficiency, and military weakness shattered those illusions. China seemed destined to sink into internal conflict after the war, and a resumption of warlord politics seemed possible. The best that FDR could do was gain Stalin's agreement that the Great Powers would not seek additional advantages at China's expense. He and Stalin would stand outside the ring while the Communists and the Guomindang wrestled for the Mandate of Heaven.

Although the Yalta Far Eastern protocol provided a fairly clear indication of Roosevelt's thinking concerning the future of China, the agreement was silent on other areas of Asia. According to the Cairo Declaration the Allies agreed that Korea would become free "in due course." During the conference FDR clarified his thinking on the subject only slightly. The president told Stalin that, after forty years of Japanese rule, the Koreans would require international guidance in the form of a trusteeship, but he did not expect American troops to occupy any portion of the peninsula during that time. Roosevelt also spoke of a possible trusteeship for French Indochina, but he was short on details. More than other Western leaders, he recognized that Japan's victories had hastened the end of colonialism in Asia. The day of reckoning had not yet arrived, however, and he characteristically delayed action until it was necessary.

Roosevelt's plans for Japan followed a similar pattern. The Cairo Declaration doomed Tokyo's overseas empire, the decision on the Kuriles indicated an especially harsh territorial settlement, but the president's goals for occupied Japan remained a mystery. State Department planners, working with little guidance, concluded that in all likelihood Japan's defeat would result in the removal of the imperial dynasty and an occupation program geared toward demilitarization and political and economic democratization. Unfortunately, Roosevelt's reaction to these plans, or even if he was aware of their existence, is not known. The planners continued to churn out their position papers, but, on Japan, as with so many other issues, FDR kept his own counsel until his death on April 12, 1945.

The task of divining Roosevelt's postwar plans for Asia was only one of the many challenges awaiting Harry S. Truman, who hoped to familiarize himself with his predecessor's policies by studying FDR's wartime pronouncements and agreements. However, the new chief executive admitted that more than good work habits were needed to comprehend Roosevelt's plans. Shortly after taking office, an exasperated Truman was heard to say that every time he read the Yalta agreements he "found new meanings in them." In need of guidance, he turned to the State Department for a clear exposition of policy. Department officials provided the new president with the desired guidelines, but these bore little resemblance to the policies that Roosevelt had fashioned at Yalta. Truman learned that the United States still strongly supported Jiang as its best hope in China. On the subject of European imperialism in Southeast Asia, especially in Indochina, the State Department informed him that FDR had never challenged the right of France or the other European powers to regain their colonies. Regarding Korea, State Department officials continued to plan for participation in a four-power trusteeship with Britain, China, and the Soviet Union, but they urged the president and his new secretary of state, James Byrnes, to reach a final agreement at the upcoming summit conference scheduled for mid-July.

By the time Truman arrived in the Berlin suburb of Potsdam for the last of the Big Three wartime conferences, he knew that it would be difficult to maintain a policy of cooperation with Stalin. Soviet actions in eastern Europe, particularly Stalin's unilateral action in redrawing the Polish border, put the president on his guard. Nevertheless, Truman came to Potsdam determined to cooperate, if for no other reason than to secure Soviet assistance in defeating Japan. During the conference, however, the president received several messages vividly describing the results of the successful test of an atomic device in New Mexico. With this new weapon it now seemed possible that Japan would be defeated without Soviet assistance. After meeting with Truman upon his return to Washington, Army Chief of Staff General George Marshall instructed theater commanders to prepare for the rapid occupation of Japan and a portion of Korea. In Potsdam, over the next several days, Byrnes deflected Soviet efforts to discuss the Korean trusteeship and released, without Soviet input, a final warning to the Tokyo government. The Potsdam Proclamation threatened the destruction of Japan if it did not surrender unconditionally, spoke of a military occupation of the home islands and justice for war criminals, but made no direct mention of the atomic bomb. The warning also promised the Japanese that at some future date they would be permitted to choose their own form of government but stopped short of saying what would happen to the emperor or to the imperial institution itself.

Truman and his advisers were rethinking some of the basic premises on which American policy rested, but no clear policy had emerged to replace the alliance diplomacy of the war. The future was still too uncertain. Uppermost in the president's mind was the task of defeating Japan quickly, and with minimal casualties. For this he needed the Soviets, who still might have to contend with Japan's renegade army in Manchuria even after Tokyo capitulated. Moreover, although Truman expressed confidence that victory was at hand, some of his most respected advisers, including General Marshall, remained cautious. Some Americans believed that Japan would surrender if it were promised that the emperor would be retained, but the signals from militarists in that country were far from promising on this point. Japan's admirals and generals firmly rejected an Allied occupation and insisted on the right to disarm themselves and try their own war criminals. Under the circumstances, the most that Truman could do was to hedge his bets, plan for a sudden surrender, but do nothing to threaten Soviet cooperation. The Russians would enter the war anyway, and it was best not to provide them with a pretext for abandoning the Yalta agreements. In the meantime, American landings in Korea would place the United States in a better position to influence the future of the peninsula and prevent Soviet unilateral action, such as had occurred in eastern Europe.

The atomic blasts over Hiroshima and Nagasaki in August touched off a frenzied scramble for territory. By the time the Japanese formally surrendered on September 2, 1945, the victors had marked out their spheres. For the most part, practicality and logistical requirements determined the surrender lines. In Southeast Asia, Britain took responsibility; the United States accepted the surrender in the Pacific islands and Japan; and the Soviets, who had entered the Pacific war on August 8, assumed responsibility for Manchuria. Much to the surprise of planners in Washington, Moscow agreed to share surrender duties in Korea, even though American forces had no hope of reaching the peninsula for several weeks. The Allies ordered Japanese forces in China to surrender to Jiang's armies and prohibited them from turning their arms over to the CCP. In the final days before Japan's surrender, American officials prepared to occupy one of the southern Kuriles to strengthen their claim to landing rights somewhere in the island chain. They also planned to land forces at Port Arthur, Dairen, and Tsingtao in northern China, but the movement of Soviet troops and Stalin's reminder to Truman about the terms of the Yalta accords preempted all but the last of these operations.

Despite the mutual mistrust that surfaced at the end of the war, neither Truman nor Stalin seemed ready to abandon the alliance. Both powers had secured their primary area of interest: the United States held Japan, while the Russians settled into Manchuria. American airplanes and ships transported Nationalist troops into northern China to accept the surrender of Japanese troops, but this aid, as well as the exclusion of the Communists from the surrender terms, fell within the expectations of the Yalta agreements. However, American troops in northern China and in Korea below the 38th parallel were another matter. Stalin seems to have accepted the surrender line in Korea because it resembled the division of the peninsula by Russia and Japan earlier in the century, but the presence of between fifty and sixty thousand U.S. Marines in northern China might presage an expanded American involvement in Chinese affairs. Stalin urged the CCP's leadership to negotiate with Jiang lest the Americans intervene further. Mao Zedong (Mao Tse-tung), the CCP's chairman, resented Stalin's interference but resumed negotiations with the Nationalists. Mao and Stalin were not alone in anticipating greater American support for the Nationalists: Jiang also counted on Washington's aid in the event of hostilities.

Not surprisingly, the talks quickly stalemated. In the meantime, U.S. Marines guarded Chinese railways with assistance from Japanese troops, while Nationalist forces marched inland in pursuit of the Communists. Alarmed by the American presence, Stalin contributed to the weakening of the Yalta agreements by obstructing Nationalist landings in Manchuria. His main concern seems to have been looting China's northeastern provinces of their industrial capacity, but at times Soviet troops aided the entering CCP troops. Roosevelt's understanding with Stalin called for restraint on the part of the United States and the Soviet Union, but in the turmoil following Japan's surrender such self-discipline was in short supply.

Conditions elsewhere in East Asia were no more conducive to good relations between Moscow and Washington. To the consternation of American officials, the 38th parallel in Korea was taking on the appearance of a permanent boundary. For his part, Stalin complained bitterly to the U.S. ambassador that Soviet concerns in Japan were being ignored by the Supreme Commander for the Allied Powers (SCAP), General Douglas MacArthur. In late November, as wartime agreements frayed and started to unravel, the American ambassador to China suddenly resigned, loudly blaming Communist sympathizers in the State Department for undermining negotiations between the Guomindang and the CCP. President Truman recovered quickly from the shock of this betrayal by appointing the recently retired General Marshall as his special representative.

Marshall dutifully departed for China in early December, only days before Secretary of State Byrnes flew to Moscow for a meeting of the Council of Foreign Ministers. Byrnes sought a series of compromises with Stalin that would maintain the spirit of Allied cooperation while preserving the vital interests of both countries. As the historian Patricia Dawson Ward notes, the secretary "traded the Russians token concessions in Japan for token concessions in the Balkans, and American troops stayed in China while Soviet troops remained in Iran." Concerning Korea, Byrnes and the Soviet foreign minister agreed on a joint commission to create a provisional government to unify both the North and the South. Byrnes returned to Washington convinced that he had saved the alliance, only to encounter an irate president ready to disavow his secretary's handiwork. Soviet misconduct left Truman in an uncompromising mood. The United States should demand free elections in Romania and Bulgaria, he insisted, and the Soviet Union should evacuate Iran in accordance with its wartime promises; furthermore, "we should maintain complete control of Japan. . . . We should rehabilitate China and create a strong central government there. We should do the same in Korea." In the aftermath of Japan's surrender, Truman had come to regard Soviet activities in Asia as part of a larger pattern of subversion, opportunism, and aggression originating in eastern Europe and extending through the Middle East to the Korean Peninsula. A new policy was taking shape in Washington, and the Cold War in Asia had begun.

It was one thing for Truman to state his intentions for China and Korea, but it was quite another to act on them. General Marshall soon discovered that Jiang had little interest in negotiations and even less desire to maintain the fragile truce in China. Jiang counted on his supporters in Washington to keep supplies flowing to his government, but he nearly overreached himself in thinking that the Americans would not let the Nationalists fail. After a year's effort at mediation, a disgusted Marshall returned home to become secretary of state. He did not welcome a CCP victory, but the earlier withdrawal of Soviet forces convinced him that Stalin intended no further mischief in Manchuria. Open warfare soon commenced in China.

In response to the deteriorating situation in China and the strain on American resources created by the perceived threat of Soviet expansion in Europe and the Middle East, the United States withdrew its forces from Korea and turned the problem of unification over to the United Nations. Originally, the trusteeship plan was devised to reconcile competing great-power interests on the peninsula. Typically, however, no one had taken Korean nationalist aspirations into account. Despite the experience of the United States in the Philippines at the beginning of the century, officials in Washington were not prepared for the Koreans' hostility to outside tutelage. American authorities were even less ready for the bitter internal rivalries that they encountered on arriving in the South. In the early days of the occupation, the U.S. commander turned away from the left-wing, anti-Japanese resistance forces in the countryside and gravitated instead to the reactionary officials in Seoul, many of whom had collaborated with the Japanese. Above the 38th parallel, the Soviets backed a Communist regime under the leadership of the young resistance fighter, Kim Il Sung.

Efforts to unify the country after the Moscow conference failed, and by 1948 the United States had cajoled the United Nations into supervising elections in the southern zone. Relying on violence and intimidation, the government of Syngman Rhee captured the elections and tightened its grip on the South. American troops withdrew, leaving behind a small advisory group to train and equip Rhee's forces. Neither Rhee nor Kim considered the partition of the country final, however, and both resorted to guerrilla raids and terror to undermine the other's hold on power.

The deepening tensions of the Cold War and the outbreak of civil war in China also influenced U.S. policy in Japan. At the end of World War II the Americans decided to work through the existing government in Tokyo and spare the life of the emperor so as to ensure an orderly surrender and occupation. This decision necessitated some modification of the State Department's plans to restructure Japanese society, but the first years of the occupation produced substantial change nonetheless. Led by MacArthur, occupation authorities implemented liberal reforms in such areas as land ownership, organized labor, trust-busting, and education. MacArthur's proudest moment came with the ratification of the so-called Peace Constitution, with its famous renunciation of war as an instrument of policy.

This initial phase of the occupation made Japan safe for the rest of East Asia and produced lasting changes in its society, but its ailing economy raised concerns that for years to come American taxpayers would be called on to save the country from destitution. An impoverished Japan also seemed an inviting target for Communist infiltration. As the Nationalists careened toward defeat in China, the Truman administration looked to Tokyo as a potential ally in the Cold War. American conservatives, dismayed by the liberal economic reforms, teamed up with allies in Washington and prominent members of Japan's conservative elite to reverse course on occupation policy. Tighter restrictions on labor, the reinstating of purged leaders, the dismantling of the antitrust program, and an American-imposed fiscal austerity plan followed. This new emphasis on economic recovery sacrificed some of the liberal policies of the early occupation and imposed greater hardship on many Japanese, thereby leaving them with the bitter feeling that true democratic reform was abandoned when it suited American interests.

By early 1949, Japan's economy failed to revive while Jiang's Nationalist government seemed about to expire. The Guomindang was setting up operations on the island of Taiwan, one hundred miles from the mainland, in preparation for a final defense against the Communists. Jiang's supporters in Washington began to argue for a plan of military and economic assistance to Taiwan and Southeast Asia to stem the Red tide. Taiwan formed an important link in America's offshore defenses, they argued. Moreover, Japan would need Southeast Asia's markets and raw materials to prevent Tokyo's dependence on a Communist-controlled and presumably hostile China. Taiwan and Southeast Asia, part of the Great Crescent running from Japan down to the Indian Ocean, now seemed vital to the recovery of America's former enemy and to the stability of U.S. defenses in the Western Pacific.

To the consternation of Jiang's American supporters, Dean Acheson, the new secretary of state, dismissed these arguments about the importance of the Great Crescent. If Taiwan were a peninsula jutting out into the China Sea, he observed, no one would claim that it had any strategic value. Southeast Asia remained under European control, linked to the metropolitan economies and unlikely to support Japan's recovery. The area was devastated from the war and united only in its loathing of Japan. Moreover, having squandered American aid, Jiang seemed even less deserving of additional support. Given these circumstances as well as his overwhelming preoccupation with Europe, Acheson preferred to let the dust settle from the Chinese Communist victory and see whether the new People's Republic of China (PRC) would act independently of Moscow, much as Joseph Broz Tito had done in Yugoslavia. China might not be "lost" to the United States after all.

In the following months, Acheson came under intense pressure from critics within and outside of the administration. Even the usually supportive Truman questioned his policy. Following Chairman Mao's announcement of an alliance with the Soviet Union in February 1950, the ground began shifting under the secretary. To placate the JCS, Acheson agreed that the defense of Taiwan might be necessary in the event of a general war in Asia involving the Soviets; but since no war appeared in the offing, this seemed to be a satisfactory compromise. Having preserved the core of his policy, Acheson anxiously awaited the destruction of the Nationalists on Taiwan.

It seems safe to say that when North Korean armored units plunged across the 38th parallel on June 25, 1950, no one in Washington was more surprised than Acheson. Earlier in the year he had announced that South Korea lay outside the American defense perimeter, but he was only expressing what was agreed policy in the Pentagon and the State Department. In retrospect, the statement read like a standing invitation to invade the South, and both Stalin and Kim appear to have read it that way. Border skirmishes were common on the peninsula, but neither Rhee's nor Kim's forces could launch a full-scale invasion without offensive weapons provided by their sponsors. Much to Rhee's frustration, no such aid was forthcoming from Washington. Kim, however, succeeded in prying loose the desired armaments from the usually cautious Stalin. Previously, the Soviet leader had urged restraint on the CCP for fear of prompting American intervention in China. When the civil war broke out, Stalin's worries proved unfounded. Thus, when Kim sought Soviet assistance, Stalin agreed; surely, Korea was not as important to the United States as China.

Now it was Stalin's turn to be surprised. Within days the Truman administration, backed by a UN resolution charging North Korea with aggression, landed troops at the southern tip of the peninsula. The Korean crisis also activated Acheson's earlier promise to defend Taiwan in the event of a regional conflict. Units of the Seventh Fleet steamed between Taiwan and the mainland shielding the island from attack. Beginning in September, the UN offensive quickly regained control of South Korea up to the 38th parallel, paused, and moved northward. Flushed with victory, Truman, the JCS, and most of his civilian advisers decided to press on in the

THE KOREAN CONFLICT. General of the Army Douglas MacArthur, commander in chief in Korea, leads the saying of the Lord's Prayer at ceremonies held on September 29, 1950, at the Capitol Building in Seoul to restore the capital of the Republic of Korea to President Syngman Rhee. (U.S. Signal Corps, National Archives)

hope of unifying the peninsula under a single government. In Beijing, Mao and his advisers concluded that the UN command intended to push beyond Korea into the PRC. The long-expected American assault seemed to be at hand. Mao urged Stalin to join the fight to save North Korea if the United Nations failed to heed Beijing's warnings. Stalin appears to have assented, only to renege later. In the meantime, three hundred thousand Chinese "volunteers" entered North Korea and engaged UN troops in brief but fierce combat before pulling back. The Americans responded to Beijing's warnings to cease their campaign with assurances that the UN command desired only the unification of Korea. As the UN offensive resumed on November 24, Chinese forces reentered the fighting. The UN lines faltered and then crumbled, and by November 28 they were in full retreat.

The rout touched off a near panic at General MacArthur's headquarters, in the United States, and in the capitals of America's European allies. British prime minister Clement Attlee hastened to Washington fearful that Truman might resort to atomic weapons and expand the war into the PRC. Attlee felt certain that escalation would bring direct Soviet intervention and transform this localized struggle into World War III. By early 1951 the UN lines stabilized and slowly moved back toward the 38th parallel. As American officials regained their composure, MacArthur lost his. The general, a theater commander, failed to understand the global requirements of the Pentagon's strategic plans. When MacArthur persisted in challenging U.S. policy and calling for widening the war, Truman removed the old hero from command. Although negotiations for an armistice commenced soon afterward, the bloody stalemate continued for another two years.

Given the confusion in American policy up to that point, MacArthur's frustration seems understandable. Why did Washington first appear to write off Korea, only to intervene when North Korea was on the verge of victory? And what were its objectives in the war? Some historians have argued that the Truman administration reversed itself and entered the conflict primarily to salvage its dormant plan for increased military spending. According to this thesis, administration officials exploited the crisis created by the North Korean invasion mainly to justify adoption of a National Security Council plan (NSC-68) to triple defense spending. The real purpose of NSC-68, it is argued, was nothing less than the rescue of the U.S.-controlled capitalist world system. American taxpayers might not support the necessary reconstruction aid to Western Europe, but they would have no choice if they could be convinced that the survival of Western civilization was at stake. In taking advantage of the Korean crisis to adopt a policy of "military Keynesianism," the United States could revive the flagging economies of its allies and secure those countries of the Asian Rim that were needed as markets and sources of raw materials for Japan and the West.

America's military expenditures indeed increased rapidly as a result of the Korean War, and its allies in Europe and Asia benefited from purchases made through the newly created Military Assistance Program. But this does not mean that U.S. officials manufactured the crisis or that, as some historians have implied, Acheson actually invited the North Korean invasion and that the United States prolonged the war in order to lock in its spending programs. Proponents of this military Keynesianism thesis draw heavily on world-systems theory to make their case. They argue that in moving to prop up the international economy, the United States, as the hegemonic power in the capitalist system, acted exactly as this theory predicts it would. Such an argument assumes, however, that Washington officials comprehended the system as clearly as the theorists who wrote decades after the event. Indeed, it assumes that these policymakers even thought that a system existed and that they were in control of it. The military Keynesianism thesis also commits the fallacy of reading history backwards. Military spending increased, these scholars argue; therefore, this increase was the real reason for intervention. Perhaps the most important weakness of the world-systems approach is that it requires the historian to maintain that American officials did not feel threatened by Soviet military power in 1950.

Such complacency seems possible only from a vantage point years removed from the era in question. The Soviet explosion of an atomic bomb in September 1949, followed by the creation of the PRC in October, and the Sino-Soviet alliance in February 1950, altered the strategic setting and created a vivid impression of America's eroding position in Asia. Within weeks, Moscow and Beijing extended recognition to Ho Chi Minh's revolutionary government in Vietnam. Could Chinese assistance be far behind? Convinced that a Sino-Soviet rupture was only a matter of time, Secretary of State Acheson tenaciously held his ground against the rising chorus favoring support to Jiang on Taiwan. But others in

Washington needed only to point to a map to make their case: all of Asia was turning Red.

Operating in this atmosphere, U.S. officials initially saw the North Korean attack across the 38th parallel in June 1950 as the opening round in a new Soviet campaign of aggression. Although neither Rhee nor Kim had accepted the permanent division of the peninsula, Americans perceived the North Korean offensive as a clear-cut violation of an internationally recognized boundary. After the failure of appeasement in World War II, Americans of that generation agreed that aggressors had to be met with force. The credibility of the United Nations and of the United States seemed to be at stake. The Truman administration did not intend to abandon Rhee's regime in 1949; it had withdrawn its forces only because they were needed elsewhere. Now, the American-sponsored South Korean government was about to crumble under the weight of a Soviet-equipped army in the North. Even after officials in Washington concluded that another Soviet move was not likely any time soon, the lesson of the Korean debacle remained clear: Moscow would continue to capitalize on American weakness. The massive military buildup that had occurred during the war was intended to reassure U.S. allies and obviate the hard choices that had left South Korea exposed.

Once UN forces reached the 38th parallel, the temptation to unify the peninsula seemed irresistible. What had looked like victory in July, a return to the prewar boundary, was now perceived as a half-way measure. One can readily understand why Mao and his comrades were not persuaded by Acheson's assurances that UN troops would stop at the border with China. American intervention in that country's civil war, the sudden inclusion of Korea in the U.S. defensive zone, the movement of the Seventh Fleet into the Taiwan Strait, and the decision to advance beyond the 38th parallel all argued against accepting the Truman administration at its word. It took an act of supreme arrogance on the part of the Americans to think that Mao would take their soothing promises at face value.

Indeed, Americans, Chinese, and, most of all, Koreans paid a high price for this tragic blunder. Acheson's nuanced policy toward China also fell victim to the anti-Communist hysteria that gripped the United States following the Communist intervention. Thereafter, toughness became the watchword in American diplomacy, and talk about independent Communist movements was political suicide. The crisis atmosphere also strengthened the influence of the armed services in policy-making. Ironically, so did MacArthur's dismissal, since Truman needed to rely on his military advisers to counter the general's stinging criticisms. Military aid to Indochina and other countries in Southeast Asia also increased as a consequence of the war. The United States did not commit itself to the defense of a non-Communist Vietnam, but it took a further step in that direction by increasing aid to the French in Indochina. And finally, the Korean War hastened the end of the occupation of Japan and transformed that country into an American ally.

In the peace treaty with its adversaries signed in September 1951, Japan gave up its claims to Korea, the Pacific Island Mandates, and rights in China. Tokyo also renounced its sovereignty over the Kuriles without specifying which islands were covered by this term and without recognizing the islands as Soviet territory. The architect of the San Francisco treaty, John Foster Dulles, arranged for this provision so that the Russians would have to sign the document to obtain legal title to the archipelago. Stalin, however, was unwilling to drop his objections to the treaty, which he believed too lenient, or to abandon the PRC, which had been excluded from the conference, only to notarize the title to islands that the Soviet Union already occupied. As Dulles expected, the issue of who held sovereignty over the Kuriles became an obstacle to ending the state of war between Tokyo and Moscow.

Having maneuvered to isolate the Soviets and the PRC, Dulles completed the alliance between Washington and Tokyo with a separate security treaty signed on the same day as the peace treaty. Under the terms of the pact, the United States could maintain bases in the home islands and use its forces to quell internal disturbances, but it was under no obligation to defend Japan. As part of the price of independence, Prime Minister Shigeru Yoshida agreed to join the trade embargo imposed on the PRC during the Korean War and to establish diplomatic relations with Jiang's government instead of with the Communists. Americans justified the glaring inequality in the security treaty by pointing to Japan's inability to contribute to its own defense. The Japanese countered that their American-sponsored constitution prohibited them from rearming. More important, Yoshida reasoned that with U.S. forces in his country there was no need to divert scarce resources to rebuilding a military establishment. His critics would complain later about Japan's "subordinate independence," but the essentials of the prime minister's policy—concentration on economic recovery and alliance with Washington—remained unchanged for the rest of the Cold War.

During the presidential campaign of 1952, Republicans promised a more assertive policy in Asia to undo the years of supposed neglect under successive Democratic administrations. Nevertheless, when Dwight D. Eisenhower became president in 1953, he and Secretary of State John Foster Dulles continued the Europe-first emphasis of their predecessors. In Asia, Eisenhower showed the same predilection for holding the line that characterized his domestic policy. Other leaders were more intent on changing the international system that emerged from the Korean War.

The death of Stalin, which occurred three months after Eisenhower took office, may have been the most important harbinger of change. As Soviet leaders fought over the succession, Moscow adopted a more conciliatory approach to the outside world. One probable consequence of this thaw in relations was the completion of the armistice in Korea. Furthermore, in Britain the return to power of Winston Churchill brought surprising changes as the old Cold Warrior urged Eisenhower to negotiate with the new men in the Kremlin. Anxious about a Japanese challenge to their economic position in Southeast Asia, British officials also prodded the Americans to end the trade embargo against the PRC so that Japan might find a less threatening outlet for its goods. In Tokyo, Yoshida eventually gave way to a new government headed by Ichiro Hatoyama, one of the so-called revisionists, who hoped to alter the international regime in Asia by adopting a more independent foreign policy. Hatoyama's agenda called for increasing military spending along the lines desired by the United States, expanding trade with the PRC, and normalizing relations with the Soviet Union. Although American officials welcomed the first of these measures, the latter two proved more vexing to alliance managers in Washington.

If left to act on his own instincts, President Eisenhower would have lifted the embargo on the PRC. In this instance his anticommunism was no match for his devotion to conservative economic principles. He believed that coercing trade into unnatural patterns was counterproductive, causing friction in the Western alliance and stunting Japan's economic growth. Although Eisenhower frequently talked of ending the restrictions, opponents within his administration, especially the JCS, argued that such backsliding would demoralize America's Asian allies. Trapped by his administration's tough rhetoric and its promise to take a combative posture toward Beijing, he quietly permitted American firms in Canada to trade with mainland China and relaxed slightly the restrictions on Japanese and European trade. Otherwise, he left the embargo intact.

Eisenhower's policy toward Taiwan also reflected his preference for standing pat in Asia. As one of its first steps, the new administration symbolically "unleashed" Jiang to prey on the mainland. Privately, however, Dulles shared Acheson's contempt for the Nationalist leader. Eisenhower and his secretary of state understood that Jiang hoped to liberate China with American forces, but they were no more willing than their predecessors to fight there. Ideally, Eisenhower hoped to stabilize conditions in the Taiwan Strait and institutionalize the existence of two Chinas. As in Korea, this plan for a great-power partition ran afoul of the rivals contending for power. Jiang and Mao correctly perceived American intentions, and neither willingly submitted to the permanent division of their country.

In October 1954 artillery units of the People's Liberation Army began to shell the small islands held by Nationalist forces just off the mainland. Jiang's use of the Dachens, Jinmen, and Mazu to stage raids on the PRC and interfere with coastal trade offered justification enough for a campaign to seize the islands, but Mao also initiated this show of force to warn the Americans against making a security pact with Taibei (Taipei), which he mistakenly believed was in the offing. Once again the chairman miscalculated, bringing about the very alliance that he had hoped to prevent. For his part, Jiang wanted to lure the United States into a defense of the offshore islands, but Eisenhower did not take the bait. Instead, American naval units evacuated Nationalist troops from the indefensible Dachens. The president refused to commit the United States publicly to the defense of Jinmen and Mazu, but he admitted privately that although the islands possessed limited strategic value, they had to be held for the sake of morale on Taiwan. In March 1955, after a period of considerable tension and loose talk in Washington about the use of nuclear weapons, the PRC abandoned its campaign against the islands. Eisenhower had narrowly escaped from a dilemma of Jiang's making.

American efforts to persuade the Nationalist leader to abandon the islands once tensions had eased proved unavailing. Instead, Jiang raised the stakes in the Taiwan Strait by stationing even more troops on Jinmen and Mazu. Like Mao, Jiang rejected the idea of two

Chinas. As a consequence, America's European allies were treated to another alarming showdown over the offshore islands in September 1958. This time, Eisenhower announced that the United States would defend the islands. More threats of nuclear war issued from Washington, but American-supplied fighter planes allowed Jiang's forces to control the approaches to the islands. Mao unconvincingly declared a victory and called off the campaign, complaining all the while that the Soviets had deserted him again.

Despite the harrowing episodes in the strait, Dulles defended the administration's China policy against those who urged a rapprochement between Beijing and Washington. These critics wanted the United States to exploit the growing friction in the Sino-Soviet alliance by initiating formal diplomatic relations with the PRC. The secretary of state responded that he well understood the potential for a Sino-Soviet split. According to Dulles the American campaign of military, economic, and political pressure against the PRC was designed to drive a wedge between Moscow and Beijing by forcing China into greater dependence on the Soviet Union. Dulles predicted that the PRC would grow restive in the Kremlin's tight embrace and would eventually break out of the alliance. In retrospect, however, it seems clear that his plan was actually little more than a rationalization for continuing a politically safe but strategically bankrupt policy. Washington officials detected strains in the Sino-Soviet alliance throughout the decade, but Eisenhower and Dulles remained inflexible and unable to capitalize on the emerging schism in the socialist world.

Similarly, although Eisenhower displayed a thoughtful appreciation of Japanese concerns, more often than not he was content to let policy run in the grooves established by his predecessor. As mentioned, he recognized the importance of mainland trade to Japan. Rather than overturn the existing system of restrictions, however, the president worked on the margins, making minor adjustments where they provoked the least political opposition. Unlike Dulles, who has been immortalized in Japan for his prediction that its people would never be able to sell anything more than towels and cocktail napkins to the United States, Eisenhower understood the importance to the Japanese of an expanding American market. Despite domestic and allied opposition, he made some progress in lowering trade barriers and gained admission for Japan to the General Agreement on Tariffs and Trade (GATT), the non-Communist world's international trading regime. Although GATT members promptly invoked special protectionist provisions against Japanese competition, Japan benefited greatly over the long term by participating in the organization.

During the 1950s, U.S. efforts to encourage rearmament foundered on the issues of economic recovery and incipient neutralism. Japanese defense spending increased, but it fell far short of Pentagon recommendations. Referring to Tokyo's anemic military budgets, Dulles complained that, unlike Germany, there had been "no spiritual rebirth in Japan." His real concern, however, was that the Japanese had become born-again neutralists. Hatoyama's attempt at a rapprochement with Moscow appeared to give credence to these worries. Of even greater concern were Japanese protests over American nuclear weapons policy. The Eisenhower administration's emphasis on nuclear deterrence alarmed the Tokyo government. Dulles's combative rhetoric, and incidents such as the contamination of a Japanese tuna-fishing boat by American radioactive fallout in the Pacific in March 1954, frightened Japanese citizens for obvious reasons. In 1960, Washington officials sought to mollify their ally by revising the security treaty on terms more favorable to Tokyo. The new treaty excised some of the more obnoxious provisions in the earlier pact and made for greater reciprocity in the alliance. Nevertheless, the agreement provoked mass demonstrations in the streets and opposition in the Diet.

Although the Diet ratified the new treaty, the storm of protests that it ignited convinced the incoming administration of John F. Kennedy that the United States could not expect more than passive support from its East Asian ally. The charismatic young president and his elegant wife immediately won favor in Japan, a land where style is substance. In 1961, Kennedy appointed as ambassador Edwin O. Reischauer, the distinguished scholar of Japanese history; and he also started talks on transferring Okinawa to Tokyo's jurisdiction and negotiated more favorable access to American markets for Japanese goods. In short, Kennedy initiated a policy of asking of Japan so little that it could not refuse. That pattern would hold for the rest of the decade.

Despite visible evidence of a rupture in Sino-Soviet relations, American policy toward the PRC held to the established pattern as well. For all their enthusiasm for innovative ideas, Kennedy's New Frontiersmen continued to apply Cold War axioms to Asian politics, only now the PRC was perceived as the source of instability in the region. Although some officials urged reconsideration of the policy of nonrecognition, Washington held to the fiction that Jiang's regime was the sole government of China. As George Herring notes elsewhere in this volume, Kennedy expanded American involvement in Vietnam in part because he equated a North Vietnamese victory with the extension of Chinese influence in the region. Even more worrisome was the PRC's effort to build a nuclear arsenal. After narrowly avoiding a nuclear catastrophe in 1962 during the Cuban missile crisis, Kennedy did not relish the prospect of confronting a China armed with atomic weapons. Following the Cuban crisis, Washington officials hoped to isolate Beijing by signing a nuclear test-ban treaty with Moscow. It also appears that some people in the administration even proposed cooperating with the Soviets to "bomb China's bomb," although nothing came of these plans.

Lyndon B. Johnson in 1963 inherited Kennedy's concerns about Chinese expansionism and followed them to their fateful conclusion: full-scale intervention in Vietnam. Like his predecessor, Johnson did not want to face a partisan inquest over who "lost" Vietnam, and, like previous presidents, he was convinced that the lessons of Munich permitted no choice but escalation. Johnson, however, was also haunted by the Korean War and the specter of Chinese intervention. Consequently, he restricted American military operations so as not to provoke China's wrath. Even without direct military intervention, the People's Republic influenced the course of the war.

To their discomfort, the Japanese found the Vietnam War, with all its destruction and human loss, both troubling and immensely beneficial. Japanese firms grew fat on American war contracts, while an appalled and fascinated public watched "the fire across the sea." The war re-energized the peace movement in Japan and produced protests from officials who were concerned that the presence of American bases in their country might drag them into the conflict. Prime Minister Eisaku Sato's support for the war pleased Washington, but officials there recognized that the war was accelerating important changes in the alliance. Japan's economy boomed while the American dynamo sputtered under the burden of military spending, and American dissatisfaction with Japan's contribution to the alliance grew in direct proportion to the latter's rising gross national product. For their part, many Japanese continued to admire the United States, but they no longer saw it as unique among the nations of the world. During the war, riot-plagued America slipped from first to third place in public opinion polls, ranking behind France and Switzerland as the country most admired by the Japanese.

By the time Richard M. Nixon became president in early 1969, changes in the international balance of power highlighted the anachronistic nature of American policy in Vietnam. The previous administration already had begun the arms negotiations that would lead to a period of détente with the Soviet Union. Along the vast border between Russia and the PRC, Chinese and Soviet troops regularly traded insults and bullets, provoking two serious clashes in March 1969. Assessing these changed circumstances, Nixon, who had gained fame as a Red-baiting congressman, veered sharply from the policy of his predecessors. Whereas Eisenhower and Kennedy had assumed that cracks in the Sino-Soviet alliance could be exploited through a policy of toughness, Nixon now indicated a willingness for limited cooperation with the PRC. Gradually, as China emerged from the reign of terror known as the Great Proletarian Cultural Revolution, leaders in Beijing also took stock of the new international situation. Zhou Enlai, the PRC's experienced foreign minister, persuaded Mao that the Soviet Union loomed as the greater threat to China. An intricate diplomatic minuet followed, concluding in a summit conference in Beijing in February 1972. Nixon's visit ended with the Shanghai communiqué establishing that Taiwan was part of China but that unification would best be accomplished by peaceful means. As historian Warren Cohen notes, Dulles's two-Chinas policy was discarded for a policy of "one China, but not now."

Nixon's surprising turnaround toward Beijing stunned America's allies in Tokyo for various reasons, not least of which was the president's failure to give the Japanese advance warning of the change in U.S. policy. Moreover, his dramatic opening to China caught Japan's officials already reeling from the Nixon administration's vigorous efforts to adjust its trade imbalance. During 1971, Nixon threatened to invoke the 1917 Trading with the Enemy Act to curtail Japanese textile imports, ceased redeeming foreign-held dollars with gold, devalued the dollar to boost exports, and imposed a 10 percent surcharge on imports. As one American observer commented, "The new economic approach, coupled with the coming presidential visits to Peking and Moscow, produced the most bizarre U.S. foreign policy imaginable: war on our friends, concessions to our traditional adversaries."

The Nixon *shokus* (shocks), as they were known in Japan, appeared to signal a new era in American-Japanese relations. Officials in Tokyo moved quickly to open contacts with North Vietnam, recognized Outer Mongolia, and followed up Nixon's visit to Beijing with one of their own. Nevertheless, when all the excitement subsided, the familiar twin pillars of Japanese foreign policy—economic expansion and military alliance with Washington—remained in place. The revival of Cold War tensions with the Soviet Union in the 1980s demonstrated to Tokyo the wisdom of maintaining the American-Japanese alliance. Despite its monstrous trade imbalance with Japan, Washington had sound economic and strategic reasons for continuing "the most important bilateral relationship in the world."

During the final stage of the Cold War, American officials also had reason to be grateful for their improved relations with the People's Republic. Following recognition, these officials promoted the opportunities awaiting businessmen in the fabled China market, but it was the PRC, with its high volume of sales to the United States and its purchases of sophisticated technologies, that seemed to benefit most. It does not appear that Washington achieved very much in the way of military cooperation with Beijing. Better relations with China, however, did allow the United States to concentrate its defenses in Asia against the Soviet military buildup. If the Americans miscalculated the threat posed by the PRC in the 1950s and 1960s, it seems that in the 1970s and 1980s they also overrated the advantages that would come from playing the "China card" against the Kremlin. Numerous obstacles stood in the way of closer cooperation, but neither government wished to return to the earlier era of belligerence and nonrecognition.

The United States reached this conclusion only after years of trial and error. During World War II the pursuit of victory over Japan had led Roosevelt to frame postwar plans for Asia in terms of limits and restraint. Japan's sudden collapse in 1945 did not remove all of the barriers to an activist policy on the mainland, but it did seem to provide the United States with an opportunity to exert greater influence in the region. After the war, officials in Washington hoped to direct the transformation of China and Korea along nonrevolutionary lines even though the modernization of their own country and that of the other industrial powers had been a wrenching and disruptive process. By 1949 the chance to shape China's future seemed to vanish with the victory of Mao and the

Communists. In the ensuing debate over the precise nature of American interests in the region, Secretary Acheson took the stand that the limitations of his country's power called for a defensive position centered on Japan and a nonprovocative approach to the PRC. His policy of watchful waiting prevailed until the Korean War tipped the balance in favor of those who wished to apply the policy of containment to the PRC as well as to the Soviet Union. China's intervention in the war shattered what hope remained for a rapprochement with Beijing. The Korean War then froze Sino-American relations in a state of intense hostility for nearly two decades. The brief thaw in Soviet-American relations after Stalin's death and the splintering of the Sino-Soviet alliance did not ease tensions in the region. Neither the United States nor China seemed ready to compromise: Eisenhower remained committed to the policy of nonrecognition, and Mao showed little inclination to accept the "one China, but not now" solution that he later adopted.

Japan became the principal beneficiary of this prolonged ideological struggle, although the United States also gained economically and strategically from its alliance with Tokyo—a point all too easily overlooked at the end of the Cold War. For their part, Japanese officials accomplished much within the constraints of their "subordinate independence." A decade after the occupation they had successfully revised the security treaty. Ten years later they had assumed jurisdiction over Okinawa and placed their country on the path to achieving an unprecedented standard of living for its citizens. By the 1980s, Japan had become an economic rival of the United States even while it continued to depend on America for its security. The strains created by this dissonance in status gave rise to disturbing speculation in Washington about using China to contain Japan, thus demonstrating the wisdom of the old adage that "history does repeat itself, but not without a change of costume."

During the late 1960s defeat in Vietnam, coupled with economic stagnation, weakened America's ability to project its influence in Asia. These developments, as well as the growth of Chinese and Japanese power during the same period, forced officials to revive the diplomacy of limits and restraint. Soviet power, which at the onset of the Cold War seemed the main determinant in American policy, had become only one of several factors in Washington's calculations. Strangely, the Cold War in Asia seemed to outlive the Soviet Union. In Europe, the Kremlin released its grip on the former "captive nations," thus making possible the peaceful reunification of Germany. In Asia, however, Korea remained divided and Taiwan kept its independence from the mainland. Japan had normalized relations with the Soviet Union in 1956, but an actual peace treaty and full economic contacts with the successor Russian Republic awaited resolution of the Kuriles controversy. Twenty years after the end of the Vietnam War, the United States still withheld diplomatic recognition from the Democratic Republic of Vietnam. More than forty years after the Korean armistice, American troops guarded the 38th parallel on the peninsula. The persistence of this unsettled business seemed to underscore the extent to which nationalism and regional imperatives moved like an underground stream beneath the surface of the superpower struggle in East Asia. During the Cold War, American officials discovered this reality the hard way, through experience with Jiang Jieshi and Mao Zedong, Syngman Rhee and Kim Il Sung, and Shigeru Yoshida and Ichiro Hatoyama.

Sources and Suggested Readings

Borg, Dorothy, and Heinrichs, Waldo. *Uncertain Years: Chinese-American Relations, 1947–1950*. New York, 1980.

Chang, Gordon. *Friends and Enemies: The United States, China, and the Soviet Union, 1948–1972*. Stanford, CA, 1990.

Chen, Jian. "China's Changing Aims during the Korean War." *Journal of American-East Asian Relations* 1 (1992): 8–41.

Cohen, Warren I. *America's Response to China: A History of Sino-American Relations*. 3rd ed. New York, 1990.

——. *Pacific Passage: American-East Asian Relations on the Eve of the Twenty-First Century*. New York, 1995.

——, and Iriye, Akira, eds. *The Great Powers in East Asia, 1953–1960*. New York, 1990.

Cumings, Bruce. *The Origins of the Korean War*. Vol. 1, *Liberation and the Emergence of Separate Regimes, 1945–1947*. Princeton, NJ, 1981.

Dingman, Roger. "The Dagger and the Gift: The Impact of the Korean War on Japan." *Journal of American-East Asian Relations* 2 (1993): 29–55.

Dower, John. *Japan in War and Peace: Selected Essays*. New York, 1993.

Gallicchio, Marc S. *The Cold War Begins in Asia: American East Asian Policy and the Fall of the Japanese Empire*. New York, 1988.

Iriye, Akira. *The Cold War in Asia: A Historical Introduction*. Englewood Cliffs, NJ, 1974.

Kaufman, Burton I. *The Korean War: Challenges in Crisis, Credibility, and Command*. New York, 1986.

McMahon, Robert J. "The Cold War in Asia: Toward a New Synthesis?" *Diplomatic History* 12, no. 3 (1988): 307–27.

Schaller, Michael. *The American Occupation of Japan: The Origins of the Cold War in Asia.* New York, 1985.

Stueck, William Whitney, Jr. *The Road to Confrontation: American Policy toward China and Korea, 1947–1950.* Chapel Hill, NC, 1981.

Tucker, Nancy Bernkopf. *Patterns in the Dust: Chinese-American Relations and the Recognition Controversy, 1949–1950.* New York, 1983.

Westad, Odd Arne. *Cold War and Revolution: Soviet-American Rivalry and the Origins of the Chinese Civil War.* New York, 1993.

Zhai, Qiang. *The Dragon, the Lion, and the Eagle: Chinese-American Relations, 1949–1958.* Kent, OH, 1994.

Zhang, Shu Guang. *Deterrence and Strategic Culture: Chinese-American Confrontations, 1949–1958.* Ithaca, NY, 1992.

Nuclear Weapons and Cold War Diplomacy

Walter L. Hixson

However one interprets the history of the Cold War—whether the emphasis is on economic, geopolitical, or other forces—few would dispute the fact that nuclear weapons distinguished the conflict from previous periods of international tension. The nuclear arms race, spreading fear and uncertainty across the globe, was inextricably linked to Cold War history. The United States, first to master the technology of the atomic bomb, took the lead in escalating the weapons race. The Soviet Union strove to keep pace before finally achieving parity in the late 1960s.

Both the United States and the USSR embraced deterrence through mutual assured destruction (MAD). Each would maintain nuclear forces sufficient to absorb an atomic attack and launch a massive retaliatory strike. MAD thus would deter any use of the weapons of mass destruction. MAD could have been achieved on a basis of "finite deterrence" by maintaining only enough invulnerable nuclear weapons to ensure the capacity for a devastating retaliatory strike. Instead, however, Washington led an arms race of seemingly boundless escalation, wasting resources, heightening the danger of nuclear war, and setting a poor example for the world. The excesses of this race contributed to the economic collapse of the former Soviet Union but did not bring about the end of the Cold War.

Atomic weapons had first appeared not during the Cold War but in World War II. Fearing that Nazi Germany, which had harnessed its scientific establishment to Adolf Hitler's aggressive course, would develop and use atomic weapons, President Franklin D. Roosevelt authorized a crash course to ensure that the United States would be first to build the bomb. The Manhattan Project, as the top-secret research effort was known, began in August 1942. The $2-billion program, by far the most expensive research undertaking during the war, involved some 150,000 people operating primarily in the three "atom bomb cities" of Hanford, Washington; Oak Ridge, Tennessee; and Los Alamos, New Mexico. By relying on oral rather than written communication, the Manhattan Project remained unknown to most of the public, although Soviet spies did penetrate the program.

Before dawn on July 16, 1945, the Manhattan Project culminated in a brilliant flash of light over the New Mexico desert. The first successful test of an atomic weapon came at the very time that Harry S. Truman, Roosevelt's successor as president, British prime minister Winston Churchill, and Soviet premier Joseph Stalin were meeting at Potsdam, Germany, to make final plans to secure the unconditional surrender of Japan. After some debate, American officials resolved to employ the bomb as soon as it became available. Since Nazi Germany had been defeated by means of the Allied conventional war effort, Japan remained the only potential target of American atomic bombing. The British had been kept apprised of the Manhattan Project, but Roosevelt and Churchill decided not to inform their Soviet allies about the progress of the bomb. Finally, in the wake of the successful test blast, Truman casually informed Stalin at Potsdam that the United States had developed a powerful new weapon. The Soviet premier just as casually encouraged Truman to use it against the Japanese.

President Truman assumed responsibility for the subsequent bombing of Hiroshima and Nagasaki on August 6 and 9, but he was merely following through on a course that already had gathered momentum: a government committee charged with planning for the bomb had approved targets in Japan. Truman would have had to reverse American policy to stop the attack. In the context of the most brutal war in human history, one in which Allied bombing had already obliterated German and Japanese cities, the decision to use the new weapon did not seem out of context. Racism ran high against the "treacherous Japs" who had bombed Pearl Harbor in a "sneak attack" in 1941 and thus had unleashed a brutal imperial war, replete with atrocities and kamikaze raids, across Asia and the Pacific. The horrific destruction beneath the giant mushroom cloud over Hiroshima left some 130,000 dead and buildings leveled in Japan's eighth-largest city. The gruesome effects of radiation also attested to the destructive potential of nuclear weapons. An incomparably destructive age had begun in the history of warfare.

Was the atomic bombing necessary to secure the surrender of Japan? Were there alternatives, such as a demonstration blast on some remote Pacific atoll, that Americans rejected in favor of the awesome display of military technology? Scholars and citizens have long debated these questions. President Truman and defenders of his decision argued that the use of the bomb was necessary to prevent the thousands of American casualties that would result from an invasion of the Japanese home islands. In retrospect, however, it is clear that Tokyo faced certain defeat and that forces were at

ATOMIC BLAST. The mushroom-shaped cloud from the second atomic bomb dropped near the end of World War II rises to a height of 60,000 feet over the Japanese port of Nagasaki on August 9, 1945. (National Archives)

work in Japanese society to compel the emperor to accept that reality. The United States and its allies probably could have succeeded through diplomacy in securing Japan's defeat without using the bomb or invading the home islands—especially with the Soviet Union poised to join the United States in attacks on Japanese positions. Even after using the two atomic weapons, Washington had to agree to allow the emperor to remain in power as a symbolic figurehead before the country agreed to surrender. The policy of unconditional surrender, racism, and four years of bloody war made the decision to use the bomb expedient and popular.

The destruction evident at Hiroshima and Nagasaki made it clear, at least, that world leaders would have to find ways to prevent the use of such weapons in the future. American scientists such as J. Robert Oppenheimer, the "father" of the atomic bomb, had nurtured gnawing doubts about the development and use of nuclear weapons, and they advocated international agreements forbidding their use. American efforts to promote a system of international controls before the new United Nations fell victim to Cold War tensions. The Soviet Union, increasingly seen not as a wartime ally but as an aggressive global rival driven by Communist ideology, would not accept a 1946 American proposal (the Baruch Plan) that would have maintained the U.S. monopoly until all other nations turned over their atomic energy programs and matériel to the United Nations. Even a more equitable plan probably would have been ignored by the USSR, which was committed to its own program of atomic research and development.

By the time of the successful Soviet test of an atomic weapon in September 1949, Cold War tensions had escalated dramatically. Europe had been divided into spheres of influence, and both the United States and the USSR had begun to compete for influence in the developing world. Washington and its European allies had formed the North Atlantic Treaty Organization (NATO) to "contain" putative Soviet expansionism. Both superpowers had inaugurated a military buildup. When China "fell" to communism in 1949 and Communist and non-Communist forces went to war in Korea the next year, the Truman administration put the United States on a war footing. The decisions codified in the National Security Council's paper (NSC-68) in the spring of 1950 envisioned massive increases in military spending, which could not help but fuel the burgeoning nuclear arms race.

By 1950 both American and Soviet scientists were at work on more powerful fusion bombs. Despite the opposition of Oppenheimer and several other scientists, Truman authorized the development and testing of a thermonuclear, or hydrogen, bomb that was one thousand times more powerful than the weapons that had devastated Hiroshima and Nagasaki. The H-bomb test succeeded in November 1952, followed nine months later by another successful test that culminated in a furious Soviet effort to match American nuclear advances. Both nations began stockpiling weapons of incalculable destructive force.

Despite the potentially suicidal nature of nuclear war, the United States, especially under the Eisenhower administration, made the weapons a central component of Cold War strategy. President Dwight D. Eisenhower, a Republican and fiscal conservative, argued that nuclear weapons provided "more bang for the buck" than maintaining sprawling military bases and occupation forces overseas. Washington would contain the Soviets by threatening to unleash what Secretary of State John Foster Dulles called "massive retaliation" against either the USSR or China in the event of Communist aggression anywhere in the world. This implicit nuclear threat may have contributed to the willingness of the Communist powers to help bring about an armistice in Korea in July 1953. American officials discussed the possibility of using the bomb to aid the French, who were on the verge of defeat in Vietnam in 1954, but no such plans came close to being operational.

Rather than actually using nuclear weapons, the Eisenhower administration continued to employ the bomb as a tool of psychological warfare. Implied threats to use the weapons of mass destruction, especially when offered by outspoken anti-Communists such as Dulles, would serve to restrain presumed Soviet and Chinese expansionism and keep the Communist powers off balance. Efforts to exploit the bomb for propaganda purposes succeeded only in heightening Soviet insecurities and fueling the arms race. Both superpowers conducted research and development on intercontinental ballistic missiles (ICBMs) that could deliver nuclear warheads from land or sea, thousands of miles from their target. The recognition of American vulnerability to Soviet rockets accounts for the high level of anxiety in this country that greeted the Soviet launching of *Sputnik*, the first Earth satellite, in October 1957. Although the achievement electrified world opinion and sent tremors through the American political landscape, the 184-pound *Sputnik* actually was technologically crude and of no military significance. It became obvious, however, that if the Soviets could launch a satellite into space, they also could deliver nuclear-tipped warheads over American shores.

Sputnik precipitated a panic that gave rise to the myth of a "missile gap," which held that the Soviets had gained the strategic superiority that would allow them to launch a crippling first strike. The arms race had entered its most dangerous phase. Democrats and critics within his own party condemned Eisenhower and his administration for allowing the supposed gap to occur. Money flowed into national defense think tanks, into nuclear research and development, into public schools for scientific education, and into the political coffers of advocates of nuclear escalation. Ignoring muted calls to rein in the weapons race, the United States continued to take the lead by placing nuclear missiles targeting the Soviet Union on European territory.

Hysteria over the missile gap drowned out Eisenhower's pleas for calm. The president himself knew that there was indeed a missile gap—one weighted heavily in favor of the United States, which maintained a substantial lead in both bombers and missiles. American submarine technology was also far superior to the Soviets'. As Premier Nikita S. Khrushchev recalled in his memoirs, the men in the Kremlin plainly understood that Washington's strategic superiority—and their own vulnerability—could not be challenged for at least another decade. Unable to check the momentum for escalation in the wake of the missile gap controversy, Eisenhower warned his listeners in his 1961 farewell address to "guard against the acquisition of unwarranted influence . . . by the military-industrial complex." The existence of a vast public and private "complex" devoted to research and development of the instruments of Armageddon fueled the arms race even after new satellite reconnaisance photographs in 1961 belied reports of massive Soviet ICBM deployment.

Under pressure from the more militant Chinese as well as from his own Communist party hard-liners to respond to the American escalation, Khrushchev decided in 1962 to place Soviet nuclear missiles secretly in Cuba. This decision must be seen in the context of the breakdown of early efforts toward détente and of Soviet frustration over the inability to eliminate the Western enclave in Berlin. Efforts to ease tensions began with the "spirit of Geneva," dating from a 1955 summit in that city, and continued through Khrushchev's 1959 tour of the United States and the opening of an American cultural exhibition in Moscow that same year. Both superpowers had observed an informal moratorium on nuclear testing since 1958 and were within reach of a formal agreement until the shootdown of an American U-2 spyplane, which had penetrated 1,200 miles into restricted Soviet airspace, propelled Washington-Moscow relations into a downward spiral. Eisenhower had authorized Central Intelligence Agency (CIA) overflights in the ultralightweight spyplanes, packed with photographic equipment, in order to monitor Soviet nuclear development. Following the downing of Francis Gary Powers's U-2 on May 1, 1960, Khrushchev denounced the United States and abruptly ended a summit conference in Paris two weeks later.

The Soviet decision to place theater nuclear weapons in Cuba thus came in the midst of heightened East-West tensions over the missile gap and the U-2 incident. Newly elected president John F. Kennedy had made no progress at a tense meeting with Khrushchev in Vienna in June 1961. Moreover, two months earlier the United States had failed miserably in an attempt to topple Communist leader Fidel Castro by landing CIA-trained Cuban exiles at the Bay of Pigs. CIA assassination plots against the Cuban president continued. The Kremlin had already broken the informal moratorium on nuclear testing and now made secret plans to build the missile sites. By placing nuclear missiles targeting the United States in Cuba, Khrushchev intended to enhance Castro's ability to defend the Cuban Revolution as well as to give Americans "a little of their own medicine"—to teach them "just what it feels like to have enemy missiles pointing at you," which the Soviets knew very well from the deployment of NATO missiles in Europe and across the Black Sea in Turkey.

The Soviet action was legal under international law but dishonest, since the Kremlin had denied that the USSR intended to place nuclear missiles in Cuba. Khrushchev clearly hoped to confront the United States with a fait accompli that would strengthen his standing with the Chinese and his own Politburo hard-liners. Instead, Kennedy, having learned of the missile sites through a U-2 overflight, went on national television on October 22, 1962, to demand that the Soviets dismantle them. He established a naval blockade of Cuba to interfere with Soviet freighters but avoided calls for bombing the missile sites. The tense international crisis carried a palpable threat of a Washington-Moscow confrontation that might easily escalate to nuclear war.

Khrushchev stopped Soviet ships that were steaming toward Cuba and agreed to dismantle the missile sites, but only after Kennedy pledged publicly to respect Cuba's territorial integrity and privately to withdraw Jupiter missiles from Turkey. The crisis had the salutary effect of sobering both leaders about the real dangers of nuclear war, and it also broke the impasse in the ongoing test-ban negotiations. In 1963 the two superpowers established a hot line for instant communication in the midst of any future crisis and signed the Limited Test Ban Treaty terminating above-ground nuclear tests. A new era of détente had begun, but research, construction, and deployment of nuclear weapons and various delivery systems continued unchecked.

The Soviets embarked on a concerted effort to build large-scale ICBMs that, while less accurate, were far more powerful than the Pentagon's Minuteman missiles. The overthrow of Khrushchev in 1964 signaled the triumph of hard-liners, led by Leonid Brezhnev, who eventually would pursue détente but only while striving simultaneously to achieve strategic parity. The United States continued to assemble a massive nuclear force on the European continent, emplacing 7,200 nuclear weapons there by 1966—an absurd exercise in overkill that, as Defense Secretary Robert S. McNamara admitted, served no rational purpose. Despite the accumulation of overkill, the appropriately named system of MAD perpetuated stable, but not finite, deterrence.

Washington, backed as always by the quest for profit and influence on the part of the military-industrial complex, continued to take the lead in expanding the arms race. An exception to this role was the Soviet decision to install an antiballistic missile (ABM) system around Moscow. The weak defensive system hardly could have stopped a nuclear onslaught against the capital, but it strengthened the case of American proponents not only of ABMs but also of the new, far-reaching innovation of multiple independently targetable reentry vehicles (MIRVs). Under this technology, individual nuclear warheads could be released from a missile at various times and angles with the ability to reach multiple targets.

The Soviets, previously reluctant to sacrifice their primitive ABM system, were willing to negotiate to head off an explosive arms race in both offensive and defensive weapons against a technologically superior adversary. Washington announced and then canceled the Strategic Arms Limitation Talks (SALT), set to begin in late 1968, in response to the Warsaw Pact invasion of Czechoslovakia in August of that year. At the same time the United States had become deeply embroiled in a fruitless war in Southeast Asia. While détente lagged, the arms race, now centered around the research and development of multiple warhead missiles, gained momentum.

President Richard M. Nixon, little interested in arms control on its own merits, sought to revive negotiations in an effort to gain Soviet assistance in finding an acceptable basis for U.S. withdrawal from Vietnam. Simultaneously, he and his national security adviser, Henry Kissinger, sought to pit the now bitterly divided Soviets and Chinese against each other. Nixon and Kissinger agreed to limit ABMs in the historic 1972 SALT I Treaty, whose essence was mutual recognition of the futility of defensive systems, which could always be penetrated by an array of offensive weapons. Nixon and Kissinger threw away a golden opportunity to limit offensive MIRVs, which the Soviets soon developed in response to the American initiative and placed on their mammoth ICBMs. Similarly, Washington proceeded with the development of the Trident nuclear submarine, thus furthering its distinct advantage at sea.

With both superpowers amassing thousands of warheads within their strategic triad (land-, air-, and sea-based weapons), any international crisis carried with it the threat of a devastating nuclear holocaust. At least since the 1967 Six-Day War, the Middle East had been considered a likely site for the escalation of a regional conflict into a superpower confrontation. With the outbreak there of war in 1973, and with Washington's client Israel poised to deliver a humiliating defeat to Egypt, Brezhnev pointedly threatened Soviet intervention. Nixon, then in the midst of the Watergate scandal that later would force his resignation, ordered Defense Condition III, which put American military forces just short of full readiness for war for the first time since the Cuban missile crisis in 1962. The Middle East crisis quickly abated, however, when Egyptian president Anwar Sadat withdrew his request for Soviet support in favor of an international peacekeeping force.

Détente helped resolve the crisis in the Middle East, but the relaxation of Soviet-American relations proved short-lived. Détente broke down over a whole host of issues—East-West trade, human rights (including Jewish emigration from the USSR), and Soviet support for Marxist revolutionaries across the globe—and arms control was a casualty of this collapse. A summit meeting between President Gerald R. Ford and Brezhnev at Vladivostok in 1974 established ceilings on the number of delivery vehicles and MIRVs. Since the ceilings were actually higher than the numbers in existence, the agreement did not represent arms reductions at all, but both leaders planned a more comprehensive accord in a subsequent SALT II treaty. However, vocal critics of détente misrepresented the arms control process, arguing that it offered the Soviets a strategic advantage. Détente thereafter became a dirty word, and Ford held off on SALT II until after the 1976 presidential election, which he lost.

By the time Jimmy Carter came to the White House in 1977, the escalatory spiral continued. Pentagon planners had already authorized a new B-1 bomber, and cruise missiles that could be launched from land, air, or sea. These low-flying missiles were small, relatively cheap, and easy to hide, all of which made them destabilizing and an impediment to arms control. As was often the case, the United States initiated a new weapons system that contributed nothing to deterrence and therefore represented a pointless escalation that the Soviets were sure to match. Once the Pentagon and private defense contractors—the military-industrial complex— committed to a new system, however, its momentum could scarcely be stopped.

Criticism of détente and arms control mounted under Carter, whose focus on human rights abuses angered the Soviets as much as his cancellation of the B-1 bomber infuriated American hawks. He did go ahead with the cruise missile program while shelving SALT in the first half of his presidency. By the time Carter signed a SALT II treaty with the Soviets, he had already spent most of his political capital in the Senate to gain approval for the 1978 Panama Canal Treaty. To restore a consensus for arms control, he had to appease the critics who argued that the latest Soviet ICBM, the more accurate and heavyweight SS-18, could serve as a first-strike weapon. The fictional "window of vulnerability," reminiscent of the missile gap, held that the Soviets might wipe out the Minuteman force in a first strike, thus subjecting the United States to blackmail or nuclear devastation before it could react. This absurd scenario, aside from viewing the Soviets as suicidal, ignored some 7,000 American warheads at sea as well as bombers that might respond from scores of U.S. bases. The Kremlin leaders were hardly in a position to ignore those weapons even if they had been as demonic as Washington's hawks liked to picture them. But as arms-race historian John Newhouse has noted, "Common sense was no match for the minatory bolt from the blue; it had become the fashionable anxiety."

To appease his critics and build consensus, Carter authorized the MX, or experimental missile, which the Congressional Budget Office estimated would cost $60 billion. In 1979, NATO approved the deployment of 464 ground-launched cruise missiles and 108 Pershing II missiles throughout Western Europe, including West Germany. In that year the American political atmosphere turned sharply to the right. While hawks made an issue of the existence of a fictional Soviet "combat brigade" in Cuba, moderates withdrew their support for the SALT II treaty. Giving up on détente, the Soviets lent credence to worst-case scenarios in the West by invading Afghanistan in December 1979. A month earlier, Iranian militants had taken Americans hostage at the U.S. embassy in Tehran, initiating an agonizing crisis that strengthened the appeal of those who argued that the United States had become weak in defending its national interests. Carter's presidency collapsed in an overwhelming reelection defeat at the hands of Republican conservative Ronald Reagan.

Long considered too far to the right to gain the presidency, Reagan not only won two landslide elections but also became one of the most popular chief executives in American history. In a nation wounded by defeat in Vietnam, humiliated by the Iranian hostage crisis, and no longer the dominant superpower, Reagan's optimistic appeal to traditional values, including military supremacy, enjoyed broad support. The California Republican labeled the USSR an "evil empire" whose machinations were at the root of "all the unrest that is going on" in the world. Openly declaring that the United States would not settle for parity with the USSR, Reagan set off a paroxysm of military spending that threatened to destabilize the arms race. Like his hawkish subordinates Alexander Haig (State), Caspar Weinberger (Defense), and William Casey (CIA), Reagan believed in the "window of vulnerability" as well as that the Soviets were preparing to fight and win a nuclear war. Shunning all negotiations, the president committed the United States to a massive rearmament campaign reminiscent of NSC-68 in the Truman years.

The Reagan military buildup received much popular support, but it also alarmed many Americans and NATO allies. Antinuclear demonstrations erupted throughout the West, while the nuclear freeze movement—advocating an immediate halt to the rampaging arms race—gained momentum. Under public pressure, Reagan initiated the Strategic Arms Reduction Talks (START) and opened negotiations on intermediate-range nuclear forces (INF) in Europe in the midst of American plans to deploy new Pershing missiles. Negotiator Paul Nitze, a veteran Cold Warrior who had written NSC-68 more than thirty years before, came to terms with his Soviet counterpart during the famous "walk in the woods" in 1982, but Secretary Weinberger and his aides sabotaged what would have been a significant agreement requiring the Soviets to remove 80 percent of their mid-range missiles targeting Europe.

Brilliant as the "Great Communicator" but often out of touch on specific issues, Reagan took the lead on nuclear weapons only when some particular aspect struck his fancy. Such was the case with the Strategic Defense Initiative (SDI), promptly dubbed Star Wars after a popular science-fiction movie, which proposed to employ lasers, particle beams, and interceptors to shoot down incoming Soviet missiles, thus rendering nuclear weapons, as the president put it, "impotent and obsolete." Reagan stunned the public with his glib, but entirely sincere, announcement of the program in March 1983. The problem with SDI, besides its inherent impracticality, was that the ABM Treaty—probably the most successful U.S.-Soviet agreement in arms control—forbade testing and deployment of the type of defensive systems envisioned by Reagan. SDI would replace deterrence with an unworkable defensive system whose costs would far exceed any other program in the history of the weapons race. Soviet leader Yuri Andropov reacted sharply in *Pravda* four days after Reagan's speech, declaring that SDI would "open the floodgates of a runaway race of all types of strategic arms, both offensive and defensive. . . . Engaging in this is not just irresponsible, it is insane."

If SDI was one nail in the arms control coffin, then the shootdown of Korean Airlines Flight 007, which had strayed hundreds of miles into Soviet airspace on September 1, 1983, was another. The Soviets apparently mistook the jetliner for an American RC-135 spyplane, but the Reagan administration wasted no time in asserting that the Kremlin knowingly had shot down the civilian plane, killing all 269 passengers on board. Reagan used the incident to bolster his "evil empire" thesis and to lobby Congress for MX funding. Two months later the United States began deploying Persh-

ing II missiles in the NATO countries, prompting bitter denuncia-
tions from Moscow and mass demonstrations in Western Europe.
The USSR suspended all arms control talks. At this time, the popularity of the ABC television movie "The Day After," which depicted
the devastation of nuclear war, and books such as Jonathan Schell's
The Fate of the Earth attested to mounting anxieties. Veteran Cold
Warriors Robert McNamara, George Kennan, McGeorge Bundy,
and Gerard Smith—dubbed the Gang of Four by critics—launched
a campaign against the NATO policy of "first use," which envisioned using nuclear weapons in a conventional war. The Soviets
had previously renounced first use.

Following his overwhelming reelection in 1984, Reagan took
the advice of moderates such as Secretary of State George Shultz
as well as his wife Nancy to soften his hard line and leave a more
peaceful legacy. British prime minister Margaret Thatcher, herself
a staunch conservative, also urged Reagan to pursue arms control.
By far the most important development in the revival of a consensus for arms control, however, was the rise to power of a new Soviet leader, Mikhail Gorbachev. Committed to revolutionary changes
in world politics, he displayed an openness to accommodation with
the West and a flair for public relations that shattered all stereo-
types about the succession of dour Kremlin leaders. Gorbachev
hoped to forge a peaceful relationship with the West in order to
devote Soviet resources to deep-seated economic and political
problems.

Gorbachev urged massive reductions in military forces, including, above all, the superpowers' nuclear arsenals. He proved his
sincerity with concrete actions that could not be dismissed as typical Communist machinations. The Soviet leader denounced the war
in Afghanistan as a "bleeding wound" and initiated the withdrawal
of the Red Army from that country. He made dramatic unilateral
cuts in Soviet Warsaw Pact forces while allowing the Baltic republics and East European satellites to go their own way. Deemphasiz-
ing class struggle against capitalism, Gorbachev withdrew support
from Third World revolutionaries, including longtime clients such
as Cuba's Castro, and championed the United Nations as a forum
in which to settle international conflicts.

In no area did Gorbachev move more swiftly or decisively than
in his calls for reining in the nuclear arms race, which he denounced
as dangerous and excessive. Soon after taking power in 1985, he
unilaterally suspended nuclear testing, halted deployment of middle-

range weapons in Europe, and proposed mutual on-site inspections of each superpower's weapons installations, a move long resisted by previous Kremlin leaders. Gorbachev made a favorable impression on Reagan, as he had on Thatcher, in meetings at Geneva in 1985 and at Reykjavik in 1986. America's *Challenger* space shuttle and two rockets had exploded shortly after takeoff that year, which also included the worst nuclear disaster in history at Chernobyl, in the Ukraine. Such technological failures soured world opinion even further on nuclear devices and made a mockery of the concept of perfecting a space-based defense system.

These developments argued powerfully for a breakthrough in the arms control impasse, but Reagan's commitment to Star Wars remained the chief obstacle. Much to the chagrin of his advisers, the president was actually a radical who favored absolute solutions on arms control. The former actor sought a happy ending to the arms race saga. To Reagan, the ideal solution was either a perfect defense (which he promised to share with Moscow) through SDI, or an abolition of nuclear weapons. He and Gorbachev nearly agreed to the latter during fifteen hours of conversations at the Reykjavik summit, but the abolition option collapsed over Gorbachev's insistence on reaffirmation of the ABM Treaty and Reagan's refusal to refrain from SDI testing.

American hawks and European allies made it clear that abolition was going too far and that deterrence through MAD, the foundation of postwar defense, had to be maintained. As Secretary Shultz put it, "Reykjavik was too bold for the world." Although they failed to agree at Reykjavik, Reagan and Gorbachev now trusted one another sufficiently to take a small step forward in 1987 with the INF Treaty on forces in Europe. The agreement, signed in Washington in December 1987, included unprecedented Soviet accommodation on verification, allowing for the inspection of more than eighty East Bloc nuclear facilities compared with some thirty in Western Europe. Like past arms-control agreements, the INF Treaty was more symbolic than real, with the weapons destroyed amounting to less than 4 percent of the fifty thousand then in existence.

By the end of the Reagan administration, Gorbachev withdrew his opposition to SDI testing, perhaps realizing that the cost and impracticality of the program would eventually cause its own quiet death. Indeed, such has been the case. In the meantime, stunning political events—the East European revolutions of 1989, German reunification in 1990, and the collapse of the Soviet Union in 1991—

overshadowed arms control efforts. Following the disintegration of the USSR, Washington's policy focused on supporting Russian democracy and promoting solutions that would allow for stable command and control of the former Soviet Union's nuclear arsenal. Russian President Boris Yeltsin assured the West that he had established such control, but in a nation desperate for hard currency and riven by corruption a real danger existed of Russia's nuclear weapons technology being sold abroad.

The collapse of the Soviet Union gave rise to an interpretation vindicating American nuclear weapons policy, particularly during the Reagan years, and including most especially SDI. According to this interpretation, the arms race had forced the Soviets to spend themselves into oblivion, thus leading to the collapse of the USSR and the end of the Cold War. The Soviet economic collapse stemmed from an emphasis on heavy industry, armaments, and a large standing army. Not only the nuclear arms race but also the Cold War as a whole asked too much of the Soviet Union—hardly an "Upper Volta with rockets," as one wag once put it, yet in certain fundamental respects still a developing country.

More than the pressures of the Cold War, the collapse of the Soviet Union stemmed from the unworkability of, and inability to reform, a command economy that dated to Stalin's "revolution from above" in the 1920s and 1930s. That system produced an unwieldy, corrupt bureaucracy, offering little incentive or individual reward. Defense spending amounted to as much as one quarter of annual disposable income over the course of the Communist regime's history. The East-West conflict placed heavy demands on the Soviet system, but the system itself was flawed. Gorbachev's efforts to reform the Stalinist structure and revivify socialism encountered insuperable economic, ethnic, and political obstacles, leading to his own fall from power. Nevertheless, his statesmanlike pursuit of accommodation with the West, including a series of unilateral concessions and the repudiation of class struggle, led to the end of the Cold War.

Some scholars have viewed the arms race in a benign light, arguing that nuclear weapons have been responsible for the "long peace" (as John Lewis Gaddis describes it) that has prevailed between the Cold War adversaries. They argue that deterrence backed by MAD helped ensure that the great-power conflict remained "cold," rather than escalating into a "hot" shooting war. This argument may contain some truth, yet it is flawed on at least two counts.

First, even though the superpowers themselves never fought directly, the Cold War exacerbated scores of regional conflicts, causing destruction and millions of casualties in Korea, Southeast Asia, parts of Africa, and Central America. These regions witnessed no "long peace." Second, rather than the existence of nuclear weapons, memories of the horrors of World War II and the knowledge that another conventional war would be devastating were sufficient to keep the peace between the Soviet Union and the United States. The simplest explanation for the "long peace" is the best one: East-West ideological conflict, including economic and political competition, could exist without a military conflict. The superpowers remained at peace because there was insufficient cause for war. Rather than keeping the peace, the arms race destabilized relations, as in the Cuban missile crisis, when nuclear weapons were at the center of anxieties that nearly brought about a devastating war. Once the atom had been split, the arms race became inevitable. It would not have been possible for the superpowers to refrain from devising new and more powerful weapons as well as the means of delivering them to their targets. Given these realities, deterrence through MAD was inevitable.

The tragedy of the weapons race, for which the United States must take primary responsibility as its undisputed leader, was not only its existence but also the excesses that characterized it. A prudent policy based on finite deterrence backed by, let us say, two hundred nuclear warheads that could be delivered by various means from air, land, and sea would have comprised a sufficient, invulnerable retaliatory force. As long as the Pentagon maintained such a force—which it possessed through the strategic triad and especially through its untrackable nuclear submarines—MAD would be assured. In other words, the American-led escalation beyond that sufficient, invulnerable retaliatory force wasted resources, institutionalized the military-industrial complex, and promoted international instability. Offensive first-strike weapons, such as MIRVs and cruise missiles, which were inherently escalatory, could have been proscribed by treaty. Washington could have joined Moscow in accepting the limitations inherent in finite deterrence, renouncing first use and refraining from developing "war-fighting" weapons, all in recognition that "limited nuclear war" was the ultimate oxymoron. Had both sides agreed upon MAD (backed by finite, rather than infinite, deterrence) and pursued arms control more diligently, the arms "race" need not have occurred at all. Neither side intended to unleash nuclear war, yet both sides lacked the courage, at least until Gorbachev came to power, to attempt to rein in the spiraling competition. Meaningful East-West arms control agreements based on finite deterrence would have saved billions of dollars, reduced global anxiety, and, perhaps most important of all, provided a basis for limiting the proliferation of the weapons of mass destruction.

Instead, the poor example set by the superpowers has encouraged other nations to develop nuclear weapons of their own. Britain, France, and China quickly followed the U.S.-Soviet lead in the 1950s and early 1960s before the superpowers made efforts to contain a global arms race. The 1968 Nonproliferation Treaty failed, however, to gain the adherence of "threshold" states such as Argentina, Brazil, India, Israel, Pakistan, and South Africa. Today, nations with demonstrable hostility toward the West—including Iran, Iraq, Libya, and North Korea—are on the nuclear threshold.

The end of the Cold War has not brought a resolution of the nuclear arms race. If the United States intends to remain a leader of the post-Cold War world, it should adopt a policy of finite deterrence and make an international cause célèbre of its willingness to destroy thousands of superfluous nuclear weapons in the interests of a more peaceful world. Only then can it attempt, without hypocrisy, to encourage other states to refrain from deploying their own nuclear forces.

Sources and Suggested Readings

Alperovitz, Gar. *Atomic Diplomacy: Hiroshima and Potsdam*. New York, 1985.

Baucom, Donald R. *The Origins of SDI, 1944–1983*. Lawrence, KS, 1992.

Blight, James G., and Welch, David A. *On the Brink: Americans and Soviets Reexamine the Cuban Missile Crisis*. New York, 1990.

Bundy, McGeorge. *Danger and Survival: Choices about the Bomb in the First Fifty Years*. New York, 1988.

Craig, Paul P., and Jungerman, John A. *Nuclear Arms Race: Technology and Society*. New York, 1986.

Divine, Robert A. *Eisenhower and Sputnik*. New York, 1993.

Freedman, Lawrence. *The Evolution of Nuclear Strategy*. New York, 1989.

Gaddis, John Lewis. *The Long Peace: Inquiries into the History of the Cold War*. New York, 1987.

Garrity, Patrick J., and Maaranen, Steven A. *Nuclear Weapons in the Changing World*. New York, 1992.

Garthoff, Raymond. *Détente and Confrontation: American-Soviet Relations from Nixon to Reagan*. Washington, DC, 1985.

George, Alexander L., and Smoke, Richard L. *Deterrence in American Foreign Policy: Theory and Practice*. New York, 1974.

Gorbachev, Mikhail. *Perestroika*. New York, 1985.

Herken, Gregg. *The Winning Weapon: The Atomic Bomb in the Cold War, 1945–1950*. New York, 1980.

———. *Cardinal Choices: Presidential Science Advising from the Atomic Bomb to SDI*. New York, 1992.

Hersey, John. *Hiroshima*. New York, 1946.

Holloway, David. *The Soviet Union and the Arms Race*. New Haven, CT, 1983.

———. *Stalin and the Bomb: The Soviet Union and Atomic Energy, 1939–1956*. New Haven, CT, 1994.

Kaplan, Fred. *The Wizards of Armageddon*. New York, 1983.

Kennan, George F. *The Nuclear Delusion: Soviet-American Relations in the Atomic Age*. New York, 1983.

Lebow, Richard Ned. *We All Lost the Cold War*. Princeton, NJ, 1994.

Newhouse, John. *War and Peace in the Nuclear Age*. New York, 1990.

Schell, Jonathan. *The Fate of the Earth*. New York, 1983.

Seaborg, Glenn T. *Kennedy, Khrushchev, and the Test Ban*. Berkeley, CA, 1981.

Sherry, Michael. *The Rise of American Air Power: The Creation of Armageddon*. New Haven, CT, 1987.

Sherwin, Martin A. *A World Destroyed: Hiroshima and the Origins of the Arms Race*. New York, 1987.

Smoke, Richard L. *National Security and the Nuclear Dilemma*. New York, 1983.

Talbott, Strobe. *Deadly Gambits: The Reagan Administration and the Stalemate in Nuclear Arms Control*. New York, 1985.

Union of Concerned Scientists. *The Fallacy of Star Wars*. New York, 1983.

The Vietnam War

George C. Herring

The Vietnam War had profound consequences for the United States. The American phase of the conflict lasted for twelve years (1961–1973), longer than any other war in which the nation has been involved. It took the lives of more than fifty-eight thousand Americans and cost, by some estimates, more than $167 billion. The war set off a runaway inflation that devastated the U.S. economy in the 1970s. It divided Americans as no other event since their own Civil War a century earlier. It brought fundamental changes in Washington's foreign policy, discrediting the policy of containment, undermining the consensus that supported it, and leaving it at least temporarily in disarray.

Understanding Vietnam requires addressing two fundamental questions. First, why did the United States commit billions of dollars and a large part of its military power to an area so remote and seemingly so insignificant? And second, why, despite this huge commitment, did the world's richest and most powerful nation fail to achieve its objective—the preservation of an independent, non-Communist South Vietnam?

The question of causation in war is always complex, and in the case of Vietnam it was especially so. America's direct involvement spanned the quarter century between its decision in 1950 to aid France in suppressing the Vietnamese revolution and the fall of Saigon to the North Vietnamese in 1975. Over a period of years the commitment expanded incrementally from aid to France, to support for an independent South Vietnam after the 1954 Geneva Conference, to the pledge of U.S. military power in 1965. America went to war not from one major decision but rather as the result of a series of separate, seemingly small decisions over the period between 1950 and 1965. Amid this complexity, it is necessary to try to single out the common threads, the patterns of thought that determined the fateful course chosen.

In the broadest sense, U.S. involvement in Vietnam stemmed from the interaction of two major phenomena of the post-World

War II era: decolonization—the breakup of the old colonial empires—and the Cold War. The rise of nationalism and the weakness of the European colonial powers combined at the end of World War II to destroy a system that had been an established feature of world politics for centuries. Changes of this magnitude do not occur smoothly, and in this case the result was turmoil and, in some areas, war. In Asia, the British and Dutch grudgingly recognized the inevitable and granted independence to their colonies within several years after World War II. The French, on the other hand, refused to concede the inevitability of decolonization. They attempted to regain control of their Indochinese colonies and to put down the Vietnamese revolution by force, sparking in 1946 a war that in its various phases would not end until the fall of Saigon in the spring of 1975.

What was unique—and from the American standpoint most significant—about the conflict in Vietnam was that the nationalist movement, the Vietminh, was led by Communists. The father of the revolution, the charismatic Ho Chi Minh, was a longtime Communist operative who had devoted his life to gaining independence and national unity for his country. Well organized and tightly disciplined, the Communists took advantage of the fragmentation among the other nationalist groups to establish their own preeminence. During World War II they exploited popular opposition to the French and to Japanese occupation forces to build support for the revolution, and they moved adeptly to fill the vacuum when the Japanese surrendered in August 1945. During the ensuing war with France, the Vietminh solidified its claim to the mantle of Vietnamese nationalism. In all the former European colonies in Asia, only in Vietnam did Communists direct the nationalist movement, and this would have enormous long-range implications, transforming what began as a struggle against French colonialism into an international conflict of vast proportions.

At the very time that the Communist-led Vietminh was engaged in a bloody struggle with France, the Cold War was assuming global dimensions, and from an early stage Washington perceived the war in Vietnam largely in terms of its conflict with the Soviet Union. As early as 1946, Americans viewed Ho and the Vietminh as instruments of the Soviet drive for world domination, directed and controlled by the Kremlin. This view was not seriously questioned in or out of government until the United States was involved in full-scale war in Vietnam.

Reality was much more complex than Americans perceived it. Ho and his top lieutenants were Communists committed to establishing in Vietnam, at the first opportunity, a state based on Marxist-Leninist doctrine. In addition, from 1949 onward, Communist China and the Soviet Union aided the Vietminh and later North Vietnam in various ways. This being said, the view that the Vietnamese revolution was a mere extension of the Communist drive for world conquest needs qualification at several points. Ho initiated the revolution without any explicit direction from Moscow, and he sustained it until 1949 without any external support. The revolution grew in strength because it was able to identify with Vietnamese nationalism and had a dynamism of its own quite apart from international communism. Moreover, the support provided by the Soviet Union and China was neither unlimited nor unequivocal, and there is ample evidence that the three nations did not share unanimity of purpose. At the Geneva Conference in 1954, for example, the two major Communist powers, for their own reasons, forced upon the Vietminh a settlement with France that provided for the partition of Vietnam, and they gave nothing more than lip service to the provisions of the Geneva Agreements that called for elections to unify the country.

The Vietnamese were therefore keenly aware that they could not always depend upon their allies. In the case of China, moreover, they feared that dependence could lead to domination. "It is better to sniff French dung for a while than eat China's all our life," Ho had said in 1946, rationalizing his efforts to strike a deal with France and expressing in graphic fashion Vietnam's historic fears of its huge northern neighbor. Thus, the relationship between the Vietnamese Communists and their allies appears to have been based on a normal pattern of relations among nation-states rather than on ideological harmony and shared goals. America's assessment of the dynamics of the conflict in Vietnam was wide of the mark.

From 1949 onward, U.S. policy in Vietnam also was based on the premise that the fall of Vietnam to communism would threaten vital interests. There is more than a bit of irony here, for at least until the 1940s Vietnam had never been of any significance to the United States. To understand why it suddenly became so important, it is necessary to look at the reorientation of Washington's foreign policy after the fall of China to the Communists in 1949 and to the emergence of a worldview best expressed in the National Security Council study, NSC-68. Drafted in early 1950 in response to the debacle in China and the Soviet Union's explosion of an atomic weapon, NSC-68 set forth as its fundamental premise that the USSR, "animated by a new fanatical faith," was seeking to "impose its absolute authority on the rest of the world." It already had achieved major conquests in Eastern Europe and more recently in China, and American policymakers, in the frantic milieu of early 1950, concluded that Soviet expansion had reached a point beyond which it must not be permitted to go. "Any substantial further extension of the area under the control of the Kremlin," NSC-68 warned, "would raise the possibility that no coalition adequate to confront the Kremlin with greater strength could be assembled."

In this context of a world divided into two hostile power blocs in a fragile balance, a zero-sum game in which any gain for communism was automatically a loss for the United States, areas such as Vietnam, which had been of no more than marginal importance, suddenly took on great significance. The onset of the Korean War in June 1950 seemed to confirm the assumptions of NSC-68 and also suggested that the Communists were now prepared to use military invasion to upset the balance of power. Faced with this challenge, the Truman administration in 1950 extended to East Asia a containment policy that had been restricted to Europe. The first American commitment to Vietnam, a commitment to assist the French in suppressing the Vietminh revolution, was part of this broader attempt to contain Communist expansion in Asia.

There were other, more specific reasons why U.S. policymakers attached growing significance to Vietnam after 1950. The first, usually called the "domino theory," was the idea that the fall of Vietnam could cause the fall of Indochina and then the rest of Southeast Asia, with repercussions extending west to India and east to Japan and the Philippines. This fear of a chain reaction in Southeast Asia was initially set forth by the Joint Chiefs of Staff in 1950, and events in the late 1940s and early 1950s seemed to give it credence. Mao Zedong's Communists had just taken over in China. The departure of the colonial powers left a vacuum in Southeast Asia; Indochina, Burma, and Malaya were swept by revolution; and the newly independent government of Indonesia seemed highly vulnerable. Because of its location on China's southern border and because it appeared in the most imminent danger, Vietnam was considered the most important—"the keystone in the arch," as Senator John F. Kennedy put it, "the finger in the dike." If it fell, all of Southeast Asia might be lost, costing the United States access to vital raw materials and strategic bases. Primarily for this reason the United States went to the aid of France in 1950, despite its compunctions about supporting colonialism, and it stepped into the breach when France was defeated in 1954.

The domino theory was reinforced and in time supplanted by the notion that the United States must stand firm in Vietnam to demonstrate its determination to defend vital interests across the world. Acceptance of this principle of credibility reflected the intensity of the Cold War, the influence of certain perceived lessons of history, and the desire on the part of American policymakers to find a means of averting nuclear catastrophe. During the most intense period of Cold War confrontation, these policymakers felt certain that what they did in one area of the world might have a decisive impact in others. If they showed firmness, it might deter Soviet or Chinese aggression; if they showed weakness, the adversary would be tempted to take steps that might ultimately leave no option but nuclear war. The so-called Manchurian or Munich analogy—the idea that the failure of the Western democracies to stand firm against Japanese or German aggression in the 1930s had encouraged further aggression—reinforced the idea of credibility. The obvious lesson was that to avoid war a firm stand must be taken at the outset.

Even after the Sino-Soviet split dramatically altered the traditional contours of the Cold War in the mid-1960s, the notion of credibility seemed valid. Of the two Communist powers, China appeared to be the more militant and aggressive, the more deeply committed to world revolution. It was closely allied with North Vietnam, and indeed some U.S. policymakers viewed Hanoi as essentially an instrument of Beijing's policy. North Vietnam had to be deterred to prevent the expansion of Chinese influence in Asia. Even in the case of the Soviet Union, which appeared to be passive and generally innocuous in the aftermath of the Cuban missile crisis, there seemed good reason for the United States to display firmness. Rivalry with China might force the Soviets once again to assume an aggressive posture. A firm stand in Vietnam, it was reasoned, would discourage any tendency toward a return to adventurism and reinforce the trend toward détente. It also might discourage other potential troublemakers, such as Cuba's Fidel Castro, from attempting to disrupt world order.

In searching for the roots of commitment in Vietnam, a second factor deserves attention: the assumption shared by administrations from Truman to Johnson that the fall of Vietnam to communism would have disastrous consequences at home. This assumption also stemmed from perceived lessons of history, in this case the rancorous and divisive debate following the fall of China in 1949 and Republican exploitation of it at the polls in 1952. Again, the conclusion was that no administration could survive the loss of Vietnam. Although a Democrat, President Kennedy had attacked Harry S. Truman for losing China. He had been a participant in the debate and vividly remembered it. He seems to have been sufficiently frustrated by Vietnam in late 1963 that he at least considered the possibility of withdrawal, but he was convinced that he could not do so until after he had been reelected. "If I tried to pull out now," Kennedy said, "we would have another Joe McCarthy Red Scare on our hands." Lyndon B. Johnson shared similar fears on numerous occasions, exclaiming that he was not going to be the president who saw "Southeast Asia go the way China went."

In analyzing the sources of American involvement in Vietnam, several comments seem in order. First, Vietnam was not deemed significant in and of itself for its raw materials, its naval bases, or other tangible reasons. It was considered vital primarily because of the presumed effects its loss would have on other areas and for its symbolic importance. Still, the more that Washington's policymakers stressed its significance, the more important it grew until it actually became a test case of American credibility to opponents, to allies, and to the United States itself. The fact that the nation's commitment became increasingly a matter of prestige had important, although seemingly paradoxical, consequences. On the one hand, it made extrication all the more difficult. Interests may be easier to compromise than prestige. On the other hand, the absence of any compelling intrinsic significance in Vietnam or any direct threat to American security made it more and more difficult to justify the sacrifices that the nation was called upon to make. This paradox was at least partially responsible for the division and frustration that accompanied the war.

The containment policy now seems misguided, both generally and in its application to Vietnam. Soviet goals were more the product of traditional Russian nationalism than ideology. The so-called Communist bloc was never a monolith; it was torn by division from the start, and the fragmentation became more pronounced. There was never a zero-sum game. What appeared to be a major victory for the Soviet Union in China in 1949, for example, turned out to be something quite different. In most parts of the world neither the Soviet Union nor the United States prevailed, and pluralism was the norm.

In applying containment to Vietnam, the United States drastically misjudged the internal dynamics of the conflict. It attributed to an expansionist communism a war that began as a revolution against French colonialism. It exaggerated as well the consequences of doing nothing. There is reason to doubt whether the domino theory would have operated if Vietnam had fallen earlier. Nationalism has proven the most potent and enduring force in recent history, and the nations of Southeast Asia, long suspicious of China and Vietnam, would have resisted mightily. Moreover, by making the war a test case of American credibility, U.S. policymakers may have made its consequences greater than they would have otherwise. In short, by rigidly adhering to a narrow, one-dimensional worldview, without taking into account the nature and importance of local forces, the United States placed itself in an untenable position in Vietnam from the start.

Another perplexing question is: Why, despite its vast power, did the United States fail to achieve its objective? It became fashionable in the aftermath of the war to argue that it failed because it did not use its military power wisely and decisively. Johnson and Defense Secretary Robert S. McNamara placed restrictions on the military that prevented it from winning the war. Such an argument is shortsighted in terms of the long history of U.S. involvement in Vietnam. It ignores the fact that the military solution sought after 1965 followed fifteen years of policy failure. It is therefore necessary to look to the period from 1950 to 1965 to understand fully America's ultimate failure in Vietnam.

During those years, U.S. policy went through three distinct phases. Between 1950 and 1954 the United States supported French efforts to suppress the Vietminh revolution, to the extent by 1954 of paying close to 80 percent of the war's cost. From 1954 to 1959, America helped ease the defeated French out of Vietnam, served as midwife for the birth of South Vietnam, and, violating the letter and spirit of the Geneva Accords, tried to sustain an independent government below the 17th parallel. From 1959 to 1965, through increased economic and military aid and eventually thousands of military "advisers," the United States tried to help the South Vietnamese government put down the insurgency, which began in the South and by 1965 enjoyed large-scale support from North

Vietnam. With each step along the way, its policy failed to produce the desired results, leading to escalation of the U.S. commitment. In July 1965, Johnson was left the unpleasant choice of calling in American combat forces or accepting a South Vietnamese defeat.

In the case of the French, the so-called First Indochina War, the explanation for failure seems reasonably clear. France's goal, the retention of some level of imperial control in Vietnam, ran against one of the main currents of post-World War II history. Throughout Asia and Africa, nationalist revolutions eventually prevailed, and even when imperial nations were able to win wars against insurgencies, as the French later did in Algeria, they were forced to concede independence. American policymakers understood the problem all too well, but they could find no way to resolve it. They pressed the French to fight on to victory in Vietnam while at the same time urging them to leave as soon as the war ended. This contradiction made little sense from the French point of view, and, when faced with the choice of fighting for Vietnamese independence or withdrawing, the French chose the latter. After their disastrous defeat at the battle of Dienbienphu in May 1954, they agreed at Geneva to a negotiated settlement that provided for their ultimate withdrawal from Vietnam.

While Paris was negotiating, Washington was planning ways to create a bulwark against further Communist expansion in Southeast Asia by making permanent the temporary partition of Vietnam. For a variety of reasons this effort to create an independent, non-Communist South Vietnam also eventually failed. First, and probably most important, was the magnitude of the challenge itself. Had the United States looked all over the world it might not have found a less promising place for an experiment in nation building. The economy of South Vietnam was shattered from ten years of war, the departure of the French had left a gaping political vacuum, and France had destroyed the traditional structure of Vietnamese politics but had left nothing to replace it. As a result, there was no firmly established political tradition, no institutions of government, and no native elite capable of exercising effective leadership. In addition, South Vietnam was fragmented by a multitude of conflicting political, religious, and ethnic groups, and the emigration of nearly one million Catholics from North Vietnam after 1954 added to the already complex and conflict-ridden picture. Under these circumstances, there may have been built-in limits to what the United States or any nation could have accomplished in South Vietnam.

Second, America's nation-building policies were often misguided or misapplied. In the early years, U.S. advisers concentrated on building a South Vietnamese army to meet the threat of invasion from the North, a logical step in terms of the situation in Vietnam and earlier experience in Korea but one that left the South Vietnamese poorly equipped to cope with the developing insurgency in the late 1950s. By contrast, too little attention was devoted during these years to mobilizing the peasantry and promoting pacification in the countryside. When the United States attempted to deal with these problems in the early 1960s, it applied methods that had worked elsewhere but adapted poorly to Vietnam. The strategic hamlet program, promoted by the Kennedy administration with great enthusiasm, is a case in point. The idea of bringing peasants from isolated villages into settlements where they could be protected from insurgents had worked earlier in Malaya. However, in Malaya the insurgents were Chinese, and it was relatively easy to guard against infiltration; in Vietnam the insurgents were Vietnamese who had lived and worked with the villagers for years, and the hamlets were infiltrated with ease. In Malaya, moreover, the peasants were resettled without major disruption, but in Vietnam they had to be removed from lands on which their families had lived for centuries and that were regarded as sacred. Sometimes they had to be forcibly removed and their old homes burned behind them. They were left rootless and resentful, easy prey for recruiters from the insurgency.

A third important reason was South Vietnam's leadership, a problem all too clearly revealed in the frustrating and ultimately tragic American partnership with its first president, Ngo Dinh Diem. In terms of his anticommunism and his nationalism, Diem appeared to fit Washington's needs perfectly, and in his first years in power he seemed to be a miracle worker, stabilizing a chaotic South Vietnam in a way no one had thought possible. In time, however, his deficiencies became all too apparent. It was not simply that his government was corrupt and undemocratic. Such governments have survived for years, and Diem may have had logic and history on his side when he insisted that democracy would not work in Vietnam. The problems were more basic. He was a poor administrator who tolerated far too much from his family, particularly his notorious brother, Ngo Dinh Nhu. Most important, Diem lacked any real blueprint for Vietnam. He seemed content simply to preside over the government, but he proved incapable of leading his country, mobilizing the peasantry, or coping with the insurgency.

Diem was also fiercely independent, and this attribute posed a dilemma that the United States never resolved. Americans came in time to see his weaknesses, but they could not persuade him to change or impose their will on him. They saw no alternative to Diem, however, and feared that if he were removed it would only lead to greater chaos. Thus, the United States, with some reluctance, stood by him for nine years as the political and military situation in South Vietnam deteriorated. "Sink or swim with Ngo Dinh Diem," a critical journalist summed up American policy. It was only when Diem's actions produced a full-scale political upheaval among Buddhists in South Vietnam's major cities in 1963, and when it was learned that he and his brother were secretly negotiating with North Vietnam, that the United States finally concluded that he must go.

As many observers had predicted, the overthrow of Diem in November 1963 offered no real solutions, only more problems. The army generals who replaced Diem were, for the most part, Western educated. They lacked close touch with their own people and even less than Diem had the capacity to unify a fragmented society. Divided among themselves, they spent their energy on intrigue, and one coup followed another in such rapid fashion that it was almost impossible to keep up with the daily changes in government. Thus, by mid-1965 the United States found itself in a position that it never really had wanted and whose dangers it recognized—that of an imperial power seeking to fill a political and military vacuum.

Focusing on American and South Vietnamese failures provides only a partial picture. It is also necessary to analyze why the South Vietnamese insurgents and their northern supporters had reached the verge of victory by 1965. It is now evident from captured documents that, by 1957, Diem had nearly exterminated the remnants of the Vietminh in South Vietnam. Alarmed by their plight and the growing certainty that the elections called for at Geneva would not be held, they began to mobilize to salvage the revolution of 1945. The insurgents effectively exploited the unrest caused by Diem's heavy-handed methods. In many areas they implemented land reform programs and lowered taxes, policies that contrasted favorably with those instituted by the government. They also skillfully employed selective violence by assassinating unpopular government officials and also mobilized the peasantry. Organizing themselves into the National Liberation Front (NLF) in 1960, the insurgents not only controlled large segments of the land and the population but developed a formidable army as well.

North Vietnam's role remains a matter of controversy. It seems clear that Hanoi did not instigate the revolution in the South, as the U.S. government claimed at the time, nor did it remain an innocent and even indifferent bystander, as American critics of the war insisted. The revolution did begin spontaneously in the South, perhaps even against Hanoi's instructions. Once it started, however, Hanoi did not stand by and watch. Fearful that the southern revolutionaries might fail—or succeed—without its help, it began to send cadres into the South to assume leadership of the insurgency. In 1959 the Democratic Republic of Vietnam approved the initiation of "armed struggle" against the Diem regime. In the aftermath of the overthrow of Diem, North Vietnam decided to undertake a major escalation of the conflict, even to the point of sending its own military units into South Vietnam to fight intact. It apparently took this step in the expectation that the United States, when faced with certain defeat, would withdraw as it had in China in 1949 rather than risk its own men and resources.

The North Vietnamese gravely miscalculated. Confronting the collapse of South Vietnam in 1965, Johnson never seriously considered withdrawing. Determined to uphold a commitment of more than a decade's standing and certain that tiny North Vietnam could not defy the will of the world's greatest power, the president in February 1965 initiated a regular systematic bombing of the North and then in July made what amounted to an open-ended commitment to use whatever ground combat forces were needed to determine the outcome of the war. In making this latter commitment, Johnson also miscalculated. He rejected the proposal of Joint Chiefs of Staff to mobilize the reserves. To avoid any risk of confrontation with China and the Soviet Union and, more important, to prevent what he called that "bitch of a war" from interfering with "the woman I really love"—the Great Society reform program at home—he escalated the war quietly while imposing the lightest possible burden on the American people. He did so in the expectation that the gradual increase of military pressure on North Vietnam would persuade it to abandon the struggle in the South. "I'm going up old Ho Chi Minh's leg an inch at a time," he explained.

Johnson's strategy of gradual escalation did not work. The United States expanded the tonnage of bombs dropped on North Vietnam from 63,000 in 1965 to 226,000 in 1967, inflicting an estimated $600 million in damages on a primitive economy. The gradualist approach gave the North Vietnamese time to disperse their vital resources, repair the damage, develop an effective air defense system, and adapt in other ways. It encouraged—and probably permitted—them to persevere, and China and the Soviet Union helped make up the losses that they sustained. As a result, the bombing did not decisively affect North Vietnam's will to resist, and its very intensity and the fact that it was carried out by a rich, advanced nation against a poor, small one gave the North Vietnamese a propaganda card that they played with consummate skill. In the United States, and indeed throughout the world, the bombing became a major target of criticism and a symbol of the alleged immorality of American intervention in Vietnam.

The strategy of attrition implemented by General William C. Westmoreland on the ground in South Vietnam also failed. The availability of sanctuaries in Laos, Cambodia, and across the demilitarized zone permitted North Vietnam to control its losses, dictate the pace and intensity of the war, and hold the strategic initiative.

VIETNAM, 1966. President Johnson and General William Westmoreland review U.S. troops. (Lyndon B. Johnson Library)

If at any point losses became excessive, the enemy could withdraw and take time to recover. If, on the other hand, it wished to step up the war, it could do so at times and places of its own choosing. It even had the ability to control the level of American casualties, and in time this became of considerable importance. The attrition strategy thus represented an open-ended commitment that required increasing manpower and produced growing casualties without any signs of victory. By the end of 1967 the United States had more than 500,000 troops in Vietnam and nothing to show for it except a bloody stalemate.

At the same time, Americanization of the war was counterproductive in terms of the fundamental goal of building a self-sustaining South Vietnam. The South Vietnamese army was relegated to pacification duty, which many good soldiers considered demeaning. The United States dropped more bombs on South Vietnam than on the North, and the heavy bombing, along with massive artillery fire, laid waste much of the countryside and made refugees of more than one-third of the population. The infusion of hundreds of thousands of men and billions of dollars into a small and backward country had a profoundly destabilizing effect. It was as though the United States was trying to "build a house with a bulldozer and wrecking crane," one American official later observed.

As the war dragged on, opposition in the United States assumed major proportions. "Hawks" protested President Johnson's policy of gradual escalation, urging the use of any means necessary to achieve victory. On the other side, a heterogeneous group of "doves" increasingly questioned the wisdom and morality of the war and began to conduct protest marches and encourage draft resistance and other forms of antiwar activity. The mounting cost of the conflict was more important than the antiwar movement in causing opposition among the general public. Increased casualties, indications that more troops would be required, and Johnson's belated request for new taxes combined by late 1967 to produce a sharp decline in public support for the war and the president's handling of it.

The Tet offensive of 1968 brought Johnson's gradual escalation of the war to an inglorious end. In a strictly military sense, the United States and South Vietnam prevailed, repelling a series of massive NLF assaults against the urban areas of the South and inflicting huge casualties. At the same time, Tet had a tremendous psychological impact in the United States, raising serious questions about whether anything could be achieved that would be worth the cost. In March 1968, responding to growing signs of public frustration and impatience, Johnson rejected General Westmore-land's request for an additional two hundred thousand troops and for expansion of the war, cut back the bombing of North Vietnam, launched a diplomatic initiative eventually leading to peace negotiations in Paris, and withdrew from the presidential race.

It would be seven more years before the war finally ended. Recognizing that public frustration required him at least to scale down U.S. involvement, Johnson's successor, Richard M. Nixon, pursued an approach that he called Vietnamization, initiating a series of phased withdrawals of American troops while expanding aid to the South Vietnamese army to prepare it to take over the brunt of the fighting. Nixon also escalated the war by authorizing "incursions" into the North Vietnamese sanctuaries in Cambodia and Laos to bolster Vietnamization. When the North Vietnamese in the spring of 1972 launched a major offensive against South Vietnam, he resumed the bombing of North Vietnam and mined Haiphong harbor. Nixon was able to save South Vietnam, but opposition at home continued to grow. In 1973, without resolving the fundamental issue of the war—the political future of South Vietnam—he was forced to agree to a settlement permitting extrication of U.S. forces. That issue was settled two years later when North Vietnam launched a massive conventional invasion of the South. By that time, Nixon had resigned as a result of the Watergate scandal, and the United States stood by helplessly while an ally of twenty years went down to defeat.

Although American strategies in Vietnam were clearly flawed, the argument that an unrestricted use of military power could have produced victory at an acceptable cost is not persuasive. The capacity of air power to cripple a preindustrial nation was probably quite limited, and there is considerable evidence to suggest that, even though its cities and industries were destroyed, North Vietnam was prepared to fight on, underground if necessary. Invasion of the sanctuaries and ground operations in the North might have made the strategy of attrition more workable, but they also would have enormously increased the costs of the war at a time when American resources were already stretched thin. Neither of these approaches would have solved what was always the central problem: the political viability of South Vietnam. Each ran serious risks of Soviet and Chinese intervention. Also, even if the United States

DISCUSSING VIETNAM STRATEGY. President Johnson confers in February 1968 with Special Assistant for National Security Affairs Walt W. Rostow. (Lyndon B. Johnson Library)

had been able to subdue North Vietnam militarily without provoking outside intervention, it still would have faced the dangerous and costly task of occupying a hostile nation along China's southern border while simultaneously containing an insurgency in South Vietnam.

In the final analysis, the causes of American failure must be found as much in Vietnam as in Washington. In South Vietnam the United States attempted a truly formidable undertaking on the basis of a very weak foundation. For nearly twenty years, Americans struggled to establish a viable nation in the face of internal insurgency and external invasion, but the rapid collapse of South Vietnam after their withdrawal suggests how little was really accomplished. The United States could never find leaders capable of mobilizing the disparate population of South Vietnam. It launched a vast array of ambitious and expensive programs to promote sound government, win the hearts and minds of the people, and wage war against the insurgents. When its client state was on the verge of collapse in 1965, it filled the vacuum by putting in its own military forces. The more it did, however, the more it induced a state of dependency among those whom it was trying to help. Tragically, right up to the fall of Saigon in 1975, South Vietnamese leaders expected the Americans to return and save them from defeat.

The United States also drastically underestimated the determination of its adversary. The North Vietnamese made huge blunders of their own and paid an enormous price for their success. At the same time, they were tightly mobilized and regimented, and they were fanatically committed to their goals. They were fighting on familiar soil and used methods perfected in the war against France. They skillfully employed the strategy of protracted war, perceiving that the Americans, like the French, could become impatient and that, if they bled long enough, they might grow weary of the war. "You will kill ten of our men, but we will kill one of yours," Ho once remarked, "and in the end it is you who will tire." The comment was made to a French official on the eve of the First Indochina War, but it just as easily could have been said of the American phase.

The circumstances of the war thus posed a dilemma that Washington never really understood, much less resolved. The attainment of American goals would probably have required the physical annihilation of North Vietnam, a distasteful and extremely costly course of action that held out a serious threat of Soviet and Chinese intervention. The only other way was to establish a viable South Vietnam, but, given the weak foundation it worked from, not to mention the strength of the internal revolution, this course was probably beyond its capability. The United States very well may have placed itself in a no-win situation.

For Vietnam, the principal legacy of the war was continued human suffering. The greatest losers were the South Vietnamese. Many of those who remained endured poverty, oppression, forced labor, and "re-education" camps. More than 1.5 million so-called boat people fled the country after 1975. Some perished in flight; others languished in squalid refugee camps in Southeast Asia. Between 750,000 and 1 million South Vietnamese eventually resettled in the United States.

Even for the winners, victory was a bittersweet prize. The Hanoi regime attained, at least temporarily, its goal of hegemony in Indochina but at an enormous cost. In time, it became bogged down in its own "Vietnam" in Cambodia, waging a costly and ultimately unsuccessful counterinsurgency against stubborn Cambodian guerrillas. Its long-standing goal of a unified and independent Vietnam was achieved in name only. Historic differences between the North and the South were exacerbated during three decades of war, and even the most heavy-handed methods could not force the freewheeling and resilient South into a made-in-Hanoi mold. Most mortifying for many Vietnamese, for more than a decade after the war their country remained dependent on the Soviet Union.

For all Vietnamese the most pressing legacy of the war was grinding poverty and economic deprivation. Thirty years of conflict left the economy in shambles, and continued high military expenditures and the government's ill-conceived efforts to force industrialization and collectivize agriculture made the situation worse. A *doi moi* (renovation) program launched in the mid-1980s introduced free-market incentives and brought significant gains, especially in agriculture, and the end of a U.S. embargo in 1994 promised an infusion of investment capital and expanded trade. Even then, Vietnam remained one of the world's poorest countries, and an antiquated infrastructure, pervasive corruption, and a population explosion posed major obstacles to economic growth.

Although the United States emerged physically unscathed, the Vietnam War was among the most debilitating in its history, triggering an inflation that helped undermine its dominant position in the world economy. The war also had a high political cost, along with Nixon's Watergate scandal increasing popular suspicion of government, leaders, and institutions. It crippled the military, at least for a period, and temporarily estranged the United States from much of the rest of the world.

Somewhat like World War I for the Europeans, Vietnam had an enormous impact in the realm of the spirit. As few other events in our nation's history, it challenged Americans' traditional beliefs about themselves—that in their dealings with other people they had generally assumed a benevolent role, that for them nothing was beyond reach. It was a fundamental part of a much larger crisis of the spirit that began in the 1960s, raising profound questions about America's history and values. The war's wounds continued to fester among some of its 2.7 million veterans. The persisting popularity of novels, movies, and television shows about the Vietnam War suggests the extent to which it is etched in the nation's consciousness.

Nowhere was the impact greater than on the nation's foreign policy. The war destroyed the consensus that had existed since the late 1940s, leaving Americans confused and deeply divided on the goals to be pursued and the methods used. From the Angolan crisis of the mid-1970s to the Central American crisis of the 1980s and the Persian Gulf, Bosnian, and Somilian crises of the 1990s, foreign policy issues were viewed through the prism of Vietnam and debated in its context. The world changed drastically after the end of the Cold War. The conflicts that provoked debates over U.S. intervention were fundamentally different from those of the Cold War era, and the debates centered around different issues. The influence of Vietnam persisted, however, and America's involvement there should stand as an enduring testimony to the pitfalls of intervention and the limits of power.

Sources and Suggested Readings

Appy, Christian. *Working Class War: American Combat Soldiers and Vietnam*. Chapel Hill, NC, 1993.

Bergerud, Eric. *The Dynamics of Defeat: The Vietnam War in Hau Nghia Province*. Boulder, CO, 1991.

Caputo, Philip. *A Rumor of War*. New York, 1977.

DeBenedetti, Charles, with Chatfield, Charles. *An American Ordeal: The Antiwar Movement of the Vietnam Era*. Syracuse, NY, 1991.

Duiker, William. *The Communist Road to Power in Vietnam*. Boulder, CO, 1981.

Fall, Bernard B. *The Two Vietnams: A Political and Military Analysis*. New York, 1971.

Hayslip, Le L. *When Heaven and Earth Changed Places: A Vietnamese Woman's Journey from War to Peace*. New York, 1989.

Herring, George C. *America's Longest War: The United States and Vietnam, 1950–1975*. New York, 1986.

Kahin, George McT. *Intervention: How America Became Involved in Vietnam*. New York, 1986.

Karnow, Stanley. *Vietnam: A History*. New York, 1983.

Kolko, Gabriel. *Anatomy of a War: Vietnam, the United States, and the Modern Historical Experience*. New York, 1986.

Race, Jeffrey. *War Comes to Long An: Revolutionary Conflict in a Vietnamese Province*. Berkeley, CA, 1972.

Sheehan, Neil. *A Bright Shining Lie: John Paul Vann and America in Vietnam*. New York, 1988.

Truong, Nhu Tang. *A Vietcong Memoir*. Boston, 1985.

Latin America in the Cold War and After

Lester D. Langley

In the fall of 1939, as Europe plunged into the Second World War, there existed on the surface a solidarity in the Western Hemisphere. In the past decade, Herbert Hoover and Franklin D. Roosevelt had done much to alter the image of the United States as a predatory Anglo-Saxon nation in Hispanic America. Under Hoover the country had dramatically retreated from the empire that it had created in the Caribbean after the war with Spain; under Roosevelt it had repudiated intervention as a means of settling its disputes with hemispheric countries and to some degree accommodated its policies to nationalistic Latin American governments seeking greater control over foreign companies operating in their domain. Roosevelt became a popular figure in Latin America. "Some of them," he once declared, referring to its people, "think they're just as good as we are—and they are!"

In 1938, at the Pan-American Conference in Lima, delegates who a decade before had condemned U.S. intervention in Nicaragua supported a vaguely worded resolution calling for a united hemisphere (Canada excepted) to meet any external threat. Shortly after the outbreak of the European war in the following year, they met again in Panama to deal with the economic problems brought on by the war, and, following Roosevelt's personal recommendation, to declare the Western Hemisphere south of the 49th parallel off limits to belligerent activity. As Hitler's armies swallowed up western Europe in the summer of 1940, hemispheric conferees met in Havana and announced that European possessions in the Western Hemisphere could not be transferred to a non-American state. Already the United States had undertaken a vigorous defense program for the vulnerable Caribbean and its strategic lifeline, the Panama Canal. After Pearl Harbor yet another special conference was called to line up Latin American nations behind the United States against its global enemies—Germany, Italy, and Japan. By then, most already had broken diplomatic relations with the Axis powers and would shortly declare war.

Beneath this apparent harmony there were discordant signs. The United States declared that its purpose in waging war was the elimination of dictatorial regimes such as Hitler's Germany, Mussolini's Italy, and Hirohito's Japan, yet its Latin American allies were hardly examples of "decent democratic regimes" committed to Roosevelt's Four Freedoms (of speech and worship, from want and fear). In the Caribbean, which almost slavishly followed American policy, strongman governments prevailed in Cuba, the Dominican Republic, and Nicaragua. In the larger countries, whose commitment was even more crucial to American policy, there were blatantly anti-democratic governments. Although supportive of the war effort to the extent of sending an expeditionary force to Europe, Brazil had in Getulio Vargas what some American observers considered a "Brazilian Mussolini"; and Argentina, which did not join the Allies until the war was virtually over, exhibited a defiantly pro-German stance.

Generally, the United States obtained what it wanted from Latin America in World War II: subordinate economies and states in the Caribbean and defense sites from Panama to the bulge of Brazil. In the beginning it had justifiable concerns about Latin America's solidarity behind the American cause, but, by the end, when the United States stood militarily and economically supreme, the entire hemisphere appeared to stand solidly behind it. Then Washington committed what in retrospect has been judged a grievous error when it neglected its Latin American allies.

The United States and Latin America emerged from the war with different political perspectives on world affairs and strikingly disparate economic prospects. More concerned with the Soviet challenge in Europe, U.S. policymakers considered Latin America of lesser importance in their global calculations. To be sure, the United States committed itself to regional defense and organization at the Chapultepec Conference in Mexico in 1945, in the Inter-American Treaty of Reciprocal Assistance (Rio Treaty) signed in Rio de Janeiro in 1947, and, one year later, in the restructuring of the old Pan-American system into the Organization of American States (OAS) at Bogotá. During the Bogotá meeting there were serious riots in the city (in which Fidel Castro participated) brought on by the assassination of a popular Colombian politician, Jorge Eliécer Gaitán. In the United States the *bogotazo*, as the riots were called, took on little more significance than an isolated case of public unrest in the Hispanic world. To the Latin American left, however, it represented a deep dissatisfaction with the continent's economic decline and an opportunity for a more drastic solution. The United States, it was argued, had profited by its victory; it was restoring world capitalism and revitalizing its markets abroad and, by the end of the decade, reaping the benefits.

Latin America, which had dutifully subordinated its economies to American interests in the war, had emerged from the global conflict with expectations of sharing in the postwar prosperity. Instead, its economies had suffered from wartime inflation and loss of world markets. Expecting something on the order of the Marshall Plan, by which the western European economies had been restored, Latin America received comparatively little public assistance from the United States and considerable advice on how to run its political house. When John F. Kennedy commented in the presidential campaign of 1960 that since 1945 the U.S. government had provided more public aid to Yugoslavia, a socialist state, than to all of Latin America, he was making a grim statement on the status of inter-American affairs in the postwar era.

The U.S. government usually got what it wanted in the region during the 1950s: a collection of client states among the smaller countries, and among the larger ones, such as Mexico, Colombia, Venezuela, Brazil, and even Argentina, whose economic nationalism under Juan Perón was not perceived as a Third World challenge, more ambitious governments eager to expand their economies to bring about a more consumer-oriented society on the American model. The adoption of the socialist model by Latin America as an acceptable solution to the economic problems wrought by the war and the "revolution of rising expectations" remained forbidden.

Most Latin American governments played the American game by Washington's rules. Even Mexico, which before the war had antagonized the United States by nationalizing its foreign-owned oil industry, elected a businessman's president (Miguel Alemán) and embarked on a vigorous expansion of the national economy that earned the plaudits of New York bankers. Cuba became a marketplace for American goods, and its new leader, Fulgencio Batista, a once lowly sergeant in the army who had become a general, president-maker, and finally president of his country in 1940, threw out the civilians in a bloodless coup in 1952, turning the country into a reliable anti-Communist bastion. In the Dominican Republic, Rafael Trujillo ruled like the "little Caesar of the Caribbean" in his personal fiefdom, reassuring Washington with his anti-Soviet

"PRESIDENTS COME AND GO, BUT WE'LL NOT DESERT YOU, SEÑOR!" (*Kansas City Star*)

rhetoric. Nicaragua, another client state, was the domain of the Somoza family, installed in power by the Americans a generation before. The tyrants of the Hispanic world, whom the moralistic Cordell Hull had condemned as "proto-Fascists" before the war and whom the United States, under Latin American liberal pressures, was urged to turn out in 1945, had achieved by the mid-1950s a certain respectability in Washington's judgment.

Perhaps no event of the decade more accurately reflected America's priorities in Latin America than its ouster of the leftist government of Jacobo Arbenz in Guatemala in 1954. Ten years earlier, a coalition of Guatemalan reformers had turned out the dictator Jorge Ubico. Under Juan José Arévalo (who years later would write a bitterly anti-American manifesto, *The Shark and the Sardines*), Guatemala embarked on an economic and social modernization program. After 1950, when Arbenz took over, the government began moving against the most powerful foreign firm on the isthmus, the United Fruit Company (UFCO). In the process, Arbenz had to rely more and more on the Guatemalan trade unions and other leftist groups. To Secretary of State John Foster Dulles, who had once been associated with the New York law firm representing UFCO, Guatemala was fast becoming an agent of Soviet imperialism. With President Dwight D. Eisenhower's approval, the Dulles brothers (Allen was chief of the Central Intelligence Agency, or CIA) crushed Arbenz—John Foster by extracting from the Latin American governments at the Tenth Inter-American Conference at Caracas a pledge that "communism was incompatible with the hemisphere," and Allen by using the CIA to help finance, under Colonel Carlos Castillo Armas, an anti-Arbenz movement operating out of Honduras. The affair was thoroughly and inexpensively carried out.

The compliant Latin American governments, expecting Washington to be grateful for their support by opening its coffers, learned shortly afterward from Secretary of the Treasury George M. Humphrey that they must still look to private investment for their needs. The continent received some public aid, but it was a pittance compared to the millions poured into Western Europe. In 1952, when revolutionaries took over Bolivia and nationalized the tin mines, the Eisenhower administration subsidized the new government in large part to prevent a sharper turn to the Left. A few years later Eisenhower responded favorably to Panama's pleas for greater economic benefits from the canal. Not until after Vice President Richard M. Nixon was stoned and spat upon by leftist demonstrators in Lima and Caracas in 1959 did the U.S. government finally acquiesce in the region's insistence on an inter-American development bank, a proposal that it had been making for twenty years.

On January 1 of that year, Castro had triumphed in Cuba. From its beginning, the Cuban Revolution became intricately intertwined with U.S. policy toward Latin America. Ultimately, it would dramatically affect the Soviet-American relationship as well. Ironically, when Castro first came to power, many observers in this country welcomed the political change. After all, the end of the 1950s in Latin America looked like the "twilight of the tyrants": Perón had fallen in a military coup in Argentina in 1955; Manuel Odría, the Peruvian chieftain, in 1956; and Gustavo Rojas Pinilla and Marcos Pérez Jiménez, Colombian and Venezuelan strongmen, in 1957 and 1958, respectively. Even the supreme tyrant of the Caribbean, "El Benefactor" Trujillo of the Dominican Republic, although still in power in 1959, had virtually exhausted his once considerable influence in Washington. Only the Somozas in Nicaragua seemed secure, having survived the assassination of the patriarch by a madman in 1956 and the opposition of Costa Rica's leader José "Pepe" Figueres. Throughout the region it appeared that a new generation of civilian leaders, who believed in political honesty and progressive rule, was taking over. Even under Eisenhower, and certainly under Kennedy, the United States realized that its policies must accommodate these changes. In this view, then, Castro looked very much like the guerrilla warrior fighting for the restoration of constitutional rectitude in a corrupt society.

In Cuba, unlike any other Latin American country, the triumph of the revolution meant ultimately not only a break with the old order but also something more significant: a break with the United States. How this came about is still a controversial story. Castro's detractors—those Americans such as Vice President Nixon, or the professional classes that fled the island in the early 1960s—argued that he was, as he declared in late 1961, always a Marxist-Leninist and fully intent on communizing the island. In a variation on this theme, tough-minded liberals who saw Castro as a social reformer contended that he betrayed his own revolution by letting ideologues such as Ernesto "Che" Guevara chart Cuba's course. His defenders in the United States—mostly academics—and elsewhere in Latin America argued just as vehemently that the American decision to use economic and, ultimately, military measures to overthrow Castro drove him into the waiting arms of the Soviets.

Washington closely monitored the course of the revolution from the circus-like public trials of former Batistianos to the succession of economic measures leading inexorably to the nationalization of U.S. companies. Throughout the period the official and unofficial American response was one of virtually unqualified disapproval, coupled with a determination to retaliate. Yet in the same era—the first two years or so of the revolution—Castro cleverly exploited in Cuba the latent anti-Americanism wrought by sixty years of dependency, and he unconscionably drove into exile many thousands of middle-class Cubans who found fault with his revolution. In short, the U.S. government made Castro pay a high price to carry out his revolution, but he was determined to pay it in order to alter Cuba internally and to change its relationship with the United States.

At least to realistic observers of the cyclical shifts of Washington's interest in hemispheric conditions, it was clear that the grandiose plans of the Alliance for Progress, a Latin American idea picked up by Kennedy in the 1960 campaign and dramatically set into motion early in his administration, were inseparable from America's fear that the Cuban Revolution was exportable. "Those who make peaceful revolution impossible," Kennedy was fond of saying, "will make violent revolution inevitable." He was referring to the fact that in 1961, when so much American attention was directed toward the Western Hemisphere, Latin America was still a rigidly structured society ruled by social and military elites. Kennedy was brutally realistic. While he was extolling the new civilian rulers such as Rómulo Betancourt in Venezuela and the Alliance goals of industrialization and agrarian reform, at the same time he seemed determined to punish Castro for defying the United States.

Kennedy inherited the plan, concocted by Nixon in 1959 and transmuted by the CIA and Joint Chiefs of Staff into Operation Zapata, for the invasion of Cuba in April 1961. Although the liberating force was composed mostly of Cuban exiles and Kennedy himself declared that no Americans participated, U.S. involvement in what turned out to be a political and military disaster ran deep. Castro's reputation soared, both in Cuba and throughout the world.

After the Bay of Pigs debacle in 1961, when the CIA believed that it could stage "another Guatemala," American prestige plummeted, but Kennedy did not back off. During the summer there was another confrontation, this time outside Montevideo at a plush resort in Uruguay called Punta del Este, where Kennedy's alert crew of Latin Americanists exchanged sharp challenges with Guevara. "Look at Latin America a decade from now," he roared, "and then at Cuba and see which has achieved the goals of the Alliance for Progress!" Delegates went back home counting proffered American aid and calling it "Fidel's money." Early in 1962, again at Punta del Este, under severe American pressure they voted Castro's government out of the OAS. During these years, as the Church Committee Report on CIA operations revealed much later, several assassination plots against Castro were linked to the U.S. government.

All the while the Cuban-Soviet connection grew stronger. The first ties, cemented in 1960, were essentially economic agreements whereby the Soviets took the Cuban sugar that the Americans no longer wanted. One year before, during his visit to the United States, Castro had boasted that his country had no ties with the Soviets, but in his second, more dramatic sojourn he and Premier Nikita Khrushchev had embraced at the United Nations, and the Cuban flew back to Havana aboard a Russian jet. In Washington, the Cuban-Soviet relationship was disquieting, but it produced no serious alarm until the summer of 1962 when Cuban exiles and a prominently outspoken senator, Kenneth Keating, charged that the Soviets were up to suspicious military activity at isolated sites in Cuba.

The missiles destined for these sites—missiles capable of carrying warheads to virtually every major city in the Western Hemisphere—did not arrive until September. They were not discovered until mid-October, but their presence triggered two harrowing weeks in the Cold War during which the two superpowers seemed bent on nuclear annihilation. Cuba lies far from the Soviet Union, however, and the Russians, who still did not possess the sea power to challenge the U.S. Navy, dared not risk a nuclear exchange in which they held an inferior position. Khrushchev, who would pay for this embarrassment two years later with his ouster from power, did secure a pledge from Kennedy that there would be no invasion. Angry over the Soviet-American deal carried out without his approval, Castro refused to let UN observers verify the removal of the missiles. For over a year he flirted with the Chinese, who were vilifying the Soviets as "accommodationists," and dispatched Guevara to Bolivia to create "one, two, many Vietnams," but the Russians atoned for their disgrace by giving Cuba a more important place in the socialist system. At one time after Castro's later involvement in

Africa's troubles, the Kremlin wearied of his disruptive proselytiz-
ing and looked to his more trustworthy brother, Raúl, as its choice
for Cuba's Sovietized bureaucracy. Fidel, truly the symbol of the
revolution bearing his name, survived, however, by toning down
his rhetoric and promoting closer relations with other hemispheric
nations, including the United States. By then Kennedy was dead,
and America, mired in a jungle war in Southeast Asia, was rapidly
losing interest in Latin America. In his brief presidency, Kennedy
had erred often in dealing with hemispheric problems, but his instincts had been right. Even Castro recognized that, beyond serving America's strategic and economic interests, the Alliance for
Progress, despite its shortcomings, offered hope for the millions of
Latin Americans trapped in poverty.

In the early 1960s, Washington's amenable attitude toward military governments and dictators had noticeably cooled. What the
United States wanted—and what Latin America needed—were left-
of-center civilian governments, but there was a limit to how far left
a country might shift before it incurred America's displeasure.
Kennedy set the priorities early on after the assassination of Trujillo
in the Dominican Republic. Our choices, he told an aide, are "a
decent democratic regime, a continuation of the Trujillo dictatorship, or a Communist takeover. We should strive for the first, but
we can't rule out the second until we're sure we can avoid the third."
Using such logic, he condemned the military when it took over in
the Dominican Republic, Honduras, Peru, and Argentina in 1962–
63, but in the same period he quietly acquiesced in its seizure of
control in Guatemala, where Arévalo was on the verge of returning
to power, and in British Guiana, scheduled for independence, where
the United States had to choose between a popular pro-Soviet leftist, Cheddi Jagan, and an anti-Soviet leftist, Linden Forbes
Burnham. Kennedy met with Jagan but remained suspicious and
persuaded the British to delay their departure until 1966 when
Guyana, with Burnham as leader, became independent.

Lyndon B. Johnson inherited not only Kennedy's Vietnam policy
but his hemispheric policy as well, and, as in Southeast Asia,
Johnson put his own peculiar imprimatur on it. Of all recent American leaders, Johnson should have been the best informed about
Latin America's political, economic, and social problems, about
the Hispanic psyche and its values, and about the U.S.-Latin American relationship. After all, he had grown up in the hill country of
south central Texas only one hundred miles or so from the Mexican

border in a state heavily influenced by Hispanic culture. Still, his was a warped cultural education; he saw Mexicans harassed for years in a political and economic system that regarded them mostly for their cheap labor and their votes in an election. In the campaign of 1960, Kennedy had won by a razor-thin margin. In Texas, Mexican voters in the southern counties had been hastily corralled by rural Democratic bosses and transported to the polls to give Kennedy and Johnson a victory. In dealing with Hispanics, Kennedy, who had been virtually uninformed about Latin America before the 1960 campaign, was noticeably *simpático*. His successor once laid out his philosophy with, predictably, an anecdote that was vintage Johnson: "I know Mexicans," he declared, "they're good neighbors. But you've got to lay down the rules when they get to the front gate. If you don't, before you know it they're up on the front porch."

Johnson acquired a reputation as a "great persuader" among fence-straddling congressmen on Capitol Hill who had to be threatened, cajoled, and sometimes physically intimidated to approve his programs. He demonstrated much the same approach toward Latin Americans. After only a few months in office he plunged into a major diplomatic crisis in Panama brought on by age-old resentment over American jurisdiction of the Canal Zone. After a series of riots in 1964, Panama suspended diplomatic relations and took its case to the rest of the region. Johnson decided to deal with the Panamanian leader as if he were some recalcitrant Democratic politician: "Get me the president of Panama—what's his name—on the phone!" Months of tedious diplomatic negotiations followed, but in the end Johnson was able to employ his carrot-and-stick approach. On nationwide television, sitting in front of a map of the entire isthmus, he dramatically announced that his administration and Panama were working on new treaties that would one day transfer the existing canal to Panama, provide a new defense agreement, and, more important, arrange for the construction of a new sea-level canal which, the president said, "may be built in Panama." Three years later, long after Johnson had forgotten about tiny Panama and its monomania, the canal, the three treaties finally appeared, but they were assailed in Washington by the then-powerful canal lobby and in Panama by anti-American nationalists.

Johnson had come into political prominence during the bitterest years of the Cold War; he was defiantly anti-Communist and thus, unlike Kennedy, did not make subtle distinctions among varying brands of Latin American leftism. Castro was anathema. America had lost Cuba to the Communists, Johnson said, but under him it would not "lose" another hemispheric country to them. Therefore, in late April 1965, when a reformist element in the Dominican Republic moved to reinstall former President Juan Bosch, whom the generals had tossed out two years before, Johnson acted. Declaring that he was not going to permit "another Cuba" in the Caribbean, the president dispatched twenty thousand crack troops into Santo Domingo. Although the force was later expanded to include troops from several other Latin American countries, notably from those with rightist regimes, the United States was clearly in charge when it determined that Bosch, whom Washington officials considered too tolerant of Communists in his brief presidency, would not be reinstalled in power. Throughout the hemisphere, Johnson was accused of reverting to gunboat diplomacy. If a country in the Western Hemisphere appeared ready to fall to the Communists by violent means, the Johnson Doctrine declared, the United States had the right to intervene to prevent it.

Johnson has been harshly judged by Latin Americans not only for his role in the Dominican intervention but also for his uncritical response to the military takeover in Brazil in 1964, which demonstrably slowed that country's spiraling inflation but did so at a noticeably severe political price. Investors who had grumbled for years about inefficient Alliance programs and inept leftist governments welcomed Johnson's appointment of Thomas Mann as coordinator of hemispheric policy because Mann had a businesslike approach to the region's issues. Yet it must be remembered that Johnson maintained financial commitments to the Alliance even as the Vietnam War was annually consuming more and more of his budget and time. He could be charitable with Hispanics, such as at the Chamizal ceremony that took place on a strip of land between El Paso and Juárez that after a century of dispute was being turned over to Mexico, or as spokesman for the International Great Society as he stood under a blazing border sun with the president of Mexico and talked about some vast cooperative program for the Mexican and American peoples, to the noticeable indifference of the Mexican leader.

When Nixon became president in 1969, the country's Latin American policy was in shambles. The Alliance for Progress, essentially still functioning, already had come under harsh congressional scrutiny for its demonstrable failures. Critics were saying that the average Latin American now lived under more repressive regimes and poorer economic circumstances than in 1960, when reformers heralded the Alliance as the hemisphere's salvation. In any event, Nixon seemed determined to kill it off, claiming that the Latin Americans really did not want the Alliance anymore. "What they want," said Nixon, echoing the collective sentiment of the Viña del Mar Conference of the region's leaders, "is trade, not aid." His special emissary to the hemisphere, Nelson Rockefeller, the owner of a hacienda in Venezuela, already had returned after a whirlwind trip. In his sometimes frankly realistic report, Rockefeller had written that the prospects for upheaval throughout the continent were greater than ever. He recommended the creation of a secretariat of Western Hemispheric affairs and an inter-American police force. The first never came into being; the second ran afoul of Latin American nationalistic sensibilities, although rightist regimes were cooperating by exchanging information on leftist organizers and its armies now had a generation of young officers drilled at the counterin-surgency school in the Canal Zone.

Nixon referred to his Latin American policy as the "new partnership." Economic barriers began to fall as he announced that a new General System of Preferences (GSP) would govern inter-American trade. For the hard-pressed Caribbean nations, which usually exported one or two products, GSP meant greater access to the vital U.S. market. Much of the goodwill was offset, however, when Congress, infuriated over the 1973 oil embargo, took revenge on all members of the Organization of Petroleum Exporting Countries, including Venezuela and Ecuador, by denying them trade preferences. The effect on Venezuelan-American relations was predictably harsh.

Nixon could not readily comprehend how a military government such as that in Peru could espouse populist programs; but, when the Peruvian generals took over an American oil company, he did not invoke the Hickenlooper Amendment, which called for shutting off aid to any government that nationalized U.S. companies without adequate compensation. If a Latin American government offered a direct challenge, as did Salvador Allende's socialist regime in Chile, Nixon did not hesitate to retaliate. There was no military crusade against Chile like the one unleashed by Kennedy against Castro, but Nixon used American influence with International Telephone and Telegraph, which had extensive operations in

Chile, to distribute funds to Allende's opponents in the 1970 presidential election. When Allende won anyway, Nixon undertook a campaign waged largely through American-dominated international lending institutions to harass him for the next three years. By then Allende's appeals to Chile's lower classes had so frightened the middle class that the country had plunged into civil war, a struggle in which the military, alert to Washington's disapproval of Allende's socialism, triumphed.

Thus, Nixon and Secretary of State Henry Kissinger, who had done so much to reshape U.S. policy elsewhere in the world, relegated Latin America to a secondary position in their global priorities. Retreating from the Asian mainland, the United States appeared to retreat from the Western Hemisphere as well. At important OAS sessions the Latin Americans began meeting privately and, after agreeing among themselves, summoned the U.S. representative to listen. In 1975, under Mexican, Venezuelan, and Cuban guidance, twenty-five governments in the region founded a separatist hemispheric organization, the Latin American Economic System, which excluded the United States. A former adviser to Kennedy on Latin American affairs, William D. Rogers, noting the growing gulf between his country and Latin America, recommended that the United States pull out of the OAS.

One year or so before Nixon resigned there was a thaw in Cuban-American relations brought on by Castro's irritation over skyjackers and, more important, by Congress's urging. Nevertheless, relations deteriorated just as quickly when Cuba dispatched troops into Angola and Ethiopia. Rebuffed by congressmen alarmed over "another Vietnam," Kissinger announced that Cuba was simply doing Moscow's bidding in Africa. This statement was only partially correct. True, the island nation had been fully incorporated into the Soviet bloc, but its role in Africa went beyond the carrying out of the Kremlin's designs. Cuba's cultural background is African as well as Hispanic; thus, Castro declared that Cuba must participate in liberating African peoples from the last "grasp of imperialism." (In 1979 the Cubans began dispatching the first contingents of troops to Angola, thus creating a force there eventually numbering more than twenty thousand, with half of them black.) To Washington, these words were very much Marxist rhetoric, but they had a noticeable impact in the Caribbean, where "black power" movements had surfaced in the early 1970s and people were becoming more sensitive to their African past. Cuba's relations with the Lesser Antilles, negligible in 1970, grew rapidly in the course of the decade.

Even those countries once considered surrogates defied the United States. Tiny Panama, under Omar Torrijos, threw out the 1967 canal treaty proposals and demanded a new agenda. He united all Latin Americans against the United States on the canal issue and even brought the UN Security Council to Panama to deliberate on the subject. Although every president since Kennedy had declared that one day the canal should be Panama's, there was still the issue of dealing with the powerful canal lobby. Before the fight was over and President Jimmy Carter and Torrijos were sitting side by side to sign new treaties providing for ultimate Panamanian ownership, the canal's defenders fought a final battle to preserve the most visible symbol of America's imperial past.

In Panama, Carter did what he thought was right; elsewhere in the region he directed U.S. policy toward protecting human rights. The results were mixed. In Brazil, Chile, and especially Argentina, where military governments cracked down severely on political enemies of the regime even to the point of using torture, American condemnation probably saved lives, but the policy inevitably brought countercharges that the president was not uniform in applying his human rights prescription, and relations with these countries worsened. In Nicaragua, where America traced its considerable influence back to a time before World War I, the ruling Somoza family, overthrown in a bloody civil war in 1979, blamed many of its troubles on Carter's insistent pressures for human rights. This accusation was absurd, but Anastasio Somoza did have a point when he protested that he had faithfully stood by the Americans in the Cold War and now they were letting him down.

The overthrow of the Somozas, whom the Americans had put into power a half century before, marked the end of an era in which the United States relied on Caribbean surrogates to keep order and promote economic development along Washington's guidelines. Ironically, it had been in Nicaragua that the policy of military intervention and gunboat diplomacy had succumbed in 1933 to Augusto Sandino's jungle war and a collapsing international capitalist structure.

By 1979, American leadership in the Western Hemisphere had slipped badly. The new rulers in Nicaragua, a curious mixture of socialists and middle-class reformers, were not impressed by

America's arrangement of Somoza's departure and embarked on a course of national economic policy that for Washington resembled too closely Castro's economic experiment in Cuba. When in American estimation the Nicaraguans began helping the guerrillas in El Salvador where a frightfully bloody civil war had broken out, the United States started applying severe pressure on Nicaragua, thereby shutting down the flow of aid to its hard-pressed government and stepping up its military support to the shaky Salvadoran government of José Napoleón Duarte, a Christian Democrat caught between a murderous right wing and a fanatical left, and to Nicaragua's northern neighbor, Honduras.

The "loss" of Nicaragua did not figure prominently in Ronald Reagan's defeat of Carter in 1980, but Reagan's North American "continentalists" made it clear that in championing human rights Carter had alienated America's friends. The truth was less palatable: the United States, mired in economic difficulties, its embassy personnel held hostage in Iran, was a wounded giant no longer able to chart the future of the Western Hemisphere. The ultimate proof of its impotence came in the 1982 war over the Malvinas Islands (Falklands) between Argentina and Great Britain when the politically harassed Argentine military government, virtually indifferent to the moral blandishments of Washington, attacked the British-controlled Malvinas in the South Atlantic and Great Britain reacted with force, in the process demanding—and getting—American support.

The Malvinas war, which for a few weeks alerted the American people to the hemispheric crisis, just as quickly passed into obscurity. The dramatic U.S. invasion of Grenada in October 1983, presumably undertaken to prevent over six hundred American medical students from becoming hostages to a radical regime that had seized power from pro-Cuban governments, also did not convince Americans that they must shift away from globalism. These events, however, illustrated Washington's dilemma in dealing with Latin America. In the late 1930s, as war approached in Europe, the Roosevelt administration had exploited public fears about German influence in Latin America to break down isolationist sentiment. Defense of the hemisphere became a popular theme during the war, but the United States had a different purpose than had Latin America in promoting inter-American unity. It was moving toward globalism, and it needed reliable allies in the region for its future commitment in the world. Their country's fundamental political, economic, and cultural interests lay with Western Europe, Americans decided, even as it participated in the Rio Treaty and the OAS. Obsessed with the Soviet threat in the postwar years, the United States relinquished much of its commitment to the "Western Hemisphere" idea, the cumulative beliefs of generations that held that the future of the hemisphere lay in republican governments whose goal was the betterment of their own people's lives. As Kennedy said, the United States must strive for "decent, democratic regimes." He believed that the American political and economic system, despite its flaws, offered the developing Latin American nations a preferable alternative to Castro's Cuba.

In some respects the 1984 Kissinger Committee report on the Central American crisis restated Kennedy's priorities of democracy, economic development, and social justice, yet, as he himself had shown in his dealings with Latin America, the top priority in U.S. policy was "strategic denial." In other words, the U.S. approach to the Western Hemisphere sought always to deny, or at least to limit, the influence of nonhemispheric powers. After the 1960s strategic denial declined in importance in U.S. calculations. The Nicaraguan Revolution and the guerrilla insurgency in El Salvador, profoundly influenced by the Cuban Revolution, challenged U.S. hegemony in a region historically considered our own "backyard." In the 1980s, however, the Reagan administration's efforts to achieve a military solution (usually expressed as "low-intensity warfare") ran afoul of contradictory and even hostile counterforces. The Sandinistas in Nicaragua proved that they could defy the United States; the Salvadoran guerrillas demonstrated that they could hold their own against a government heavily dependent on U.S. military support; most Latin American and even usually sympathetic European allies were opposed or indifferent to what they considered a misplaced U.S. preoccupation with Central America; and, most important, Congress (doubtless expressing widespread public doubts) grew disenchanted with the hard-line approach. In the late 1980s, Central Americans began to take control of their own destiny with high-level negotiations to end the decade-long strife. In 1990 the Sandinistas lost the Nicaraguan presidency with the surprising electoral victory of Violeta Chamorro, and a few years later a fragile cease-fire came about in El Salvador.

By then the Soviet Union had collapsed, and with its demise the Cuban challenge rapidly weakened. And although his decision to invade Panama in December 1989 (Operation Just Cause) to oust dictator Manuel Noriega looked like a reprise of the Reagan formula for Latin America, President George Bush made it clear that his administration intended to address other issues. Taking advantage of the resurgence of democracy and the decline of military governments throughout the region in the 1980s—a trend for which Reagan took credit, but it was in actuality a legacy of Carter's influence—and, especially, the demands of Latin Americans themselves, Bush established harmonious relations with several leaders. He responded favorably to Mexican president Carlos Salinas de Gortari's proposal for the economic integration of Mexico and the United States (North American Free-Trade Agreement, or NAFTA, approved by Congress in 1993) and called for new trade initiatives for the entire hemisphere (Enterprise for the Americas).

As President Bush turned over Latin American policy to Bill Clinton, the prospects for a democratic and prosperous hemisphere were, paradoxically, both heartening and ominous. Unlike the 1960s there was no Soviet or Cuban challenge, and authoritarian governments had given way to democratic regimes espousing pluralistic politics and free-market economic models. Yet, despite the promise of a new era, Latin Americans in the 1990s confront social inequities in many ways as grievous as those denounced by Kennedy in 1960, as the economic reforms have produced limited results. Populist appeals, whether from the Right or the Left, resonate in such circumstances. Narcopolitics is as threatening to democracy as Marxist ideology ever was. In Peru and Haiti, harassed governments defy the international community, the OAS, and the United Nations. In the summer of 1994, as desperate Cubans piled on makeshift rafts to leave a failed socialist economy where nutritional levels have fallen to precarious levels, Castro proved again (as he had during the 1980 Mariel boatlift) that the Cuban government, however weakened, could nonetheless exercise influence over U.S. immigration policy.

What the United States confronts in Latin America, then, is an opportunity to join with other governments in dealing with these issues and, in the process, to forswear the unilateral solutions of the past for a reasoned, collective strategy. What both the United States and Latin American governments may face by the year 2000, however, is a hemisphere riddled with seemingly intractable problems—economies that cannot be managed by traditional political means; societies of misery in the midst of progress; governments whose policies are determined less by purpose than by budgets;

and nation-states so fragmented by racial, ethnic, and cultural divisions that social cohesion and attachment to country are as fragile as they were at the moment of independence. In such circumstances the democratic, prosperous Latin America imagined by the proponents of a North American developmental policy after World War II may remain a fanciful dream.

Sources and Suggested Readings

Atkins, G. Pope, ed. *The United States and Latin America: Redefining U.S. Purposes in the Cold War Era.* Austin, TX, 1992.

Blasier, Cole. *The Giant's Rival: The USSR and Latin America.* Pittsburgh, 1983.

———. *The Hovering Giant: U.S. Responses to Revolutionary Change in Latin America.* Rev. ed. Pittsburgh, 1985.

Carothers, Thomas. *In the Name of Democracy: U.S. Policy toward Latin America in the Reagan Years.* Berkeley, CA, 1991.

Conniff, Michael L. *Panama and the United States: The Forced Alliance.* Athens, GA, 1992.

Desch, Michael. *When the Third World Matters: Latin America and United States Grand Strategy.* Baltimore, 1994.

Haglund, David G. *Latin America and the Transformation of U.S. Strategic Thought, 1936–1940.* Albuquerque, NM, 1984.

Immerman, Richard H. *The CIA in Guatemala: The Foreign Policy of Intervention.* Austin, TX, 1982.

LaFeber, Walter. *Inevitable Revolutions: The United States in Central America.* Rev. ed. New York, 1993.

———. *The Panama Canal: The Crisis in Historical Perspective.* Rev. ed. New York, 1989.

Langley, Lester D. *America and the Americas: The United States in the Western Hemisphere.* Athens, GA, 1989.

———. *The United States and the Caribbean in the Twentieth Century.* 4th ed. Athens, GA, 1989.

———, ed. *The United States and the Americas.* Athens, GA, 1989.

Leonard, Thomas M. *Central America and the United States: The Search for Stability.* Athens, GA, 1991.

Levinson, Jerome, and De Onis, Juan. *The Alliance that Lost Its Way: A Critical Report on the Alliance for Progress.* Chicago, 1970.

Maingot, Anthony. *The United States and the Caribbean: Synergies of a Complex Interdependence.* Hampshire, England, 1994.

Pastor, Robert A. *Whirlpool: U.S. Foreign Policy toward Latin America and the Caribbean.* Princeton, NJ, 1992.

Paterson, Thomas G. *Contesting Castro: The United States and the Triumph of the Cuban Revolution.* New York, 1994.

Pérez, Louis A. *Cuba and the United States: Ties of Singular Intimacy.* Athens, GA, 1990.

Plummer, Brenda G. *Haiti and the United States: The Psychological Moment.* Baton Rouge, LA, 1992.

Raat, W. Dirk. *Mexico and the United States: Ambivalent Vistas.* Athens, GA, 1992.

Rabe, Stephen G. *Eisenhower and Latin America: The Foreign Policy of Anticommunism.* Chapel Hill, NC, 1989.

Randall, Stephen J. *Colombia and the United States: Hegemony and Interdependence.* Athens, GA, 1992.

Sater, William F. *Chile and the United States: Empires in Conflict.* Athens, GA, 1990.

Smith, Gaddis. *The Last Years of the Monroe Doctrine.* New York, 1994.

Stallings, Barbara, and Székely, Gabriel, eds. *Japan, the United States, and Latin America: Towards a Trilateral Relationship in the Western Hemisphere.* Baltimore, 1994.

The Middle East, Oil, and the Third World

James W. Harper

After World War II, Americans became accustomed to new words
describing the world in which they lived. During the late 1940s
they learned that they inhabited a "bipolar world" dominated by
the United States and the Soviet Union. In the mid-1950s the phrase
"Third World" crowded its way into the headlines. The Third World
countries, most of them located in Africa or Asia and most of them
former European colonies or spheres of influence, sought a neutral
or nonaligned path following neither the United States and its allies nor the Soviet bloc. Dominated by a consuming desire for full
national independence, often facing staggering economic problems,
and having regional rather than global interests, these nations posed
major challenges for American foreign policy.

No region of the globe was more typical of the Third World or
more challenging than the Middle East. Before World War II most
of the region had been under various forms of European control,
and even nominally independent nations such as Saudi Arabia and
Iran often felt the pressure of outside influence. Economically, most
of the region was backward, underdeveloped, and feudal, and it
depended on foreign economic assistance. Even the newly discovered oil wealth went largely into foreign hands. After World War II
the nations of the Middle East moved rapidly from political dependence to independence, and the formerly subsidized Arab oil states
emerged as one of the world's dominant economic forces. Most
important, the region's chief political conflict—the Arab-Israeli
confrontation—dominated all diplomacy and helped to transform
the United States into a Middle Eastern power.

In the last fifty years the United States has become the major
foreign participant in Middle Eastern affairs. This transformation
in policy constitutes one of the most dramatic changes in modern
American diplomacy and a major chapter in its relations with the
Third World. In 1900, America's interests in the Near East were
modest. Its limited trade centered on exports of petroleum, chiefly

kerosene, to a region whose vast oil deposits had not yet been discovered. Its diplomacy focused on protecting American nationals, securing opportunities for Christian missionaries to proselytize in the Moslem region, and supporting American Jews who wished to spend their last years in Jerusalem. In all matters political and economic, the nation's diplomacy took a backseat to European activity. Although America's involvement increased between 1900 and 1945, as manifested by oil concessions in Saudi Arabia and growing support for a Jewish national homeland in Palestine, it deferred to Britain in the region until after World War II.

Several factors intensified this involvement after 1945. One was the growing importance of Middle Eastern oil. Fearing a postwar shortage of oil, State Department officials, during World War II, had moved to increase U.S. influence in the region. The February 1945 meeting between President Franklin D. Roosevelt and King Ibn Saud of Saudi Arabia symbolized America's growing interest in this strategic and oil-rich region. Moreover, it became apparent that Britain, weakened by the war, would be unable to perpetuate its dominance in the area after the global conflict. As in other areas of the world, the United States took steps to replace Britain as the stabilizing force.

The Cold War also helped to alter traditional American policy. Tension between the United States and the Soviet Union first occurred in the Middle East during 1946 when Soviet troops refused to honor a wartime agreement to evacuate the northern third of Iran, which they had occupied during the war. The Russians demanded oil concessions similar to those that Iran had granted to Britain, aided Iranian Communists in the Azerbaijan region, and threatened to make the country a Soviet sphere of influence, if not a satellite. The United States moved quickly to support the Tehran government, and eventually the twin pressures of American opposition and Iranian resistance forced a Soviet retreat. For U.S. policymakers, however, the Middle East had become yet another region threatened by Soviet expansion. A second Iranian crisis occurred in the early 1950s when Premier Mohammed Mossadegh sought to nationalize the British-owned oil fields. Britain threatened an invasion, and the Western oil companies initiated a boycott of Iranian oil that threw the country's economy into chaos. Fearful that Mossadegh was a front for Soviet influence, the United States responded to the crisis with a Central Intelligence Agency intervention that led to

Abdul-Aziz Ibn Saud (1888–1953), King of Saudi Arabia. (Saudi Arabian Embassy, Information Office, Washington, DC)

his overthrow. The agency helped to restore Shah Mohammed Reza Pahlavi to power in 1954. Thereafter, American policy was aimed at bolstering the shah as an anti-Communist bulwark in the region. Spurred by visions of restoring Persian greatness, Reza Pahlavi cooperated with the Western powers, working out an oil-takeover agreement with the British in 1954 and joining defense arrangements such as the American-supported Central Treaty Organization (CTO) in 1956.

Perhaps the most important cause of increased U.S. involvement in the region was the creation of the state of Israel in 1947. This dramatic event aroused the deepest animosities of the peoples of the Middle East, caused four major wars and hundreds of incursions and terrorist attacks, and spun a web of diplomatic problems still not untangled. The Holocaust had galvanized Western opinion behind the old idea of a homeland for the Jewish survivors of the ghastly Nazi exterminations. As Seth Tillman has noted, however, this support for Zionism conflicted with America's economic stake in Arab oil and its strategic interests in aligning the Arab states against the Soviet Union. Moreover, when the Palestinians dispossessed by Israel made their own demands for nationhood, they, like the Israelis before them, appealed to the venerable American principle of self-determination.

On November 29, 1947, the UN General Assembly, as a first step toward the creation of a Jewish state, voted to partition the former British mandate of Palestine into Jewish and Arab sections. After some initial opposition within his administration, President Harry S. Truman threw his full support behind Israel, recognizing the state within ten minutes of its proclamation of independence on May 14, 1948. American recognition was followed by a warm reception for Israeli president Chaim Weizmann two weeks later, and within one year the United States had facilitated a $100-million loan to the infant republic.

Bitterly hostile to what they regarded as a new form of Western colonization in their region, the Arab states of Egypt, Syria, Jordan, and Lebanon declared war on Israel. However, the Arab effort was poorly planned and coordinated. The Westernized, disciplined Israeli army with superb leadership, many soldiers who had served in European and American armies, and modern tactics smashed the Egyptian and Syrian invasions. Israeli units also fought the British-trained Jordanian army to a draw before an armistice ended the fighting in July 1949.

The 1948–49 war caused much turmoil in the Middle East. Huge numbers of Arab refugees either fled Israel or were driven out. Over 200,000 left before May 14, 1948, and by the war's end over 600,000 Palestinians had settled on the West Bank of the Jordan River or in the Gaza Strip in Egypt. Despite UN pleas, Israel refused to take back the refugees, preferring to preserve as much land as possible for the large number of new Jewish immigrants, while Arab nations demanded a homeland for the Palestinians. This unresolved question has caused, and continues to cause, enormous tensions in the Middle East. The humiliation of the Arab states also contributed to increased political instability, and revolutions took place in both Egypt and Syria within the next decade.

In defeat, the Arabs naturally blamed outsiders, especially the United States, for supporting Israel. However, during the five years after 1949 the Arab states were impotent, and crises in China and Korea dominated Washington's attention. Even during this period of relative calm, the commitment to Israel increased. Although the United States initially refrained from giving military assistance to Israel, public and private economic aid was substantial during the 1950s. In the 1960s the United States began providing considerable direct aid, and by 1980 military assistance totaled $13 billion and economic aid $5.5 billion. This increasing assistance was supported by large sections of the American population, led by Jews and fundamentalist Christians.

During the Eisenhower administration, the Middle East became the scene of superpower rivalry. After the death of Joseph Stalin in 1953, the new Soviet leadership began major efforts to increase its influence in the underdeveloped world. Apparently the Soviets saw the decline of Western influence in the Third World as an excellent opportunity to enhance their political and ideological standing and to secure strategic and economic gains. The United States faced considerable difficulties in competing for influence. Arab states continued to blame America for the creation of Israel, a source of humiliation, political instability, and revolution. In addition, its alliance with Britain and France associated the United States with past European imperialism. These problems were complicated by the moralistic approach of Secretary of State John Foster Dulles, who suspected Arab nationalist leaders such as Gamal Abdel Nasser, who came to power in Egypt in 1954, of being tools of the Soviets. Dulles failed to understand why these nationalists did not share his fear of Russia and communism.

Initially, President Dwight D. Eisenhower and Secretary Dulles sought to use Britain and France as the leaders in organizing the region against the Communist menace. The three nations continued their Tripartite Declaration limiting arms shipments to the belligerents of the 1948–49 Arab-Israeli War. More dramatically, Dulles encouraged Britain and France to form a defensive alliance—a Middle Eastern NATO—called the Baghdad Pact, or CTO. This link of Britain, France, Turkey, Iran, and Pakistan secured the membership of only one Arab state, Iraq, and excited fears in Syria, Egypt, and Jordan that it was simply a device for renewed colonialism. The Arabs were more concerned with Israel and their own internal development than with the Cold War, and their opposition to the Baghdad Pact typified the inclination of most Third World states to stay free of East-West alignments.

The efforts of Eisenhower and Dulles to align the Arab states against the Soviets revealed the preoccupation with the Cold War and the insensitivity to nationalism that typified America's response to the Third World. By the 1950s these "emerging nations" were seeking to act collectively as a third force in a seemingly bipolar world. In 1955 they held a major conference in Bandung, Indonesia. Led by Egypt's Nasser, India's Jawaharlal Nehru, and Yugoslavia's Marshal Tito, they sought to create a collective neutralist posture toward Soviet-American competition. The Soviets were quick to seek favor with the neutralists with a series of showy foreign aid projects and persistent anticolonial rhetoric. The People's Republic of China was perhaps even more effective in this endeavor because it was underdeveloped and nonwhite like the great majority of nonaligned countries. The West also recognized the strategic and economic importance of Third World areas, and the United States and Europe responded with billions of dollars in economic assistance to win the support of the neutrals.

The American response to the emergence of the Third World was often ambivalent and contradictory, however. Stemming from its own revolutionary past, the United States had ideological sympathy for countries seeking national independence, but this sympathy was often overridden by strategic and economic concerns. In the era of containment it had allied itself with the very European countries that had colonized much of the Third World. While Washington officials considered economic and military aid to countries such as Belgium, Portugal, and France vital to the success of containment in Europe, such assistance was often viewed by newly emerging nations as aimed at keeping them under the European yoke. Even U.S. support of independence movements, such as that in Indonesia in the late 1940s, was obscured by the heavy political commitment to European governments elsewhere. This contradiction in goals was sharpened when the Korean War pushed the United States into a worldwide effort to contain communism.

Secretary Dulles typified the strong inclination in the United States during the 1950s to view communism as immoral and to be distrustful of countries that did not think likewise. To neutralist states far more concerned with removing the last vestiges of colonialism, gaining national self-respect, and seeking rapid economic development, Dulles's rhetoric seemed irrelevant and insulting. Further complicating American efforts was the secretary's tendency to support any government that parroted his anti-Communist line, regardless of how undemocratic, brutal, or corrupt it was.

Many Third World countries, from India to Algeria, eventually turned to a form of authoritarian socialism in the belief that state-directed economic planning would offer the fastest route to modernization. This revolutionary socialism considered foreign business interests as exploitative and in many cases proceeded to nationalize foreign holdings. Such threats to American economic interests did not win support in Washington; and, when revolutionary socialism propagated anti-American rhetoric and behavior in forums such as the United Nations, it caused many Americans to see the neutralists as Communists in disguise and to insist on firm anti-Communist credentials as the price for their support. In the Third World some conservatives such as Premier Nuri Sa'id of Iraq, King Idris of Libya, and President Ngo Dinh Diem of South Vietnam effectively used anti-Communist rhetoric and policies to gain U.S. support to maintain the status quo in their lands. Over the long haul, however, they were all toppled by authoritarian socialist revolutionaries.

America's domestic racial problems were another obstacle in dealing effectively with the countries of the Third World. These nations were largely nonwhite; and during the 1950s and 1960s, when the plight of black Americans gained international attention, racism at home undercut U.S. efforts to pose as the champion of freedom, equality, and democracy abroad. Moreover, racial prejudice, combined with economic and political considerations, made the United States slow to condemn racism in nations such as South Africa and contributed to a tendency to disparage Asians and

Africans in general. With regard to the Middle East, this attitude could be seen in a consistent and often distorted portrayal in the American press of Arabs as backward, primitive desert dwellers who were not as entitled to Palestine as the progressive, Westernized Israelis.

The Suez crisis of 1956 and the resultant Anglo-French invasion of Egypt in October of that year ended any American hopes of using England and France as anti-Soviet surrogates in the Middle East. Furious at Nasser's nationalization of the Suez Canal, in part caused by an American refusal to sell arms to Egypt or finance the Aswan Dam, England and France plotted a joint invasion with Israel. The European states intervened under the pretext of protecting the canal. Israel, eager to avenge escalating guerrilla raids that had been launched from Gaza, swept toward Suez, but the Anglo-French effort was plagued by poor planning, inept leadership, and uncertain objectives. The invasion foundered when the United States publicly criticized its allies and the Soviet Union threatened to rain down rockets on the European attackers.

The Suez fiasco marked the end of Anglo-French control in the region and forced Eisenhower to play a much more active role there. The president took the lead in effecting a British and Israeli withdrawal and, with the Eisenhower Doctrine of 1958 (congressional authorization for the United States to aid any country in the Middle East threatened by communism), sought to enhance his authority to act in the area. Nevertheless, Eisenhower's preoccupation with Soviet intentions caused him to forego any serious effort to negotiate an Arab-Israeli settlement in the wake of Egypt's military humiliation by Israel and Arab appreciation of America's condemnation of the Israeli attack. The result instead was an uneasy truce with UN peacekeeping forces separating the Israelis and Egyptians.

During the remainder of his administration, Eisenhower actively sought to align the United States with the pro-Western governments in Jordan, Saudi Arabia, and Iran. He invoked the Eisenhower Doctrine on only one occasion—in 1958 in the wake of a successful anti-Western coup in Iraq and an abortive one in Jordan. Later that year the pro-Western Lebanese government claimed that it was threatened by outside aggression. When battle-equipped U.S. Marines hit the beaches near Beirut, however, they found only bikini-clad swimmers and hot dog vendors. It became clear that the conflict in Lebanon was a result of internal strife, and the troops were withdrawn. Despite his administration's attempts at peacefully bolstering its influence in the Middle East, by the time Eisenhower left office in 1961 it was apparent that Moscow's weight in the area had grown. Soviet military advisers with the armies of Egypt, Syria, and Iraq had replaced those from the West, and Soviet funds financed the Aswan Dam and propped up the Syrian economy. Moreover, the revolutionary nationalism so loathed by Dulles was a growing force from Algeria to Yemen.

Under John F. Kennedy and Lyndon B. Johnson, American policy toward the Third World changed. Whereas Eisenhower had often granted economic aid in hopes of securing short-term political support in selected neutralist countries, Kennedy and Johnson sought to provide economic assistance with less regard for the recipient's ideology, with the intention that by promoting independence and nationalism Soviet influence might be checked. Both presidents intended to show that assistance came without strings and was aimed at the betterment of the people. The most dramatic example of this approach was the Peace Corps, which sent thousands of young Americans to underdeveloped areas to attempt to improve living standards. Also, during the 1960s the commitment of the U.S. government to rights for its own minorities blunted much of the earlier criticism of the country as a racist society. Meanwhile, as Russian contacts with people from the nations of Asia and Africa increased, stories of Soviet maltreatment of Third World students and brutish behavior in these areas made Russians appear no more free of racial prejudice than Americans.

During the Kennedy and Johnson years, Middle Eastern developments were overshadowed by the Cuban missile crisis and the Vietnam War. The region was far from calm, however. Israel concentrated on building its economy and military with the support of the more sympathetic Democratic administrations in Washington. Beneath the surface Arab resentment seethed, and American dependence on cheap Middle Eastern oil rose during a period of unparalleled economic growth. This uneasy political status quo was shattered by the Six-Day War of 1967. A variety of events including the removal of UN observers, border incidents, and threats to shipping prompted Israel to launch a full-scale attack against Egypt, Syria, and Jordan. In less than a week (June 5–10), Israeli troops routed all three rivals, seizing Gaza and the Sinai from Egypt, the West Bank and East Jerusalem from Jordan, and the Golan Heights from Syria. Despite massive military aid and training provided by the Soviets, the Egyptians and the Syrians were crushed.

Apparently, political pressure from the United States and a need to consolidate its conquests stopped Israel from taking the capitals of all three Arab nations. Now their humiliation was complete, leaving a legacy of jokes about Arab incompetence and causing Americans wistfully to contrast the decisiveness of Israel's victory with their own quagmire in Vietnam.

In the aftermath of the Six-Day War the UN Security Council on November 22, 1967, enacted Resolution 242. It called for Israel to withdraw from the newly occupied territories and for the establishment of a permanent peace based on the recognition of the prewar boundaries of all nations within the area. Writer Jon Kimche and political scientist William Quandt have argued that a major opportunity for permanent settlement was lost in the aftermath of 1967. Unfortunately, the United States, under Johnson and then Richard M. Nixon, was preoccupied with Southeast Asia, and the Middle Eastern countries distrusted each other too profoundly to formulate a permanent settlement on their own.

On October 6, 1973, a new era began with the Middle East's fourth major war since 1945. Egypt and Syria attacked a surprised Israel, and at first Egyptian forces successfully crossed into the Sinai. Quickly the Israelis counterattacked, bolstered by rush de-

KING HUSSEIN OF JORDAN AND PRESIDENT JOHNSON. The two leaders met in 1967 to discuss Middle East affairs. (Lyndon B. Johnson Library)

liveries of over $2-billion worth of U.S. arms. When the resurgent Israeli forces threatened to envelop the entire Egyptian Third Army on the west bank of the Suez Canal, the Soviet Union hinted that it would intervene. The Watergate-troubled Nixon administration responded with a worldwide alert of its nuclear and conventional forces. Although Nixon may have overreacted for both diplomatic as well as domestic political reasons, the alert caused the Soviets to act more cautiously. A subsequent Israeli pullback and agreement to implement a cease-fire ended the most dangerous big-power confrontation of recent Middle Eastern history.

The October War had profound implications. The initial, temporary Egyptian military success gave a psychological lift to that oft-defeated nation and enhanced the prestige of Anwar Sadat. The Egyptian president had expelled his Soviet advisers in 1972, apparently because they opposed his plans for a new conflict with Israel and intrigued with his domestic opponents. Free of the stigma of the total defeats of 1948, 1956, and 1967, Sadat first accepted the step-by-step disengagement agreements worked out by the tireless shuttle diplomacy of Secretary of State Henry Kissinger and then prepared for his own peacemaking efforts in the late 1970s.

To the average American the most alarming result of the October War was the Arab oil embargo of 1973–74. In reaction to the massive U.S. military resupply of Israel, the Arab oil producers, led by Saudi Arabia, banned oil shipments to states that had supported Israel. Americans soon had to adjust to long lines at gasoline stations, changes in speed limits, and lowered thermostats in winter. The embargo lasted only until July 1974, and sizable American oil reserves made its effect less painful in the United States than in Europe or Japan. It was obvious that oil was a new Arab weapon that might threaten traditional American policy.

The embargo highlighted a profound revolution in the control of oil. In the late 1940s the major Western oil companies (Anthony Sampson's Seven Sisters) had set the price and quantity of Middle Eastern production. The position of the American-owned companies was enhanced by a cozy relationship with the Truman and Eisenhower administrations, which blocked antitrust suits and allowed them to count taxes paid to Middle Eastern countries as operating costs. When an oil country such as Iran sought to challenge this control, the companies blocked the sale of Iranian oil with such devastating effect that other producers thought twice before considering nationalization.

Slowly during the 1950s and 1960s the Middle Eastern oil producers ended their subservience to Western capitalists. Thousands of young Arabs and Iranians who had received their education in the West returned home to enter the petroleum industry, where they gained experience and expertise. Independent Western oil companies sought new concessions in the region, offering the Arabs higher royalties that the older major companies soon had to match. Middle Eastern efforts to control oil led to the formation in 1959 of the Organization of Petroleum Exporting Countries (OPEC), and during the next decade this group secured information, access to company records, better prices, and, most important, cooperation and united action among the producers. However, this activity went largely unnoticed in the West as cheap oil fueled the boom of the 1960s.

In 1968, OPEC began to flex its muscles, obtaining access to accounting records from the majors, limiting the size and number of Western concessions, and creating nationally owned oil firms within each member country. In 1971 the organization pushed through substantial price increases, cost-of-living attachments, and other concessions. Against the united front of OPEC and amid a burgeoning demand for the 12 million barrels of oil produced by OPEC annually, the Western concessionaires had little choice but to yield. When the Nixon administration sought to counter the price increases by devaluing the dollar, the chief oil currency, OPEC retaliated with another round of price increases.

In 1972, OPEC insisted on the right of member nations to buy out the foreign companies. Abetted by rising revenues resulting from higher prices, most OPEC countries had taken control of all their domestic oil industry by 1980. The price of a barrel of oil rose 400 percent in the two years after 1973, and by 1980 it was 1600 percent greater than the 1960 price. The OPEC revolution closed factories and contributed to record inflation in the United States, put the reins on the European economic boom, and, most dramatically, created a $600-billion oil revenue surplus, thereby giving OPEC members incredible political power and a stake in the finances of the Western countries where the surplus was invested. U.S. conservation efforts, threats of armed intervention, and attempts at collective action by petroleum consumers failed to reverse OPEC's course.

Only rising production and Saudi moderation restrained oil prices until the mid-1980s, when producers such as Iraq and Iran increased their output levels beyond OPEC limits. By 1985 divisions within OPEC and competition from non-OPEC producers such as Britain resulted in increased output and a significant reduction in crude oil prices, which declined by as much as 30 to 40 percent from 1980 to 1986. Ironically, the lowering of prices on Middle Eastern crude decreased conservation and exploration outside OPEC and increased dependence on Middle Eastern production.

Oil dependence and the serious confrontation with the Soviets in 1973 sparked major efforts by the Nixon administration to serve as a peacemaker in the Middle East. In the immediate aftermath of the October War, Secretary Kissinger initiated a series of diplomatic efforts that produced cease-fire agreements between Israel, Egypt, and Syria and a consequent lifting of the oil embargo. Kissinger excluded the Soviets from any role in the peace process, a diplomatic achievement that bolstered American prestige in the region but one gained at the price of making the United States solely responsible for peacemaking. Perhaps most important, Kissinger's shuttle diplomacy paved the way for more dramatic steps.

In November 1977, Egyptian president Sadat stunned the world by flying to Jerusalem to discuss peace with Israeli leaders. Convinced that his country needed to focus on domestic developments, Sadat risked his prestige and the scorn of fellow Arab states by gambling that he could reach an agreement with the Israelis. He was warmly received by the hard-line prime minister, Menachem Begin, a terrorist in the early Arab-Israeli conflict and, like Sadat, a fighter against the British still earlier. Sadat's trip sparked hopes for a cessation of the hostility between the two adversaries. The Jerusalem visit and a subsequent trip by Begin to Egypt started a process aimed at a comprehensive settlement. Such an agreement had obvious advantages for the United States, and President Jimmy Carter threw his support behind its negotiation. Carter's full energies were required because the issues dividing Egypt and Israel were immense: the time schedule of Israel's withdrawal from Egypt, Israeli security, and the status of the West Bank and Jerusalem.

In the two years following the Sadat visit, negotiations threatened to break down several times, and by mid-1978 many observers believed that the process had failed. At this point President Carter invited Begin and Sadat to Camp David, Maryland, where he jawboned both leaders, especially the irascible, tough Begin, into a preliminary settlement known as the Camp David agreement. When old animosities and new irritants threatened to shatter this preliminary accord, Carter risked his own prestige in the following March in a peacemaking visit to Israel and Egypt, where he attempted to remove obstacles in the path to agreement. The efforts bore fruit on March 26, 1979, when both countries signed a formal peace treaty.

The Egyptian-Israeli treaty provided for a phased withdrawal by Israel from all of the Sinai Peninsula, coupled with the establishment of full diplomatic relations between the two nations. The pact invited other Arab states to join in an effort to create a general Arab-Israeli peace. This hope was dashed by Arab suspicions and by a failure of the negotiations to produce a workable settlement of the Palestinian question. Yet, even though the treaty failed in its wider goals, the separate peace between Israel and Egypt was the most important step toward Middle East stability since 1945.

Just as the Egyptian-Israeli treaty was being hailed as a major triumph, American diplomacy suffered a stunning reverse in Iran. After the restoration of the shah in 1954, U.S. relations with Tehran had grown increasingly close. The shah seemed like "the kind of Moslem we could live with"—his oil flowed west, he joined pro-Western military alignments, and he even maintained diplomatic relations with Israel. Even when the shah took positions in conflict with American interests, such as his leadership in establishing OPEC, he compensated by spending much of his oil revenues in the United States. Richard Nixon was determined to make Iran the linchpin of his administration's Near Eastern policy. The shah was encouraged to purchase huge quantities of the latest U.S. weapons, American businessmen rushed in to build new Iranian cities, and U.S. intelligence agencies placed some of their most important installations in his country. Reza Pahlavi was delighted to cooperate, regarding American support as the key to establishing his country's dominance in the Persian Gulf, if not the entire region.

The shah's newfound prominence obscured the wrenching changes taking place within Iran as oil wealth and foreign development propelled the country from backwardness to modernity in the space of two decades. This rapid growth provoked both leftists and rightists. Leftists, educated in the West, deplored the shah's authoritarian rule and called for a popular-based government. On the Right, Moslem leaders deplored the erosion of traditional values and the secularization that appeared indistinguishable from Westernization. By the end of the 1970s these forces burst forth into what became one of the bloodiest revolutions in modern times. The shah was deposed, and the charismatic Moslem fanatic, the Ayatollah Khomeini, gained control of the government.

Initially, the Carter administration misread the depth of opposition to the shah. As the revolution grew, memories of the Vietnam experience led the United States to refrain from massive intervention in support of the shah and to seek contacts with the revolutionaries. Unfortunately, U.S. ties to the past were all too visible in Iran, and the revolutionary rage was virulent in its anti-Americanism. This rage erupted in November 1979 with the seizure of the American embassy in Tehran and the kidnapping of over fifty U.S. diplomats and embassy employees. The ensuing hostage crisis poisoned the American mind against Iran. As diplomacy dragged on and a rescue attempt failed, the crisis undermined the ability of the Carter administration to continue the Camp David process. It also played a major role in the defeat of Carter in the 1980 election. When the hostages were finally released, Americans seemed disposed to let the dust settle and await further developments within Iran.

The hostages were released as Ronald Reagan took the presidential oath in January 1981, thus freeing his administration to return to the central question of Arab-Israeli relations. Although Reagan had campaigned on a platform of closer support for Israel and much of his rhetoric resembled that of Dulles, his administration was soon pursuing essentially the same approach as that of Kissinger and Carter. Dependence on Arab oil and a desire to support anti-Communist Arab states such as Egypt, Jordan, and Saudi Arabia balanced the political commitment to Israel, and the new administration was soon supporting a policy of major arms sales to Egypt and Saudi Arabia as well as to Israel.

Reluctantly, the United States was forced to confront what had become the major block to Arab-Israeli peace—the problem of the Palestinians. The 600,000 refugees of 1948 had become the 4 million Palestinians of 1980, spread throughout the Arab world and vehemently insistent in their demand for their own homeland. The Palestinians had first relied on Arab states such as Egypt to champion their cause, but by the end of the 1960s they became more self-assertive. By 1968 the Palestine Liberation Organization (PLO) under Jerusalem-born Yassir Arafat emerged as the leader of their nationalism. Dedicated to an Arab state in Palestine and hostile to the very existence of Israel, the PLO resorted to terrorist attacks on Israel and Israelis to gain attention to its cause. By 1974, Arab states recognized the PLO as the sole representative of the Palestinians, and Arafat made a dramatic appeal at the United Nations, which accorded his organization observer status during the same year.

Palestinian nationalism forced U.S. leaders to weigh the old American principle of self-determination against the nation's traditional policy of support for Israel. Complicating the foreign policy debate was strong domestic political support for Israel. Well-educated, influential, and with a high voting rate in key states, American Jews consistently pressured legislature and executive alike on behalf of Israel's position and contributed impressive amounts of private financial aid. By the 1980s, as noted earlier, these Jews were joined by Protestant fundamentalists who saw the Jewish state as a fulfillment of biblical prophecy and urged virtually unquestioned support for Israel. Bolstered by such powerful allies in America, successive Israeli governments refused even to consider negotiations with the PLO, and American leaders who sought to support or even establish contacts with the PLO risked the full fury of politically powerful Israeli supporters within the United States. Increasingly in the 1980s some Palestinian settlement seemed a keystone of any durable Middle Eastern peacemaking.

Although the Iranian hostage crisis and the Palestinian question captured American public attention, the 1979 Soviet invasion of Afghanistan held far greater international and strategic implications and accelerated what historian H. W. Brands aptly characterizes as "full immersion" by the United States in the region during the 1980s. The Carter Doctrine of January 23, 1980, warned that outside attempts to control the Persian Gulf menaced vital U.S. interests. It implied that nuclear weapons might be used to block threats to crucial areas such as Saudi Arabia. Carter backed his doctrine with a much higher defense budget, the creation of the Rapid Deployment Force, and covert assistance to the Afghan rebels. Reagan continued these policies. As the decade unfolded, the USSR's unsuccessful war against the Moslem *mujahideen* and growing internal weaknesses undercut its influence in the Middle East just as the U.S. profile rose.

President Reagan initiated his "full immersion" with the rhetoric of a renewed Cold War. Unfortunately, his approach suffered from his inexperience and from divisions among his key advisers. In 1982 the Palestinian issue led to Reagan's first crisis in Lebanon. This once-peaceful nation had become the major PLO base during the late 1970s. Palestinian raids, Israeli retaliation, and fragile cease-fires followed in rapid succession. Lebanese sovereignty succumbed to raids by guerrillas against Israel and strong Israeli counterstrikes against guerrilla bases in Lebanon. Moslem-Christian hostility ignited a bloody civil war while a Syrian occupation (originally aimed at ending the civil strife) became itself a source of instability. The final blow fell in June 1982 when Israel, determined to end the use of Lebanon as a base for terrorism and seeking to defuse growing Palestinian unrest on the West Bank, launched a full-scale invasion driving all the way to Beirut. The resultant civilian deaths caused by American-made Israeli weapons and the massacre of Palestinian noncombatants by Israel's Christian Lebanese allies prompted a major negotiating effort by Washington and the dispatch of U.S. Marines to Lebanon as part of an international peacekeeping force.

Neither the Israeli invasion nor U.S. intervention brought peace to Lebanon: cease-fires, truces, conferences, and fighting followed in seemingly endless succession. Unable to bring its power to bear and stung by incidents such as the terrorist bombing of the U.S. Marine headquarters in Beirut in 1983, the Reagan administration withdrew its forces in 1984. Israel did likewise in 1985. The Lebanon episode left a weakened PLO, further fractionalized by the growing appeal of Islamic fundamentalism. Most disturbing to Reagan himself, whose election had owed much to the hostage humiliations of 1980, U.S. intervention provoked new terrorist incidents and captures of Americans. Terrorism was so rampant that *Time* magazine considered the masked terrorist as its symbolic Man of the Year in 1984.

Rhetorically, Reagan denounced terrorism, opposed deals with terrorists and their sponsors, and condemned nations such as Syria, Iran, and Libya for supporting killers and hostage takers. Several incidents with Libya, culminating in a bombing attack in 1986, amplified the tough, no-deals line. Secretly, however, the administration had embarked on one of the most bizarre dealings in recent diplomacy. Hoping to open a door to Tehran and free American captives, officials led by National Security Council operatives William McFarlane and Oliver North facilitated the sale of hundreds of missiles to Iran and provided intelligence information on its enemy, Iraq. In return, Tehran was to persuade its terrorist allies to release the hostages. The effort drew the opposition of the secretaries of State and Defense and liberated only three hostages in exchange for hundreds of missiles. The initiative, however, persisted for nearly two years, partially because the participants secretly and illegally diverted funds from the arms sales to aid the Contras, a rightist group opposing the Sandinista government in Nicaragua. The exposure of this "Irangate" episode forced the resignation of several key Reagan advisers, sparked congressional hearings reminiscent of Watergate, and left serious doubts about the president's competence in international affairs, if not his leadership and memory.

Irangate also clouded Reagan's last initiative in the area. By 1987, Iran and Iraq had been at war for seven years. Their bitter struggle spilled over into the Persian Gulf when Iranian gunboats began attacking Iraqi tankers. Kuwait sought foreign assistance to convoy its oil shipments, and soon U.S., British, and French naval forces escorted the tankers.The convoying inevitably led to incidents, including an Iraqi attack on a U.S. warship costing thirty American lives and an accidental U.S. downing of an Iranian passenger plane causing three hundred deaths. Despite these incidents, allied convoying continued until the end of the Iraq-Iran War in July 1988. There followed the largest U.S. involvement ever in the region.

In July 1990, smarting from failure in his war with Iran and disturbed over low oil reserves, Iraqi dictator Saddam Hussein mobilized his forces to threaten the tiny but oil-wealthy emirate of Kuwait. On August 2 over 100,000 Iraqi troops attacked and conquered the country within twenty-four hours. Prices soared at the prospect of Iraq's adding Kuwait's oil to its own and the specter that Saddam next might overwhelm Saudi Arabia to become the world's premier oil power.

President George Bush rushed forces to Saudi Arabia to prevent further Iraqi aggrandizement, and he led UN efforts that condemned Iraqi aggression on August 2 and invoked economic sanctions against Iraq on August 9. Bush feared that its control of Kuwait's oil would harm the economies of Western Europe and Japan and indirectly destabilize the global economy. Moreover, Iraq had been seeking to join the nuclear club since the 1970s, sparking an Israeli raid on its nuclear facilities in 1981. Kuwait's wealth might buy nuclear weapons for a nation that had used biological weapons against Iran and boasted of its growing missile capability. Finally, Iraq's invasion blatantly flouted international law. With the Cold War over, Bush and other officials in Washington realized that conditions existed for a stable, liberal-capitalist internationalism, the dream of American leaders since Woodrow Wilson. Bush would not permit Saddam, whom on occasion he compared to Hitler, to thwart this "new world order."

Unlike Reagan, Bush had extensive international experience and presided over a unified foreign policy team. He masterfully organized a coalition of thirty states that contributed armed forces and another eighteen that provided financial aid. The end of the Cold War assisted the coalition's success. Soviet premier Mikhail Gorbachev desperately needed U.S. support for his policies of *glasnost* and *perestroika*. Accordingly, the Soviet Union backed anti-Iraqi resolutions and cut off arms to its former client. Bush also persuaded China not to veto UN actions. When American forces in the region reached 125,000, administration policy switched from blocking future Iraqi expansion to liberating Kuwait.

On November 29, 1990, the UN Security Council authorized the use of force against Iraq if it did not evacuate, eventually setting January 15, 1991, as the deadline for compliance. Bush found securing congressional support difficult as fears of "another Vietnam" abounded. However, the tradition of rallying behind the president in a crisis ran strong, and, on January 12, Congress by a narrow majority added its endorsement to Bush's course of action. Upon the expiration of the January 15 deadline the coalition opened a five-week air war against Iraq. The most sophisticated conventional weapons, including Stealth aircraft, laser-guided bombs, and cruise missiles, spearheaded this attack. In response to the bombing, Iraq launched Scud missiles against Saudi Arabia and Israel. By attacking the Jewish state, it hoped to provoke a military response that would cause Arab members to leave the coalition. American officials, however, skillfully persuaded the Israelis to keep out of the conflict.

Coalition forces launched their land campaign, Operation Desert Storm, on February 24. Within one hundred hours it swept to victory, liberating Kuwait, crushing Saddam's vaunted Republican Guard, and killing perhaps as many as 100,000 Iraqis. Allied forces stood poised on the road to Baghdad. Iraq accepted a cease-fire on February 28 that continued sanctions and promised reparations and restrictions on weapons.

Americans had viewed much of the war via the satellite technology of CNN and other news networks. The victorious images offered a tonic to memories of Vietnam—the Iraqis had proved to be far less formidable opponents than the Vietnamese. The short, conventional war had a clear, obtainable objective of ousting the enemy from a specific territory rather than attempting to win anyone's hearts and minds. Widespread support included military contributions from Moslem countries such as Egypt, Syria, Morocco, the Gulf States, and Pakistan as well as from traditional allies France and Great Britain. Another eighteen countries, including Japan and Germany, provided financing amounting to perhaps 60 percent of the cost of the war. Mindful of the importance of petroleum prices, Saudi Arabia dramatically increased its oil production to compensate for the loss of Kuwaiti and Iraqi outputs.

Operation Desert Storm combined with the end of the Cold War to usher in one of the brightest periods in Arab-Israeli relations. U.S. prestige reached an all-time high, and Soviet aid to Arab states and Palestinian groups ended. Israel's restraint despite Iraqi provocations improved the diplomatic climate. In 1993, Israel and the PLO reached a stunning agreement promising Palestinian self-rule in exchange for peace and recognition. Like the Begin-Sadat moves twenty years earlier, much of this activity was the result of the parties themselves, leaving the Clinton administration happy to provide its good offices. On September 13, Israeli premier Itzak Rabin and PLO leader Arafat formalized the initial agreements with a much-celebrated and photographed handshake in Washington at the White House. In the next year Bill Clinton hosted a similar meeting and handshake for Rabin and Jordan's King Hussein as those men moved toward a peaceful resolution of their disputes.

By 1994 chances for peace in the region were the best since 1945, and perhaps the best since the Balfour Declaration on Palestine in 1917. Many problems remained, however; developing and nurturing trust after decades of suspicion, violence, and hatred promised to be a slow and difficult task. The region's penchant for violence and terrorism, instability in many governments, and the still-unmeasured appeal of Moslem fundamentalism all remained reasons for caution. Yet the striking diplomatic revolution of the 1990s along with the absence of an outside power to move in troubled waters allowed ample reason for optimism.

The 1990s also marked the obsolescence of the term Third World. Even before the end of the Cold War the usefulness of the concept had waned. The striking divergence in economic status, national interests, and political alliances among the nonaligned nations made generalizations difficult and concerted policy toward them all but impossible. During the 1980s nonaligned countries had still gathered at meetings and sought unified policies in international bodies, but local conflicts often overrode common global positions. Wars and boundary disputes between countries such as Iran and Iraq, and Ethiopia and Somalia, were far more important to these nations than maintaining identical positions on Israel, nuclear arms, and economic development. China's rapprochement with the United States and its rise as an economic power had eroded its role as a spokesman for the underdeveloped lands. In areas as far apart as Angola, Kampuchea, and Afghanistan, the United States and China often adopted similar policies.

The success of OPEC, whose members had claimed emerging-nation status, created economic rifts within the Third World. Oil-rich Saudi Arabia, for example, had few economic interests in common with destitute Bangladesh. The rampant worldwide inflation of the 1970s caused largely by the astronomical OPEC price hikes produced greater economic hardship in developing countries than in the West. The very economic fragility of many nonaligned states also undermined attempts at collective positions. The collapse of common OPEC production and pricing agreements in 1985 and subsequent failures to revive the organization's power during the next decade highlighted the divisions even among oil producers.

The end of the Cold War accelerated the replacement of the term Third World with the term North-South in the international lexicon. The ideological concept of the Third World, describing those nations that wished to be nonaligned between East and West, gave way to a focus on the world's North-South economic and developmental division between the industrialized nations, mostly in the Northern Hemisphere, and the less-developed have-not states south of the Equator. This new focus promised that much diplomatic attention would concentrate on problems of environment, population growth, development, and exploitation of global resources.

American attitudes concerning the Third World had changed in the aftermath of the Vietnam War. Selected areas such as the Persian Gulf involved vital interests, but in general U.S. policy toward underdeveloped countries during the 1970s and 1980s had emphasized political activity over military intervention since any consideration of involvement in Angola, Iran, and El Salvador encountered fierce opposition cries of "no more Vietnams." The Carter administration downplayed ideology; and even the Reagan administration, whose rhetoric sounded like a return to the days of Dulles, if not John Wayne, seemed reluctant to launch a full-scale military action. Even the volatile and emotionally charged issue of terrorism evoked only limited military responses from the United States. Underscoring the diminution of American activity was the reduction of economic assistance to developing countries. By 1984 the $4.87 billion in foreign aid amounted to less in constant dollars than the $2.47 billion expended in 1974. By the 1990s even economic assistance to former Soviet Union states to help dismantle their nuclear weapons encountered difficulty as the United States grappled with its own economic stagnation and deficit. Japan, Germany, and Saudi Arabia emerged as major sources of economic aid to underdeveloped regions.

The 1990s found the United States pulled in two opposite directions. Victory in the Cold War and Operation Desert Storm had left the nation as the only global military power. The triumph of liberal-capitalist internationalism fostered a desire to engender democratic aspirations from China to Haiti. Advocates of various causes sought to enlist U.S. military support in Somalia, Bosnia, Rwanda, and elsewhere, yet the enormous economic problems within the United States and the rise of economic rivals such as Japan joined with still-strong memories of Vietnam to buttress those who called for a cautious international role. Growing diversity within American society reinforced these contradictory international impulses and gave the United States significant potential for leadership in an increasingly non-European world, but it also evoked calls from groups of Americans who wanted policy to tilt toward homelands as diverse as Armenia, Bosnia, and Cuba.

Sources and Suggested Readings

Brands, H. W. *Into the Labyrinth: The United States and the Middle East, 1945–1993.* New York, 1994.

———. *The Specter of Neutralism: The United States and the Emergence of the Third World, 1947–1960.* New York, 1989.

Bryson, Thomas A. *Seeds of Mideast Crisis: The United States Diplomatic Role in the Middle East during World War II.* Jefferson, NC, 1981.

Freedman, Lawrence, and Karsh, Efraim. *The Gulf Conflict, 1990–1991.* Princeton, NJ, 1992.

Hahn, Peter L. *The United States, Great Britain, and Egypt, 1945–1956: Strategy and Diplomacy in the Early Cold War.* Chapel Hill, NC, 1991.

Kaufman, Burton I. *The Oil Cartel Case: A Documentary Study of Anti-Trust Activity in the Cold War*. Westport, CT, 1978.

Kimche, Jon. *There Could Have Been Peace: The Untold Story of Why We Failed with Palestine and Again with Israel*. New York, 1973.

Kuniholm, Bruce. *The Origins of the Cold War in the Near East: Great Power Conflicts in Iran, Turkey, and Greece*. Princeton, NJ, 1980.

———. *The Persian Gulf and United States Policy: A Guide to Issues and References*. Claremont, CA, 1984.

———, and Rubner, Michael. *The Palestinian Problem and U.S. Policy: A Guide to Issues and References*. Claremont, CA, 1986.

LaFeber, Walter. *The American Age: U.S. Foreign Policy at Home and Abroad, from 1750 to the Present*. New York, 1989.

Lenczowski, George. *American Presidents and the Middle East*. Durham, NC, 1990.

Neff, Donald. *Warriors at Suez: Eisenhower Takes America into the Middle East*. New York, 1981.

Ovendale, Ritchie. *The Middle East since 1914*. London, 1992.

Quandt, William B. *Decade of Decisions: American Policy toward the Arab-Israeli Conflict, 1967–1976*. Berkeley, CA, 1977.

Rubin, Barry. *Paved with Good Intentions: The American Experience and Iran*. New York, 1980.

Sampson, Anthony. *The Seven Sisters: The Great Oil Companies and the World They Shaped*. New York, 1975.

Stookey, Robert W. *America and the Arab States: An Uneasy Encounter*. New York, 1975.

Tillman, Seth P. *The United States in the Middle East: Interests and Obstacles*. Bloomington, IN, 1982.

U.S. Department of State. *Foreign Relations of the United States, 1940–1961*. Washington, DC, 1949–1992.

Yergin, Daniel. *The Prize: The Epic Quest for Oil, Money, and Power*. New York, 1990.

Afterword: Facing a New World Order

George C. Herring

On the eve of the twenty-first century, Americans were wracked by uncertainty as great as at any time during the past one hundred years. The world seemed less threatening but more confusing, its contours far less distinct. There were new players, alignments, and issues but as yet no new rules. America's role in the new world order was equally unclear. Militarily, it enjoyed a preponderance of power unprecedented in modern times, but military force seemed less relevant and usable in the post-Cold War era, and, in any event, Americans were less disposed than at any time since the 1930s to employ it. Among elites, there was vigorous debate as to the principles and purposes of U.S. foreign policy in the new world order. Among the mass public, there was indifference and apathy.

For a fleeting moment in the early 1990s peace and stability seemed within reach. The end of the Cold War and the subsequent collapse of the Soviet Union removed a major cause of international tension for the past half century and eased, if it did not eliminate altogether, the dreadful threat of a nuclear holocaust. The emergence of democracies and market economies in the former Soviet satellites, Latin America, and even in South Africa offered the promise of a new age. The victory in the 1991 Persian Gulf War of a powerful allied coalition, working under the aegis of the United Nations, seemed to hail the triumph of Woodrow Wilson's dreams of collective security where peace would be maintained through international collaboration. In the aftermath of the Gulf War, President George Bush proclaimed the birth of a new world order under American leadership. State Department official Francis Fukayama went further, exulting in the "end of history," the absolute triumph of capitalism and democracy over fascism and communism and the promise of a just and peaceful world composed of stable and prosperous democracies.

It did not take long for such prophecies to be exposed as at best wishful thinking, at worst absolute folly. The end of the Cold War brought problems as well as blessings. Ironically, victory had an unsettling effect on the Western democracies, and they entered the postwar period less confident about their basic institutions and values than at any time since World War II. Demobilization in the United States brought profound difficulties of readjustment for an economy that had been geared to war for five decades. Economic stagnation among the industrial democracies posed the possibility of trade wars.

In international politics, the end of the Cold War gave birth to conflict rather than to peace and harmony. The Cold War had imposed a crude form of order on inherently unstable regions of the world, and its end unleashed powerful forces that had been constrained for years. Especially in Central Europe, the Middle East, and Central Asia, national loyalties gave way to smoldering ethnic rivalries and secessionist movements. Most prominent were the brutal war between Serbs, Croats, and Muslims in the former Yugoslavia and the conflict between Sunnis, Shiites, and Kurds in the Middle East, but the *New York Times* counted in early 1993 forty-eight such conflicts scattered across the globe. Pessimists such as Senator Daniel Patrick Moynihan of New York warned of a new era of discord and disorder. "Get ready for fifty new countries in the world in the next fifty years," he admonished, most of them "born in bloodshed." Wilson's ideal of self-determination seemed to have returned with a vengeance, threatening to tear the world apart rather than bring it together.

Other pessimists predicted even more gloomy scenarios. Some warned that the Cold War struggle between East and West would give way to a new conflict between North and South, between the haves and have-nots of the world, "the West and the rest." Runaway population growth in the developing countries portended a possibly disastrous drain on already scarce resources, enormous environmental problems that would afflict the entire globe, and the rampant spread of crime, disease, and war. Some commentators warned that international migration would be the greatest problem of the twenty-first century and foresaw an assault on the borders of developed countries through massive emigration. Others predicted that the anarchy already gripping Africa would spread across the globe, the chaos in less-developed countries eventually contaminating the developed ones. Although such scenarios appeared unnecessarily gloomy and even based on a false nostalgia for the "order" of the Cold War, it seemed clear that the end of history was not in view. Conflict and disorder would characterize the post-Cold War period.

The United States responded uncertainly to these changes. Americans recognized that there could be no return to isolationism in a world shrunken by technology and bound together by growing economic interdependence, but after forty years of international commitment and massive Cold War expenditures they yearned for relief from the burdens of leadership. As in the aftermath of World Wars I and II, they preferred to concentrate on domestic problems, and support for foreign policy ventures waned. Memories of the Vietnam debacle lingered years after the event, adding yet another restraint against global involvement. The outlines of the new world order were fuzzy at best, and Americans lacked a blueprint for dealing with it. The absence of an obvious threat to national security removed any compelling inducement to take the lead in solving world problems.

The halting response of the Bush administration to the new order that it once had hailed foreshadowed the difficulties of the post-Cold War era. If the administration looked to the future and reconsidered America's role, it did not reach any firm conclusions on how to deal with it, nor did it confront in any fundamental way such urgent issues as world population growth and the environment. After its firm leadership in the Persian Gulf War, it did little to address longer-range but still pressing problems in the Middle East. Its response to the mounting crisis in Bosnia suggested its uncertainty. Despite warnings from some quarters of a new holocaust and its own bold rhetoric, it did nothing to halt Serbia's "ethnic cleansing." State Department spokesperson Margaret Tutwiler asked, "Where is it written that the United States is the military policeman of the world?" And a top administration official added, "Do you really think that the American people want to spill their blood for Bosnia?" In his last days in office, President Bush authorized a humanitarian rescue mission in Somalia, sending troops to prevent rivalries among local warlords from causing mass starvation. But the administration appears never to have decided whether it was really committed to the new world order under American leadership that its rhetoric had proclaimed, or, because of domestic needs, it preferred retreat and retrenchment.

Much like its predecessor, the Clinton administration also found adjustment to the new world order vexing and difficult. In many ways Bill Clinton seemed more attuned to the new era, making clear his preeminent concern with domestic issues such as the economy. Having spent his entire career in state politics, he was plainly less interested in, experienced with, and informed on foreign policy issues. At least at the outset, he seemed to hope that his foreign policy team could hold the world at bay while he implemented an ambitious domestic agenda. His few pronouncements seemed to promise more forthright American leadership and a more active role in such areas as Bosnia. Yet his foreign policy advisers came out of the liberal Democratic mold—burned by Vietnam, nervous about unilateral intervention, and committed to working through the United Nations and persuading allies to share the burden of leadership.

Clinton and his advisers quickly discovered the perils of the new world order. His administration was deeply committed to promoting domestic prosperity through the expansion of foreign trade. Clinton cashed in all his political chips to secure congressional passage in 1993 of the North American Free-Trade Agreement (NAFTA). He vigorously promoted the Asia-Pacific Economic Community as a modern-day economic NATO as well as the General Agreement on Tariffs and Trade (GATT). Promoting the expansion of trade raised all sorts of problems, however. Whatever its benefits, it could also bring huge trade-offs and costly job displacements. While NAFTA promised to help many Americans, for example, it also threatened to eliminate additional jobs in the nation's already moribund manufacturing sector. In the new world economy, promotion of trade often involved unprecedented intrusion into the internal policies of other nations. The United States found itself in the unlikely position of advising Russian president Boris Yeltsin on how to construct his budget. To persuade the Japanese to reduce their trade surplus with the United States, administration officials insisted that Tokyo cut taxes to spur domestic spending so that the Japanese could purchase more American goods. A standard joke in Japan was that the United States was the only opposition party. Such intrusion risked arousing nationalist passions that could bring allies such as Washington and Tokyo into conflict, and bashers of each country in the other were ready to take up the cause.

Committed to promoting human rights as well as to expanding trade, the Clinton administration quickly discovered that the two might come into conflict. Exports were increasingly important to domestic prosperity. In the most prominent cases, the administration therefore bent to expediency without totally abandoning its principles. Two hundred thousand Americans, for example, were employed in the sale of some $9-billion worth of exports to China, yet that country's abuse of human rights offended the sensibilities of pressure groups and Washington officials. After much agonizing, the administration renewed China's favorable trade status on the condition that it act on human rights before the next renewal. Left unanswered was the question of what to do if, as it seemed likely, the Chinese failed to meet the conditions. Human rights subsequently took a backseat to conflicting economic interests when the Clinton administration threatened tough sanctions on China for refusing to observe copyright restrictions and pirating American goods.

The administration was even less surefooted on the increasingly difficult questions posed by world order: peacekeeping and intervention. In the campaign and its early days in office, it sounded at least mildly interventionist. Clinton himself scored Bush's inaction on Bosnia and affirmed that "no national security issue is more urgent than securing democracy's triumph around the world." National Security Adviser Anthony Lake coined vague phrases such as "enlargement of democracy" and "pragmatic Wilsonianism" to describe an approach that hinted at greater activism. Before its first year in office had ended, the Clinton administration had beaten a hasty retreat from whatever its rhetoric may have implied. Unable to persuade its European allies to lift the arms embargo against Bosnia, it would go no further than sanction NATO air strikes to defend embattled UN peacekeepers. It went along with expansion of the UN role in Somalia, but when eighteen GIs were killed in bloody fighting in Mogadishu in October 1993 it quickly backed off, immediately scaling down the U.S. role and assuring an anxious Congress and public that Americans would be out of Somalia by March 1994.

While rampant instability wracked the globe in 1994, the Clinton administration developed guidelines for intervention that some critics denounced as "self-containment." The United States would only intervene in cases where international security was gravely threatened, a major disaster required urgent relief, or a gross violation of human rights had occurred. Other nations would have to share the costs, but American troops would participate only under U.S. command. In response to proliferating UN commitments, the administration in May 1994 spelled out a total of seventeen even more restrictive guidelines for support of these peacekeeping operations. Making clear in the aftermath of Somalia its waning enthusiasm for such UN enterprises, it vowed that it would commit troops only in cases where U.S. vital interests were threatened. Congress would have to approve the mission, and funds would have to be available. Such missions must have a clearly stated objective, a reasonable assurance of success, and a strategy for completing the job; further, they must involve a major threat to international peace and security or gross violations of human rights. At the same time, President Clinton urged the United Nations to scale back its own ambitions: "If the American people are to say yes to UN peacekeeping, the United Nations must know when to say no." Parodying John F. Kennedy, critics claimed that in a troubled world Clinton's United States was willing "to pay only some prices, fight only some foes, and bear only some burdens in the defense of freedom." It was also admitting to potential adversaries that when Americans got killed, the United States would pull out.

The Clinton administration appeared to shift gears once again in the fall of 1994. After months of soul-searching, imposition of sanctions that hurt victims more than oppressors, and threats that were ignored, it sent troops to Haiti to remove a brutal military dictatorship and restore to power elected president Jean-Bertrand Aristide. President Clinton justified the move as necessary to "restore democracy" and, as a more pragmatic goal, to prevent a massive flight of Haitians to American shores. To the shock of some observers, U.S. troops met a joyful reception from Haitians on the island rather than resistance by force, and after tense negotiations the military government agreed to leave. Whether the intervention would contribute to the long-range goal of restoring democracy to Haiti remained much in doubt. It was also uncertain whether America's apparent success there would lead to calls for more "humanitarian" interventions.

As the administration passed its midpoint, the nation was no more settled in its response to the new world order than when Clinton first had taken office. A searching examination of the issues among foreign policy elites raised questions that went back to the birth of the Republic and resonated of earlier great debates on foreign policy. What was the proper role of the United States in the world? Were its interests and those of humanity best served by active intervention or example? When, where, and for what purpose should it intervene? The ghosts of Thomas Jefferson and Alexander Hamilton, John Quincy Adams and Henry Clay, Woodrow Wilson and Henry Cabot Lodge hovered over the nation as it discussed its international interests and obligations on the eve of the twenty-first century.

On one side, abstentionists with roots in traditional isolationism and post-World War II realism urged caution. Admitting the great temptation for the United States to brandish its power in a world where it enjoyed primacy and seemed likely to have its way, they warned of the limits on its ability to resolve intractable local conflicts and the further limits of military power to solve the most pressing problems. Acknowledging the rampant disorder and crushing human tragedy in the world, abstentionists insisted that moral outrage was not an adequate criterion for intervention. The great danger in sending armed expeditions abroad to defend the weak was that there would be no end to it. Such interventions would quickly exceed the nation's ability to support them, and, moreover, they would not ensure world order. As with Bosnia, the best solution to many crises was often a bad one. "There are a lot of tragedies in the world and we can't intervene in all of them," one abstentionist warned. American troops should be committed only when the nation's most vital interests—indeed, its survival—were at stake.

On the other side, interventionists whose mind-set and rhetoric resonated of the Cold War raised shrill alarms about the perils of inaction. Speaking in tones reminiscent of the 1940s and 1950s, they insisted that as the world became more interdependent, the United States had an even more compelling interest in containing the virus of chaos. It should work with its allies, but it must assume leadership. Interventionists feared an "endless nibbling away at our international standing that at some point makes a stark qualitative difference." The Cold War idea that the United States had to live up to its commitments and finish what it started remained valid. Interventionists became especially outspoken about Bosnia, a vivid reminder to them of the breakdown of world order in 1914 and 1938. Denouncing Western inaction as a new Munich, they warned that "genocidal aggression" must not go unchecked. The United States must ensure for the citizens of any state basic human rights. As the only superpower, it must impose order on a troubled planet.

If disorder were permitted to reign, then world peace and stability would be imperiled. America's economic interests would be undermined, and U.S. workers would lose their jobs.

Neo-Wilsonian internationalists justified intervention in different terms. Claiming that the major contribution of the United States had been the advance of democracy, they insisted that the nation continued to have a compelling interest in promoting democracy throughout the world. Such an expansion would establish among nations a greater sense of mutual respect and understanding based on common values and institutions, thereby contributing to the development of a peaceful and stable world community. To accomplish this end, the United States must take a clear and forthright stand, making plain what it expected of other nations and moving decisively to uphold its obligations. Neo-Wilsonians admitted that the United States could not do everything, but they insisted that at least in Eastern Europe, Central America, and the Caribbean it must promote its own security by vigorously defending democracy.

Somewhere between the abstentionists and interventionists were pragmatists who shared the concerns of both sides. They conceded that the country did not have the resources to intervene all over the world, but they agreed with the interventionists that it could not stand by idly in the face of genocide in places such as Rwanda. They called for a form of selective intervention in which the United States would move in where gross violations of human rights had occurred and in cases where it could make a difference at an acceptable cost.

Finally, a group of new internationalists looked more at the root causes of disorder than at the more obvious symptoms. Lamenting the outmoded thinking that drove the others, they insisted that, in the new world order, nation-states would not be the only or even the primary actors and that the line between domestic and foreign policies would become increasingly blurred. The issues that had to be addressed were global, not national: the environment, overpopulation, disease, crime, drugs, and immigration. The old threats were gone, and the large military establishments of the Cold War era were outmoded and irrelevant. The growth of trade, investment, and multilateral corporations had produced a new "mutual intrusiveness" of societies and governments that required greater cooperation. Human rights, above all, were a universal concern. These new internationalists called for new experts, a new mind-set, and new solutions to deal with the complex problems of an uncharted and dangerous era. They urged a firm commitment of aid to the developing nations, the use of scientists and engineers released by the end of the Cold War to address the problems of population and the environment, and effective measures to reduce the flow of guns.

On the eve of the twenty-first century there were thus numerous claimants for the role of another "Mr. X," the person who, like George Kennan in 1947, would set the agenda and outline the policies for a new era—but there was nothing even approaching a national consensus as to who that person should be. The world had changed dramatically since the heyday of the Cold War, but the United States had not determined how to adjust to the changes. Perhaps, as in 1939 or 1947, the rise of an external threat would forge a new foreign policy consensus. In an era when issues rather than nations appeared to pose the major threats, however, it seemed more likely that at least for the immediate future the United States would continue to improvise, reacting to events on an ad hoc basis. America faced the new world order without clearly defined notions of its international interests and obligations or how best to defend and uphold them.

Sources and Suggested Readings

Haas, Richard N. "Paradigm Lost." *Foreign Affairs* 74 (January/February 1995): 43–58.

Huntington, Samuel P. "The Clash of Civilization?" *Foreign Affairs* 72 (Summer 1993): 22–49.

Kaplan, Robert D. "The Coming Anarchy." *Atlantic Monthly* (February 1994): 44–76.

Kennedy, Paul. *Preparing for the Twenty-First Century.* New York, 1993.

Mandelbaum, Michael. "The Reluctance to Intervene." *Foreign Policy* (Summer 1994): 3–18.

Mueller, John. "The Catastrophe Quota: Trouble after the Cold War." *Journal of Conflict Resolution* 38 (September 1994): 355–75.

Waltz, Kenneth. "The Emerging Structure of International Politics." *International Security* 18 (Fall 1993): 44–79.

Index

About the Contributors

JOHN M. CARROLL is Regents' Professor of History at Lamar University in Beaumont, Texas. He is co-editor of *The American Military Tradition* (1993) and is currently working on a biography of Red Grange.

JOSEPH A. FRY is professor of history at the University of Nevada, Las Vegas. He has written *Henry S. Sanford: Diplomacy and Business in Nineteenth-Century America* (1982) and *John Tyler Morgan and the Search for Southern Autonomy* (1992). Fry is currently working on a study of the American South and U.S. foreign policy.

MARC GALLICCHIO is associate professor of history at Villanova University. He is the author of *The Cold War Begins in Asia: American East Asian Policy and the Fall of the Japanese Empire* (1988) and several articles on American-East Asian relations. His article "The Kuriles Controversy: Strategy and Diplomacy on the Soviet-Japan Border, 1941–1956," was awarded the Stuart Bernath Prize by the Society for Historians of American Foreign Relations.

JAMES W. HARPER, associate professor of history at Texas Tech University, recently completed several articles for *American National Biography* and *The Biographical Dictionary of American Sport*. He is currently working on a biography of General Hugh Lenox Scott as well as a study of baseball and television.

GEORGE C. HERRING, a specialist in the history of U.S. foreign relations, is Alumni Professor of History at the University of Kentucky. He has written widely on U.S. foreign policy since World War II, including *America's Longest War: The United States and Vietnam, 1950–1975* (3d ed., 1995) and *LBJ and Vietnam: A Different Kind of War* (1994).

WALTER L. HIXSON, associate professor of history at the University of Akron, is the author of *George F. Kennan: Cold War*

Iconoclast (1989), *Witness to Disintegration: Provincial Life in the Last Year of the USSR* (1993), and *Charles A. Lindbergh, Lone Eagle* (1996).

LESTER D. LANGLEY is Research Professor in the Department of History at the University of Georgia. His most recent book is *Mexico and the United States: The Fragile Relationship* (1991). Langley is currently working on a comparative study of the wars of independence in the Americas.

MARK H. LYTLE is professor of history and American studies at Bard College. He is the author of *The Origins of the Iranian-American Alliance, 1941–1953* (1987) and has co-authored numerous texts, including *After the Fact: The Art of Historical Detection* (1985) and *Nation of Nations: A Narrative History of the American Republic* (1991). Lytle is now working on "An Environmental Approach to American Diplomatic History."

ROBERT L. MESSER is professor of history at the University of Illinois at Chicago and is the author of *The End of an Alliance: James F. Byrnes, Roosevelt, Truman, and the Origins of the Cold War* (1982).

MELVIN SMALL is professor of history at Wayne State University and former president of the Council on Peace Research in History. Among his books relating to American involvement in war are *Was War Necessary? National Security and U.S. Entry into War* (1980), *Johnson, Nixon, and the Doves* (1988), and *Covering Dissent: The Media and the Anti-Vietnam War Movement* (1994).

JONATHAN G. UTLEY is Emeritus Professor of History at the University of Tennessee, Knoxville. His research focuses on U.S.-East Asian relations, and he has written on diplomatic and naval history, including *Going to War with Japan, 1937–1941* (1985) and *An American Battleship at Peace and War: The USS Tennessee* (1991). Utley is currently working on a biography of Cordell Hull.

JANE KAROLINE VIETH earned her Ph.D. from The Ohio State University in British history and is currently a professor at Michigan State University in the Department of History. She is the author of "Joseph P. Kennedy and British Appeasement" in Kenneth

Paul Jones, ed., *U.S. Diplomats in Europe, 1919–1941* (1983), and "Munich and American Appeasement" in David F. Schmitz and Richard D. Challener, eds., *Appeasement in Europe: A Reassessment of U.S. Policies* (1990). Vieth also has completed a manuscript on the ambassadorship of Joseph P. Kennedy at the Court of St. James's, 1938–1940.

WILLIAM C. WIDENOR is professor of the history of U.S. foreign relations at the University of Illinois at Urbana-Champaign. He is the author of *Henry Cabot Lodge and the Search for an American Foreign Policy* (1980), which won the Organization of American Historians' Frederick Jackson Turner Prize in 1981. Currently, Widenor is working on a book on the American approach to the problem of international organization.